GANDHI AND BIN LADEN

Religion at the Extremes

James L. Rowell

University Press of America,® Inc.
Lanham · Boulder · New York · Toronto · Plymouth, UK

Copyright © 2009 by
University Press of America,® Inc.
4501 Forbes Boulevard
Suite 200
Lanham, Maryland 20706
UPA Acquisitions Department (301) 459-3366

Estover Road
Plymouth PL6 7PY
United Kingdom

All rights reserved
Printed in the United States of America
British Library Cataloging in Publication Information Available

Library of Congress Control Number: 2009931982
ISBN: 978-0-7618-4766-3 (paperback : alk. paper)
eISBN: 978-0-7618-4767-0

♾™ The paper used in this publication meets the minimum requirements of American National Standard for Information Sciences—Permanence of Paper for Printed Library Materials, ANSI Z39.48-1992

Dedication

This book is dedicated to my father, for all his enthusiasm in reading my books and patience looking at my manuscripts, for my mother and her interest and inspiration in religion, and for my lovely wife, and all her support.

BL
65
.P7
R796
2009

CONTENTS

Acknowledgements	vii
Chapter 1: Introduction	1
Chapter 2: Gandhi — His Life	17
Chapter 3: Gandhi — His Beliefs	47
Chapter 4: Bio of a Jihadist	73
Chapter 5: Bin Laden's Beliefs	99
Chapter 6: Abdul Ghaffar Khan	119
Conclusion	135
Bibliography	141
Index	145
About the Author	149

Acknowledgements

I would like to thank the *Navajivan Trust* for their cooperation with the use of all materials from the works of Mohandas K. Gandhi, as well as Peter Bergen (material quoted from pages 204-205 and 291 of THE OSAMA I KNOW by Peter Bergen, © 2008 by Peter Bergen. Originally published in *The Osama I Know*, reprinted by permission of the author) and Bruce Lawrence for the invaluable works they have produced about Osama bin Laden. Additionally I extend my gratitude towards James Howarth for making translations of bin Laden's texts accessible to the English-speaking world. I would also like to thank Mr. Eknath Easwaran for his critical studies of Abdul Ghaffar Khan. Thanks to Katie Wrisley for her proofreading comments. There are additionally countless other scholars in this field who have produced fine works which I have fully referenced, and I would commend the reader's attention to these works, listed in the bibliography, for further research on Gandhi or Bin Laden. Without the work and cooperation of these fine scholars and journalists, this work would not have been possible. It is hoped that the excellence that is reflected in the best of their work also shines through here.

Chapter 1: Introduction

Satyagrahis and Jihadists

Imagine this cruel boxing match: *Gandhi vs. Bin Laden.* Gandhi appeals to Bin Laden's conscience, and stands defenseless. Bin Laden punches Gandhi in the face, drawing blood from his nose. The six-foot (plus) frame of Bin Laden towers over the five-foot-four inch Gandhi. Yet Gandhi is a physically fit man; he does not collapse on the first punch, but appeals again to the inner soul of his adversary. Bin Laden again punches him in the face. Can the power of Gandhi's non-violence find the soul and conscience of non-violence in Bin Laden? Or will the Mahatma be condemned to be beaten silly? Sickened, the audience of public opinion cannot stand by, but sends men into the ring to apprehend Bin Laden and to pull him off of his helpless target.

Of course this boxing match could never have taken place; Gandhi lived before Bin Laden's time. The forces of nonviolence and violence these two men represent, however, are still both in the world. They exist as competing ideologies. How would the one respond to the other? Can non-violence vanquish violence, or is it a doomed force? Must we always call out the armed forces to respond to malevolent threats? Gandhi and King foresaw that bullets can kill the killer, but they cannot slay hatred. Arrest, apprehend, or kill Bin Laden without defusing the Islamist anger and hatred he represents, and he will only be replaced. Gandhi believed only non-violence could dissolve the spirit of belligerence, that the silver bullet against hate is not bombs, but love. Was he right?

Mohandas K. Gandhi was one of the most famous religious leaders of the twentieth century. Gandhi made non-violence an effective technique in the modern world when so many critics thought he could not. This non-violence he dubbed *satyagraha* which he interpreted as "truth-force" or "soul-force", because he believed that the force of truth and love in politics would far outlast brute force. Rebellion by non-violence was more permanent, more lasting in Gandhi's view. What was gained by the sword could easily be taken back by the sword, but what was established on principles of truth and justice might be held and prized forever. Only non-violence could point to truth, in Gandhi's view, and a generation later another famous apostle of non-violence, Martin Luther

King Jr., made the technique of non-violence work in the United States. But sadly attention has shifted from the tactics and philosophy of Gandhi and King to those of Osama Bin Laden. Can non-violence respond to Bin Laden? Can non-violence respond to terror? If so, how?

Bin Laden's tactics of terror have cast a fell shadow on the geopolitical landscape. They seem also to have eclipsed the memory of a far nobler man and movement: Mohandas K. Gandhi. It is scarcely imaginable that the tactics of non-violence could be applied to realize a peaceful solution to political problems today, especially in the Middle East. Why is this? Is there something fundamentally different about the life and times of Mohandas Gandhi that produced a different type of person, a different type of believer, and a different context for political conflicts? Is there any chance in the future that religious movements aligned with peace could become more prevalent? These are dark and troubling times of strife for the peoples of the Abrahamic faiths — Judaism, Christianity, and Islam. Gandhi was a Hindu, and Bin Laden claims to be a Muslim. In Gandhi's own non-violent movement there were Muslims who befriended and worked with him. Can we move from these troubled times to a future illumined by a brighter and bolder religious and philosophical truth? It is hoped that we can.

Why write a book on the topic of Mohandas Gandhi and Osama bin Laden? Wouldn't such a book ultimately be comparing apples to oranges? What person could be further polarized from the Mahatma than Osama bin Laden? The fascinating conundrum here is that both of these men have been dominant leaders of political movements who claimed to be inspired by religious motivations. While one represented what many would consider to be good and admirable in the domain of religion and politics, the other is infamous for the most horrifying event that shocked Americans of the early twenty-first century.

In spite of some obvious and exceptional differences, there are distinct similarities that both Gandhi and bin Laden share. Both men were (or currently are) leaders of developing world protests against the powers of the developed world and their perceived allies. The essence and intent of Gandhi's call for *swaraj* or independence differs significantly from bin Laden's fight for *jihad*. Gandhi called for peace, and Bin Laden called for killing. It cannot be denied, however, that both Gandhi and bin Laden have had huge impacts upon religion and politics, and have set the constellations of developing eastern powers against the will and dominance of the west. Towards that end, both men in their respective times made use of religious motives to mobilize large groups of people to aid their cause. The followers of both men, additionally, have been willing to put their lives on the line or to give them up entirely. Gandhi called upon an army of *satyagrahis* (or non-violent resistors) to appeal to the conscience of their British and South African oppressors in order to effect political change and independence. Gandhi wished harm to no one, and he often fasted in repentance when his non-violent strategies went awry. Conversely, bin Laden has been able to train small cells of terrorist and suicide bombers to strike targets internationally. These "jihadists"[1] seek with full intent to harm their enemy and assure their own death in the process. Bin Laden demonstrates no remorse, but only glorifies these sacrifices.

Gandhi's *satyagrahis* differ markedly from these "jihadists" in that they intend to cause no harm (only disorder) and have at least the hopes of escaping with their lives and possibly also their liberties. They have a chance to see their cause for justice realized, here and now. Truth and justice seem to shine from their soul and their employment of "soul force" sets them apart. Yet a dark cloud of almost impenetrable psychological frustration, rage and hatred consumes the suicide bomber. The suicide bomber has no hopes of escaping with his or her life intact, only the zealous religious promise of a life in the hereafter. The suicide bomber has every expectation of being killed and of killing. Both non-violent resistors and suicide bombers are akin in their willingness to lay everything on the line, to push religion and politics to their limits. And by doing so, they have in respectively dissimilar ways had tremendous impact on the course of our history. For better and for worse, both have risked everything and made their mark.

Here we must pause for a moment for some clarification of terms. Just what do I mean by the terms "satyagrahis" and "jihadists"? Gandhi was proud of resisting non-violently, but did not like the connotations of passivity that might be imparted to his movement. Gandhi believed his non-violence did most emphatically resist. He decided to hold a contest (through his newspaper, the *Indian Opinion*) to find a name for his methods of non-violent resistance, and from the prizewinner of the contest he derived the term "satyagraha."[2] This word is formed from a combination of "satya", meaning "truth" or "love", and "agraha" meaning firmness or force. Gandhi resisted with the force of truth and the soul, not with arms or armaments. He presented his oppressors with a clearly stated case for justice (he even informed them of his civil disobedience in advance and in writing), and an adamant will to endure whatever injury or hardship was necessary in pursuit of that cause. Doing so, he hoped to hit his opponent's moral conscience with the force of his soul. Applying the force of the soul and truth to the conscience, Gandhi hoped not to conquer his enemies, but to convert them to his way of thinking. Gandhi wrote that satyagraha "is the vindication of truth not by infliction of suffering on the opponent, but on one's self." He was phenomenally successful at this — not without problems, lapses, or frustrations — but he was able to persuade by the force of his rebellious good will without inflicting violence. Non-violent disobedience was Gandhi's cause and triumph.[3]

Bin Laden, oppositely, was not an innovator of the concept of jihad. He has been seen by many to have perverted, abused, and misused the concept, but he did not invent "jihad", nor did he pioneer suicide bombing.[4] Jihad as a concept predates bin Laden by centuries, dating back to the Prophet Muhammad himself. Jihad has been interpreted in various ways. The term itself means something like "struggle" or "exertion." This struggle can be internal or external in nature. It has sometimes been divided into the concept of "Greater Jihad", which was the contest of internal will to become a better Muslim, and "Lesser Jihad", which by contrast was the military defense of Islamic territories. The Prophet Muhammad reportedly once came back from a military campaign defending Islamic territory and said that he had come from the pursuit of Lesser to Greater Jihad. At least one classically accepted interpretation of Jihad therefore implies that the moral exertion to be a better Muslim, a more moral person, was superior to that of using force of arms to defend the lands.[5] Muslims throughout history have made use of jihad, but it does not automatically carry connotations of violence, as many may think.

John Esposito and Karen Armstrong, amongst others, have defended Islam from its detractors by arguing that it is not an inherently belligerent religion and that it has in common with Christianity and Judaism the pursuit of a better life, a better morality, and a more just society. There are prohibitions in Islam against killing civilians and against murder. Terrorism and murder are generally prohibited.[6] A vast number of Muslims have come out and denounced the tactics of violence by those who practice violent jihad. Recent polls of Muslims conducted globally found only 7% who considered the 9-11 attacks to be justified, and an even smaller fraction of that percent is actually involved in terror tactics themselves.[7] Many Muslims, therefore, and many scholars of Islam, do not see that it has the militant characteristics that radicals impart to it. Yet these radicals have indeed hijacked Islam. They have taken the term "jihad" to a place of darker meaning. The radical agitators who see no life as sacred and who have been willing to sacrifice innocents, have imbued the term jihad with a bloody stain that cannot readily be removed. "Jihadists" in this sense, are indeed those who perverted Islam, and through terrorism and suicide attacks done violence to their tradition inasmuch as they have done violence to others. Islam can reclaim for itself the advocacy of peace and tolerance, but to do so it will certainly take the exertion of a great amount of "soul force." Satyagraha then, is perhaps not dead, but just waiting for a new time and place. There are countless non-violent Muslims the world over, in the United States, and abroad. The battle they face to reclaim their tradition from the extremist agitators who have attempted to hijack it is one which must be aided by Christians, by Jews, and by Hindus, who have wrestled with radical problems in their own religions.

Bin Laden and the Roots of Jihadism

The comparison of Gandhi with Bin Laden is a striking mix of similarity and stark contrasts, a myriad of puzzling questions about our human nature, our politics, and our concept and use of religion. Why is it some have been captivated by the forces of religious civil disobedience, while others are prepossessed by a dark religious rage? The answer cannot be as simple as that we are dealing with a different religion. In short, we cannot posit that Christianity and Hinduism are conducive to non-violence, and that Islam is not, because counter-examples are easily furnished to disprove this. In Gandhi's own camp he had non-violent Muslim allies, and today there are countless peaceful Muslims all over the world. We know also that there have been militant Hindus, Jews, and Christians. Gandhi himself was shot by a militant Hindu. In his own time, Gandhi wrestled with Hindus who killed Muslims, and Muslims who murdered Hindus. History is also replete with countless examples of self-proclaimed

Christians who assaulted or oppressed Jews, Muslims, or other non-Christians. Charles Kimball has pointed out that it is not so much the phenomenon of religion itself that is to blame, as it is particular characteristics that may develop within a religion. When a religion becomes absolutist, commands blind obedience, and uses any end to justify the means, Kimball believes religion as we know it becomes tainted and evil.[8]

Osama bin Laden displays many of the characteristics of religion that has become consumed by evil. Since the time of the first Gulf War and his estrangement from the Saudi elite, Osama bin Laden has become ever more radicalized in his opposition to western powers, and what he perceived to be apostate Muslim governments that were friendly to or allied with these powers. Seeing this in terms of a "Zionist Crusader alliance" which imposed an "occupation of the land of the two Holy Places" (namely, his native Saudi Arabia), bin Laden declared a Jihad against Americans in 1996 for this affront. Those Muslims who martyred themselves in this cause would receive "forgiveness with the first gush of blood" and were promised a union with seventy-two pure and beautiful "Houries" or virgins in the immediate afterlife.[9]

Standing a long-term prohibition against suicide upon its head, bin Laden has been careful never to declare sponsorship of "suicide bombings", because suicide is forbidden in Islam. The Qur'an itself condemns suicide, creating the need for those who sponsor these acts to always couch them in terms of sacrifice or martyrdom. Hamas, in sponsoring "martyrdom" (i.e. suicide) attacks against Israel has also defended "martyrdom" operations, drawing both support and criticism from the Muslim world. Indeed, the political conflict of the Palestinians with Israel was central to the genesis of modern suicide strikes.[10] The attacks on US and French barracks in Beirut of 1983 were a precursor of worse things yet to come. Violence is indeed cyclical, and more violence invites more retaliation. Gandhi and King understood this well, but jihadists seem to invite and count upon this logic for their success. The more violence, the more unstable things become, the greater the chance they have to tip the scales in their favor.

Bin Laden, however, has taken the conflict beyond Israel, and beyond Afghanistan, where he assisted the *mujahideen* in their struggle against Soviet occupation. The historical irony is that in that moment he was backing the same side as the United States (which is not to say that he was our immediate ally or sponsor), and since then he has become our greatest enemy. In 1998 bin Laden went a step further in his war against his enemies in the west and at home. Radicalized by his partnership with Ayman al-Zawahiri, and using the justification of the US occupation and dominance in Saudi Arabia, bin Laden pronounced it a duty to kill Americans. These words, ignored by too many at the time, spelled out a grim future and morbid determination:

> In the name of Allah, we call upon every Muslim, who believes in Allah and asks for forgiveness, to abide by Allah's order by killing Americans and stealing their money anywhere, anytime, and wherever possible. We also call upon Muslim scholars, their faithful leaders, young believers and soldiers to launch a raid on the American soldiers of Satan and their allies of the Devil.[11]

It was a brazen and sweeping injunction, a *fatwa* to kill Americans — both civilians and soldiers, anywhere, at any time. While it was ignored or rejected by many good and pious Muslims, by a radicalized and determined faction it was accepted, and plans were made to carry it out. Former counter-terrorism White House official Richard Clarke was alarmed and wanted to make a more immediate and aggressive response to the Al-Qaeda threat. Clarke has written books and spent a great deal of time telling us that this threat was tragically mishandled and overlooked. Instead of keeping the conflict in Afghanistan and making a full press against Al-Qaeda, he believes we have misdirected and squandered our resources in Iraq.[12] Meanwhile, Osama bin Laden is still alive; his last most potent ally was the (now deceased) Abu Musab al-Zarqawi in Iraq. If Al-Qaeda was not there before the war, it certainly became popular in response to the war. After Zarqawi's death the profile of Al-Qaeda in Iraq seems to have diminished, however. Where it stands at the moment of this publication cannot be foreseen.

Saddam Hussein was indeed a terrible dictator, though he was never a proven ally of Al-Qaeda, and never issued a *fatwa* to kill Americans, as bin Laden openly did. John Kelsay illustrates how Saddam used appeals to Islam and the issue of the Palestinians in Israel to justify his cause in the first Gulf War, against Bush senior. Saddam's rhetoric appealed for new leadership of the Arab world, a replacement for Nasser or the rebirth of Saladin.[13] Yet he never was so brazen to declare indiscriminant attacks upon American soldiers or civilians anywhere. Bin Laden did, and added the level of theological arrogance to suggest that this was "Allah's order" by which all faithful Muslim should abide. We recall Kimball's warning that claims to interpretations of absolute truth and unquestioned obedience are a sign of evil religion.

Many Islamic radicals do not and cannot view it in these terms, however. They are convinced of following an absolute truth. Living outside the tradition of a liberal western education, under adverse circumstances marked by an oppressive lack of democratic freedom, many find solace in the ideological education of radicalized *madrassas*, or Islamic seminaries. Here the teachings make them very receptive to extremes of religion and politics. They do not necessarily serve the Wahhabi doctrine of Saudi Arabia, though that is a significant contributor to radicalism, nor are they necessarily confined to the region from Egypt to Saudi Arabia and Iran. Ahmed Rashid observes these potentially explosive and oppressive political and economic conditions in the former Soviet Republics of Central Asia.[14] The region of Muslim discontent stretches all the way to Uzbekistan, a former republic of the Soviet Army.

What has caused this discontent? In part, it is a legacy of neo-colonialism and empire. The French and British had occupied territories throughout the Middle East, and when the US rose to dominance after World War Two we inherited in our sphere of influence and interest many of the burdens of their legacy. Truman's affirmation of support for the nascent nation of Israel was a significant milestone of the transition of power brokering in the area to the US. As an unintended consequence, the later burden and focus of Islamist hatred has shifted towards us. Our sponsorship of Israel has been controversial to radical jihadists. The United States has also sponsored unpopular regimes in Iran, such as the former Shah. The rebellion against the Shah there led to the ascendancy of the Ayatollah Khomeini and the birth of modern Shiite radicalism. Additionally, the first Arab leader to make an historic peace, Anwar Sadat, was assassinated for his actions.

The climate of discontent in the Middle East is not newly formed, but was brewing and waiting only for critical conditions, the end of the Cold War, to come to a boil. The end of Soviet imperialism in Central Asia is also another critical factor. It was on the battlegrounds of Afghanistan that Osama bin Laden received his first immersion into the practice of jihad. Figuring Muslim fighters were successful in ousting the Soviet Union from its seat in Kabul, bin Laden may have expected similar victory in Iraq. In the Islamic world there are some reasonable grounds for discontent with the United States, Europe and Russia, because of our actual and perceived support for regimes that have been brutal and oppressive to Muslims. Yet it may also even be simpler than this. Giants in any field with high and mighty profiles attract the ire and attention of all those with perceived problems, whether in fact the problems may be the giant's fault exclusively, or at best irrelevant or tangential to the giant's presence. And when there is a problem, the plea to solve it sticks to the giant, whether he caused it or not. Willing or no, we are also here because of our size, salience, and influence in foreign affairs, as well as our real and perceived blunders in politics.

This has become quite a swampy quagmire from which to extricate ourselves. The swamps of terrorism are in part bred by conditions of oppression and discontent, and fostered also by radical theologies born in response to modern times. Noam Chomsky has observed that to further the politics of peace, we must reduce the regions where festering problems of radical religion and politics may be born. To paraphrase his analogy, draining the swamp (of political problems) will reduce the level of mosquitoes (terrorists) bred by it. This has been and still is our greatest challenge, which has not been crowned with success. Far from having depleted or drained these swamps that may be a breeding ground for radicalism, it seems the swamp is still too full.[15]

Poverty and extreme circumstances are not, however, the major or only developmental causes of these radical jihadists. Muhammad Atta, member of the 9-11 attacks that flew the plane into the World Trade Center was not at all terribly impoverished. Nor were many of his conspirators. Osama bin Laden himself comes from circumstances of great wealth (although claims of his wealth have been greatly exaggerated in the past), yet he has exchanged a life of comparative luxury for one of subterranean revolt. This is perhaps one of his most charismatic features that appeal to disgruntled Muslims — an apparent ascetic devotion to his cause. Gandhi appealed to many also because of his asceticism and solidarity with the poor and oppressed, but the quality of his asceticism is of course of a very different nature. Bin Laden may yet have financial resources in reserve (scholars and intelligence experts disagree about how much), but we cannot stipulate that it was extreme material circumstances that drove him to this path of jihad against his enemies. So the phenomenon of "jihad" runs deeper than poverty or oppression. It runs right to the heart of the human psyche and its conception and use of religion and ideology.

Poverty itself cannot force a person to choose extremism, for that choice always lies partially in the will. Contexts and social environments can pressure and persuade a person to commit violence in the name of religion, as both Jessica Stern and Mark Juergensmeyer have shown us. The profiles of those who commit violence in the name of religion are many, but their feeling of being right in their cause is consistent.[16]

Islamic radicalism is also born of a growing belief by radicals that their religion has been abandoned and neglected in modern times. The dominance of the secular West, the legacy of neocolonialism, whether European or Soviet, is likely a serious factor here. In wide parts of the Islamic world, it is often the concept of a "neglected duty" of preserving the lands and religion of Islam that radicals have used to fuel their hatred of us. This duty is the perception that the rulers of Islamic countries, from Egypt to Saudi Arabia, to Iran, were in negligence of keeping the full spirit of *sharia* or Islamic law, and that because of this, the Muslim world has gone into comparative decline, contrasted to the West. Seeing their rulers as apostates and enemies, the war of the jihadists is an internal one against their own leadership and fellow countrymen as much as it is against the West or Israel. The crisis we are facing in the Arab-Muslim world has been long in the making, and one root of the Sunni strain of it began with Sayyid Qutb, one of the forerunners of modern extremism in Egypt. Qutb (1906-66), unlike bin Laden, had visited the United States and was repulsed by its values. His writings and his agitation in Egypt are part of the roots of radicalism today.[17] Qutb delivered a sweeping injunction that all those who did not hearken back to a strict interpretation of Islam were in a state of *jahiliyyah* (ignorance) of true Islamic principles. This has created not only a rejection of the West, but also some dissent and division within the Islamic world over who or who is not a true Muslim.[18] Qutb does not speak for all Muslims, but for a small minority, such as the 7% who accepted the 9-11 attacks, he may be very influential.

Bin Laden reportedly met Qutb's brother Muhammad when he went to school at King Abdulaziz University.[19] He also met there Abdullah Azzam, with whom he would go to Afghanistan and aid the *mujahideen* against the Soviets. Debates exist as to how involved he was in the actual fighting there. Videos of course show bin Laden firing and brandishing an AK47, but his initial role seems to be more one of leadership and organization of a radical Muslim group than of direct combat participation. Undergoing a radical transformation between his Afghan years and his return to Saudi Arabia (which we will further explore), bin Laden has become a figurehead of the jihadist movement, a Che Guevara for causes radical, Islamic, and scarred by violence.

But is this really Islam? Does bin Laden's belief in his own cause as "genuinely Muslim" give him any real claim to be called one, or even to be referred to as "religious"? It is clear a vast number of Muslims would categorically reject his claim to be a Muslim and see him as a fringe terrorist. Fareed Zakaria once called Islamic radicalism "politics wrapped in the mantle of Islam." Whether bin Laden is or is not a "true Muslim" and what the meaning of true Islam is cannot be settled here. What can be asserted, and what is important for this study, is his use of Islam to further his Jihadist cause, and how that use and characterization affects our perception of religion and our own pursuit of a greater peace.

Many evil things have been done in the name of religion. Ludwig Feuerbach once wrote, "Wherever morality is based upon theology, wherever the right is made dependent on divine authority, the most immoral, unjust, infamous things can be established."[20] Feuerbach was writing foremost about Christianity in the nineteenth century, but over a century later, we see bin Laden falling into the trap of justifying great horrors in the name of religion. Is religion itself — that is all religions — to blame as a negative influence on the human psyche? Charles Kimball points out that while there are problems in most all the world religions, we should not reify the problem in religion too much. That is we should not fool ourselves into thinking that religion is something acting externally and independently from us. Seeing the problem in "religion" as an abstract, removed and alien force neglects to remember that religion is itself a product of our own beliefs and mental activities. Quoting the Jewish scholar Abraham Heschel, who notes that "no religion is an Island"[21], we must understand that religion is a product that is socially constructed, much as our own identities are. Like us, religion is open to good and bad influences, and to change.

The truth of the matter is that the Arab Muslim world is in a period of crisis right now, and militant agitators have indeed radicalized receptive Muslims for their own purposes. The Arab Muslim world faces a complex mix of difficulties that include its problematic relation with Israel, its relation to its own sometimes brutal leadership, and its struggle to either admit or reject the hegemony of modern Western influence, values, and politics. Facing a coming of age and a new era, many Muslims themselves must decide how they wish to make or remake their own tradition, and the radical segments that have followed bin Laden wish to say an emphatic no to tolerance, inclusive religion, and non-violence. This is a disturbing trend, for Gandhi himself embodied those values to his last days. He would have been greatly pained to see the events of this day. Why was Gandhi able to see his way to peace, while others today and even in his own time, were so captivated by the implements of war?

Gandhi and Non-Violence: a Sharp Contrast

Mohandas Gandhi seems as unlike bin Laden as you could possibly imagine. Yet, like bin Laden, he was inspired by religion to pursue a cause he perceived to be just. The nature and methods by which he wished to secure that independence were different. Gandhi's campaigns were largely bound by the politics and oppression he saw in the nations of South Africa and India. His goals were clear in both contexts: rights for colored Hindus and Muslims under the apartheid of South Africa, and political independence in India. As such, his enemies were typically governments and institutions that upheld governmental policies. Bin Laden's gripe is not purely with the western world. It has been as much a contest for control of Arab-Muslim governments in countries such as Saudi Arabia and Afghanistan. In reading his demands and deciphering his intents, his goals to restore the glory of Islam are seldom very realistic or practical, yet they have a broad appeal to radicals as if they were so. Gandhi and Bin Laden both maintained that there is a very close relationship of religion and politics, which may make westerners uncomfortable who are accustomed to church-state separation.

In fact, for Gandhi, morality, religion, and politics were all necessarily interconnected. Establishing these connections, he wrote: "True religion and true morality are inseparably bound up with each other. Religion is to morality what water is to the seed that is sown in the soil."[22] Further, he wrote: "For me, there is no politics without religion — not the religion of the superstitious and the blind, religion that hates and fights, but the universal Religion of Toleration. Politics without morality is a thing to be avoided."[23] Religion was closely associated with morality in Gandhi's view, and political reform: "Religion which takes no account of practical affairs and does not help solve them is not religion."[24]

Gandhi's religion was non-violent "truth-force", the power of *satyagraha* to effect political change through the human conscience by the hand of willful disobedience and challenge. But Gandhi sought no ultimate victory of one religion over another; rather he was always adamant that tolerance and harmony of all peoples and religions result in a united and free India. His dream was only partially realized in that freedom of India from British rule became a reality. Gandhi did not, however, win his dream of an India united in Hindu and Muslim brotherhood. Muhammad Ali Jinnah had pushed hard for minority rights of Muslims and a separate electorate, and Gandhi was not able to win the hearts of a sufficient number of Muslim leaders to his cause. Pakistan became a reality.

When India won its Independence with partition into India and Pakistan, Gandhi did not celebrate. He was crushed that his message of tolerance and inclusiveness did not show in the hearts of his compatriots. Seeing the subsequent acrimonious conflict that has marred India-Pakistan relations, one could only wish he might have had more success in pushing his dream of unity. Now India and Pakistan stand as powers bitterly opposed, conflicting over the territory of Kashmir, each armed and threatening with nuclear capabilities at their command. If Gandhi had indeed had his way (he was a leader, but never a formal statesman) India would have abandoned the pursuit of armed forces altogether. Bin Laden, by contrast, has openly declared his interest in acquiring Weapons of Mass Destruction and a willingness to use them. How one wonders at the diversity of beliefs that can be exhibited by our human mind!

Gandhi once proclaimed great confidence in his vision of a more tolerant and open-minded future:

> The time has now passed when the followers of one religion can stand and say, ours is the only true religion and all others are false. The growing spirit of toleration towards all religions is a happy augury of the future.[25]

Yet his "happy augury" of the future has not come to pass, nor has inclusiveness and non-violence reigned supreme. Contrast Gandhi's above statement with the one we witnessed before from bin Laden:

> In the name of Allah, we call upon every Muslim, who believes in Allah and asks for forgiveness, to abide by Allah's order by killing Americans and stealing their money anywhere, anytime, and wherever possible. We also call upon Muslim scholars, their faithful leaders, young believers and soldiers to launch a raid on the American soldiers of Satan and their allies of the Devil.[26]

Bin Laden, and the jihadists like him, portray this war as a zero-sum contest of the just and the unjust: the forces of Allah, and those of the devil. Muslim radicals in the past have tended to see any who disagree with them as being in a state of *jahiliyyah*, or the state of ignorance of Islam. Dating from centuries past, the concept of jahiliyyah has been expounded upon and changed, much as the term jihad has. Sayyid Qutb (as reviewed earlier) in fact was one of those who applied the term to the modern West as a territory unenlightened and clouded by this ignorance.[27] Bin Laden has built upon the jihadist legacy and sees the West and its allies in not dissimilar terms. A line is drawn in the sand with this mode of thinking, one that separates us from them. How completely unlike the Mahatma it is. In an era where we have only increased access to the implements of mass destruction, we must encourage the values of men like Gandhi, while discouraging the popularity of bin Laden.

WMD in the Wrong Hands

Let me deepen the crux of this comparison by asking provocative questions: if a weapon of mass destruction were to be lost or unaccounted for, in whose custody would you rather it be found? Mohandas Gandhi or Osama bin Laden? Also — is the Muslim world ripe or receptive to the approach of non-violence? If this answer is no, or it is uncertain, we must explore it. If yes, why should that surprise us? Certainly, we would much rather foster the emergence of another Gandhi in the Muslim world than another Bin Laden. And the Muslim World has produced non-violent advocates. Abdul Ghaffar Khan, a friend and ally of Gandhi, was one very important non-violent Muslim of the past century. This book will conclude with a look at him. But today there is still profound uncertainty and ignorance in the Judeo-Christian world about the temper and problems of religion in Islam.

It is of paramount importance, then, to comparatively understand not only the disposition of these two extremely different men, but also the political and religious climate that produced them. Indeed we *must* seek to understand them, for in failing to do so, we only fall into the trap of a militaristic duel with the forces of nihilism and death; we strike, they strike back, and on ad-infinitum.

As I write these words we are already in that duel. Our armed forces have invaded Iraq and removed a brutal dictator from power, who has been tried and executed. It was thought that we would be greeted as liberators, but our popularity has waxed and waned, and it is not guaranteed to last indefinitely. Even if a majority of Iraqis welcomed our arrival, an extremely militant and dangerous minority has made our stay there a brutal and bloody enterprise. The travesty of the war is that it is an embarrassment to us and to the world because it was conducted on partially false pretexts. The weapons of mass destruction that were thought to be there by US and European intelligence agencies were not in fact there. We were sold on the fact that Iraq harbored WMD and Al-Qaeda agents before the war, when in fact Al-Qaeda agents moved in after we occupied the territory. Some have feared and speculated that Iraq might be another Vietnam, an endless fight that drains our resources and morale. From Al-Qaeda's point of view, the more correct analogy would be Afghanistan. They hope to do to us in Iraq what the *mujahideen* were able to do to the Soviets. Whether one supported or did not support the war in the first place, we as Americans must work together for the best solution to this difficult quagmire.

Both the US military and the forces of Gandhi's non-violent *satyagrahis* would find it a difficult task to respond to a covert enemy, which strikes in seemingly random and unpredictable places. We are not helpless against the tactics of terror, but we fight a difficult contest; the asymmetrical balance of power between our military and the terrorists forces them to use unconventional methods, much as Gandhi and King were forced to novel methods when faced with an overwhelming opponent. Would that the Islamic militants had only chosen the non-violent tactics of Gandhi, our conflict would have been significantly less bloody. The context and preconditions for such a non-violent rebellion seem conspicuously absent, however, and one can only foresee in the near future a daunting challenge that we must face. As of yet, no WMD has been recovered and used by terrorists, but that is not impossible.

The US and former Soviet Union, amongst other nations, have manufactured thousands of nuclear warheads and researched and/or produced chemical and biological weapons. While many of these weapons have been dismantled or destroyed, many more exist. Pakistan and India possess nuclear technologies, and some of these technologies have been sold to those willing to pay by A.Q Khan. Iran now courts the potential to make such weapons. So preoccupied we were with WMD in Iraq, we missed and were unable to thwart these transactions. The basic concepts, if not the blueprints for WMD, are available to those willing to do the research. Yet if the understanding how to build weapons of mass destruction is not too difficult to acquire, mastering the resources and tools to build them is fortunately not so easy. An invention once made, however, cannot be willed into the nether. It becomes a part of our human repertoire of knowledge, much as an evolved organ is part of our bodies.[28] The fact is that WMD exist, we the developed western powers have had a pioneering role in developing them, and we have therefore incurred a special responsibility to try to assure that they are not in fact used.

For decades, the nuclear non-proliferation treaty has attempted to keep the nuclear club limited to those who already possess the technology. Realizing that the further spread of these weapons is antithetical to the interests of safety, we have tried to prevent further nations from acquiring them. Yet this very fact creates an asymmetrical power imbalance that, in part, exacerbates their drive and desire to possess the same weapons. Because of our political, economic, and military hegemony and tense relationships, we unintentionally push extremists to use more desperate measures to hurt us. It would be irresponsible to suggest that the answer to this problem is to do away with a ban on the weapons, but it is a consummate responsibility now that we try to take a serious interest in the geopolitical climate that might cause certain parties or factions to have an increased need or desire to possess and use WMD. We have to persuade them that we are benevolent custodians of WMD ourselves if we are to dissuade them from developing those weapons for themselves. That, in any realistic assessment, will not be easy.

The crisis of our times is that the tools of WMD that we have invented, the very implements of our empire, may well be seized and used against us if we do not understand how to A) keep them secure and in safe hands, and B) better understand and transform the religious and political climate that either encourages or discourages their use. Technology has amplified our ability to create, and to destroy. If we lack the moral and spiritual temper to handle responsibly the forces of science and nature that we have unleashed, then we will be harmed by them. Unlike the optimism of the nineteenth century, the twentieth has shown us that progress (especially moral progress) is not an inevitable or inexorable fact of nature. If anything, we should have learned by now that the pursuit of good values is always in delicate hands: our own. In our negligence we too readily shatter the values which should be so precious to us. A study of Gandhi and bin Laden should, with bold clarity, indicate the heights of nobility and the depths of moral depravity that we can either rise or sink to. Such a study of ourselves is never a purely abstract and theoretical work, for it must bring us face to face with the angels and beasts in ourselves.

Gandhi was not a perfect man. Bin Laden is admired by many, as are the "magnificent nineteen" who killed themselves and thousand of other men, women and children in the attacks of 9-11. Fifteen of those nineteen were Saudi citizens, like bin Laden himself. We must seek to understand Gandhi and his context, as well as bin Laden and his times. If Gandhi had ever come into possession of an atomic bomb, he probably would have guarded it in good conscience until he could be assured it was dismantled. If bin Laden were to come across WMD, or any of the hundreds or thousands that have pledged their allegiance to him, our imagination can easily fill in the gaps. Tom Clancy has woven yarns on similar explosive situations, but this cannot trivialize or fictionalize the reality of the problem. There is indeed still a "clear and present danger" but we should look to the strength of ideals inasmuch as the strength of arms for an answer.

As individuals, it often seems that there is not much we can do to influence or change our religious and political history. Religious zealots and political demagogues seem often to dominate the power centers of decision-making and influence. Nevertheless, we must also realize that it is the sum total of our moral actions, inactions, and interactions, which add up to the unfolding of history. History is human nature in motion, later filtered by human reflective interpreta-

What We Must Learn

tion upon this motion. We owe it to ourselves then to take time to reflect upon the extremes to which our religious dispositions can take us in politics.

What We Must Learn

The juxtaposition of Gandhi and Osama bin Laden should seem both odd and unsettling. The two men never could have met, as Gandhi died long before bin Laden was born. Gandhi was born in Gujarat, a northwestern province in India, in the year 1869. His father was in civil government, and a middle-caste Hindu. Gandhi was assassinated in 1948, a tragic disproof that those who do not live by the sword cannot die by it. Bin Laden was born in 1957 in Saudi Arabia to a wealthy family that would grow to the size of 54 brothers and sisters. His father had humble origins in the Hadramawt region of Yemen, but rose quickly to great prominence and wealth in the construction business. His father regularly served the royal Saudi family, and the two families could at one time be considered very close. The religious philosophies that both Gandhi and bin Laden came to believe in are almost completely antithetical. Gandhi is tolerant and inclusive, and bin Laden exclusive and violent. Furthermore, the adoption of terrorist tactics is psychologically a mutually exclusive option to non-violent resistance. One stands out in front of his oppressor and welcomes his blows. The other hides from the enemy and strikes unpredictably. The courage it takes to suffer punishment in the cause of justice makes the stealthy strikes of suicide bombers seem comparatively like cowardice, yet suicide bombers themselves are trained to see them as pious and glorious acts of martyrdom. Martin Luther King Jr.'s resistors attended workshops on nonviolence in Birmingham and were given cards bearing ten commandments of non-violent injunction.[29] Christian values played a prominent role in preparing them for non-violence, just as a bad hybrid of Islam is being used to prepare some jihadists for terrorism and suicide bombing. Both the satyagrahi or non-violent resistor and the suicide bomber must be trained for what they do. The leaders that train them and the contexts in which they are trained differ in the extreme.

Pushing the political climate towards the complete acceptance of non-violence runs contrary to the effort to destabilize political society by violence and terror. This is one reason why Martin Luther King Jr. came into conflict with black militants who advocated Black Power or preached eye-for-an-eye justice. King did not dissent with Malcolm X so much because of the violence he perpetrated; Malcolm as a Muslim perpetrated no violence. King dissented with the Black Power group and the militants because their ideology would have pushed the political climate in a direction opposite from the one he needed to secure the success of his own non-violent campaigns. Gandhi fasted in India when Muslims and Hindus broke out into outbursts of rioting and killing, in Calcutta and elsewhere. Non-violence has to have, as a prerequisite for success, a society that at least has a healthy enough morale, a moral conscience and stability to be able to respond to its demands. Violent acts serve to constantly agitate and destabilize. Like a couple arguing and hurling more insults at one another, it accelerates the fury and temper of the overall level of rage and distrust in society. For non-violence to be successfully applied in the Middle-East today, a vast gulf has to be crossed to find the social shores upon which such a movement would find firm grounding. As difficult as this may be, this chapter has pointed out that we must attempt to find that grounding and make possible the proliferation of the shores of peace by diminishing this sea of violence. Without such an effort, we ride the tumultuous waves on a risky and uncertain course.

How did Gandhi become the Mahatma? Why is he renowned for what he did? Conversely, what produced bin Laden and the polarizing religious philosophy he epitomizes? Understanding these questions is very difficult, and this work will help serve to understand these two personalities and the precursors of culture and experience that helped make them. Something will also be said about Martin Luther King Jr. and Abu Musab al-Zarqawi along the way. Having come to better grips with understanding Gandhi and bin Laden and the contexts that created them, we will have come closer to learning some of the things we must learn. One essential thing: Islam is not inherently violent, and can be a religion of peace. The life of Abdul Ghaffar Khan helps prove this. There will still be vexing questions that remain, namely — can we really consider Gandhi and bin Laden both to be religious persons? What meaning does the term religion have if one uses it to justify murderous actions and another insists that only by abandoning violence do we further our religious journey? Possessing the devastating technologies we have devised by our science in one hand and an extreme set of choices in religion in the other, we can imagine the ideals that we should approximate, but making our feet walk in that direction is difficult. Let us first ask the question: what path is it that Gandhi would have us follow?

Notes

1. Jihad, classically, does not of course refer to suicide bombers or acts of terror, and the use of the term "jihadist" will be explored shortly.

2. Michael Nojeim, *Gandhi and King: The Power of Nonviolent Resistance* (Westport Connecticut: Praeger Press, 2004), 94.

3. Louis Fischer, *Gandhi, His Life and Message for the World* (New York: Mentor Books/ New American Library, 1982), 35-36.

4. Suicide attacks have a long history. Rohan Gunaratna points out that in the Middle East, Imad Mughniyeh, who is believed to have engineered the 1983 attacks on marine barracks in Beirut, may have also helped bin Laden with his terror tactics. See Rohan Gunaratna *Inside Al Qaeda, Global Network of Terror*, (New York: Columbia University Press, 2002), 147-148.

5. John Esposito, *Unholy War: Terror in the Name of Islam* (New York: Oxford University Press, 2002), 26-28.

6. John Kelsay, *Islam and War, The Gulf War and Beyond: A Study in Comparative Ethics* (Louisville, Westminster John-Knox Press, 1993), 57-73.

7. John Esposito and Dalia Mogahed, *Who Speaks for Islam: What A Billion Muslims Really Think* (New York, Gallup Press, 2007), 70.

8. Charles Kimball, *When Religion Becomes Evil* (New York: *HarperSanFranciso*, 2002).

9. Robert O. Marlin IV, *What Does Al-Qaeda Want?* (Berkeley: North Atlantic Books, 2004), 2-3, 13-15.

10. Esposito, *Unholy War*, 99-100.

11. Peter L. Bergen, *Holy War Inc: Inside the Secret World of Osama bin Laden* (New York: The Free Press, 2001), 96.

12. Richard Clarke, *Against All Enemies, Inside America's War on Terror* (New York: Free Press 2004).

13. Kelsay, *Islam and War, The Gulf War and Beyond,* Chapter 1.

14. Ahmed Rashid, *Jihad: The Rise of Militant Islam in Central Asia* (New York: Penguin Books, 2002), 10-11, 66.

15. Noam Chomsky in Micah L. Sifry and Christopher Cerf *The Iraq War Reader: History, Documents, Opinion*, (New York Touchstone Books, 2003), 303.

16. Mark Juergensmeyer, *Terror in the Mind of God: the Global Rise of Religious Violence* (Berkley: University of California Press, 2001); Jessica Stern, *Terror in the Name of God: Why Religious Militants Kill* (New York: Harpercollins Publishers, 2003).

17. Karen Armstrong *The Battle for God: A History of Fundamentalism* (New York: Ballantine Books, 2001), 239-244.

18. Sayyid Qutb, *Milestones* (New York, Islamic Book Service, 2005), 8-12.

19. Gunaratna, *Inside Al-Qaeda*, 17.

20. Ludwig Feuerbach, *The Essence of Christianity*, translated by George Eliot (New York: Prometheus Books, 1989), 274.

21. Kimball, *When Religion Becomes Evil*, 25.

22. Mohandas K. Gandhi, *The Selected Works of Mahatma Gandhi*, ed. Shriman Narayan, Volume 6 (India: Ahmedabad, Navajivan Publishing House,1968), 264.

23. Gandhi, *The Selected Works*, vol. 6, 435.

24. Mohandas K. Gandhi, *My Religion* ed. Bharatan Kumarappa (India: Ahmedabad, Navajivan Publishing House, 1955), 3, 4.

25. Gandhi, *The Selected Works*, vol. 6, 272.

26. Bergen, *Holy War Inc.,* 96.

27. Esposito, *Unholy War*, 42, 59.

28. An observation once made by Konrad Lorenz in his book *On Aggression.* Human social and technical inventions acquire a permanency much like evolved organs of our body.

29. Martin Luther King Jr., *The Essential Writings and Speeches of Martin Luther King Jr.*, ed. James M. Washington, (New York: Harper Collins, 1986), 537.

Chapter 2: Gandhi — His Life

Gandhi: Early Experiments With Truth

What made Gandhi a "Great Soul"? At the time of his life there were approximately 300 million Indians under British Imperial rule. Why did he stand out from the rest? Why do we remember Mohandas Gandhi as the Mahatma? It is a title he was reluctant to accept, to be sure, as he always spoke freely and openly about his own faults, yet he was the "Great Soul", or "Mahatma", the pioneer of the non-violent technique in politics during a very violent century. Marked by two World Wars, a Holocaust of the Jews, and other very horrible attempts at genocide, the twentieth century was witness to an over-abundant share of brutal dictators, their atrocities, and savage wars. How was it that this lone, frail Hindu, scarcely five and a half feet tall and not much over a hundred pounds, could bring such a monumental and heart-felt impact upon a heartless world?

In an age where we have become preoccupied with the tactics of terror and how to respond to them, we should not forget Gandhi. Gandhi once asserted "[All] terrorism is bad whether put up in good cause or bad."[1] In sharp contrast, Osama bin Laden claimed ". . .not all terrorism is restrained or ill-advised. There is terrorism that is ill-advised and there is terrorism that is a good act."[2] It is objectively absurd to claim that there is "good terrorism" and "bad terrorism." The wisdom of Gandhi here cannot be questioned.

While Bin Laden may have dominated recent headlines, and while his tactics pose a significant challenge for Gandhi's non-violence, we must not be under the mistaken assumption that our era was "more violent" and Gandhi's less so. Gandhi made his techniques work in a time marked by as much belligerence as our own. There may be (and indeed I think there are) special circumstances in which non-violence becomes more plausible, but we must not forget the behemoth challenges faced by Gandhi and ask our question again: why is he the Mahatma? In order to understand, we must conduct a biographical overview of his life, to put his mind in the context of the times he was operating in.

Mohandas Karamchand Gandhi was born in the northwest province of Gujarat India on October 2nd, 1869. Gandhi's father and grandfather had occupied the position of a local minister of government, and by all accounts Gandhi came from a middle-class and middle-caste family. His father Karamchand had married four times, and Gandhi himself was the youngest child of the last marriage. Gandhi adored his father and mother. His mother Putlibai fasted frequently as a sign of Hindu devotion. This undoubtedly left an indelible imprint on Gandhi's mind. He would later use the fast multiple times to resolve political disputes non-violently.[3]

Gandhi's *Autobiography* is titled "My Experiments with Truth", as Gandhi considered himself to be one seeking-after truth. He claimed no monopoly on truth. Gandhi believed that for him "God was Truth" and that "I worship God as Truth only." But in his youth Gandhi did not display an unusually marked interest in religion and even at one point suggested doubts about religion. Gandhi was an unremarkable yet honest student who refused to cheat even when his instructors appeared to suggest it.[4]

What was in fact remarkable about Gandhi's early life is that he was a bit of a maverick. He was willing to challenge conventional opinions and to "experiment with truth", as he called it. From an early age, Gandhi refused to see why untouchables should be ostracized. He refused to spurn the untouchable named Uka, who came to clean the latrine. Gandhi said "I told my mother that she was entirely wrong in considering physical contact with Uka as sinful."[5] This attitude did not seem to emerge from a religious conception at the time (religious conscience emerged later for Gandhi), but from Gandhi's own intuitive feel for fair play and equality. If some of us were born unprejudiced or less prejudiced than our counterparts, Gandhi was one such special child.

Sheik Mehtab, a childhood friend of Gandhi, tried to convince him that it was acceptable to eat meat. His friend Mehtab was a superior athlete, and Gandhi admired that physical prowess. Mehtab convinced him that eating meat would make him strong like the British, their dominant imperial masters. Hence, Gandhi launched into one of his early experiments of eating meat, and later smoking cigarettes. His experiments would result in his having to steal coins from his brothers and his parents. These experiments were comparatively short-lived, as Gandhi's ever-pulsing moral conscience made him feel an overpowering guilt about his actions. He confessed his deviant sins to his father, who tearfully forgave him. These events are highly significant because they show that Gandhi, from childhood, was willing to dispense with religious or social norms or customs, but was also powerfully controlled by them as well. His experiments with eating meat and his refusal to recognize the sin of untouchability clearly indicate that Gandhi was not wholly bound by social or religious convention, but would not recklessly abandon it either. His personality as a progressive but conscientious youth was beginning to take shape. It seems he had mostly his parents to thank for the moral mold of his youth.[6]

During the time of Gandhi's youth, he would experience another great trauma: his child marriage to Kasturbai at the age of 13. Gandhi later declared that he was unready for such a marriage and made it quite public that he was very opposed to child marriages. Marriage should take place at a later age in his view, and the arranged child marriage practice should be discarded. Nonetheless, and despite his "jealous and authoritative" attitude towards his young wife, they would have a relatively stable and happy marriage for some 62 years. Kasturbai would be a faithful and dependable supporter in Gandhi's many trials and tribulations throughout the years and become a mother to his four children: Harilal, Manilal, Ramdas and Devadas.[7]

Mohandas would, however, be torn between the carnal passions of his wife and his duty to nursing his ailing father Karamchand. Gandhi had a deep love of his father, but also the lust of a young husband. Routinely he would massage his father to ameliorate his painful condition, but he turned over this duty to a relative when he felt especially desirous of Kasturbai. Once in his absence his father died shortly later, and the anguish over his not being there (due to sexual craving) left a clear mark on his mind.[8]

Gandhi's attitude toward sexuality became something which most of us would regard as complex, difficult, and ultimately ascetic. Unquestionably Gandhi had strong sexual appetites — he left four children behind, and once noted a dark moment of sexual temptation in Bombay. Gandhi's views about sex and sexuality became inextricable from his religious views and social commitments. He wrestled with his role as a father and a proponent of social justice. His own sons would complain of neglect as he was often away attending to his political and religious programs and not to his immediate family. This tension was most prominent with his eldest son Harilal.[9]

Once all his children were born and his commitment to public activism was complete, Gandhi would ultimately take an oath of *Brahmacharya,* (celibacy) in 1906. Gandhi observed once "A man or woman completely practicing Brahmacharya [Chastity] is absolutely free from passion. Such a one therefore lives nigh unto God, is Godlike."[10] Gandhi came to believe that renunciation of passions and of the fruit of passions was the hallmark of one most fully devoted to truth, to love, and non-violence. Steeped in his understanding of the *Bhagavad-Gita*, Gandhi would declare in his interpretation of that work: "The renunciation of the Gita is the acid test of faith." Selflessness necessitates mastery over the physical sense, the palate, and the sexual drives — all of it. For Gandhi, complete devotion to God could not be practiced without complete mastery of the self and all its passions, and it would become his life-long goal to attain that *moksha* or liberation.[11]

Gandhi's father passed away in 1895, and at this point he did not understand all these things. He wrestled with the passion for his wife and the devotion, love and duty toward his father, and the searing pain that it caused him to feel a conflict between the two. He understood that with his father gone, someone would have to support the family. Gandhi's father and grandfather had been local ministers to support the family, but in British India, that qualification was best filled by someone with an education. A friend of the family, Mavji Dave, had encouraged Gandhi to go get his education. Gandhi had wanted to go into medicine. Law was not his first career inclination, but Gandhi felt compelled to go.[12]

There would be a problem, however. Not just one problem, but at least two. The first was that Gandhi's mother was very reluctant to let him go. She regretted parting with her youngest son but also was concerned that in a foreign culture he would not be an observant Hindu. Putlibai dreaded seeing Gandhi come back as a man transformed and beyond recognition to the Hindu fold. His mother was not the only person concerned. Local members of Gandhi's own caste met and forbade him to go, believing that such a thing would put him beyond proper caste limits for Hinduism. Gandhi, stubborn and independent, seemed unperturbed by the threat of caste ostracism and was equally determined to go with or without their blessing.

His mother would be a more formidable one to assuage, however. It was agreed, with the help and advice of a Jain monk, Becharji Swami, that Gandhi would take an oath from that monk not to touch wine, women, or meat during his entire education in England. Having the vow administered was enough to appease his mother and to allow Gandhi to go to England, provided that he stuck to his word. Gandhi did stick to his word.[13]

This in itself, however, is a fascinating moment in Gandhi's life and suggests further his inclusive attitude and unorthodox views. First, Gandhi was willing without much hesitation to ostracize his social caste to pursue an education abroad. Second, he was willing to do so by taking religious vows from a Jain monk. Jainism is a kindred religion of Hinduism, having many of the same ideas, but also differing on some key concepts. To hazard a crude but creative analogy, a religious oath administered by a Jain monk to a Hindu might be comparable to a Baptist minister administering a Bar Mitzvah or an Orthodox Jew giving Communion bread to Lutherans. The analogy is not fully square or on-target, admittedly, but it demonstratively shows the inclusive conception of Gandhi's Hinduism and the essential inter-changeable nature of religious beliefs. Gandhi later espoused the idea that all religions are universally equal paths to God. It sets his character in complete contradistinction to radical Islamists such as Bin Laden.

On September 4, 1888, Gandhi set sail for England. He would be there for scarcely two years, and he had many and mixed reactions. But he was a far cry from the latter person who would come to be known as the Mahatma.[14]

Gandhi's Education in England

Arriving in England was of course a bit of a culture shock for Gandhi. He had never seen electric lights, and elevators were also new to him.[15] Overcoming the initial disorientation, Gandhi made a point of dressing as the English gentleman and even took dancing lessons. Later, of course, Gandhi would spurn this attire completely and insist upon only homespun or home woven cloth for Indians. But at this point in his life, Gandhi was not religiously developed in mind and had not even read the *Bhagavad-Gita*, his favorite Hindu scripture. Gandhi maintained in his *Autobiography* that "one thing took deep root in me: the conviction that morality is the basis of things, and that truth is the substance of all morality. Truth became my sole objective. It began to grow in magnitude every day, and my definition of it also has been ever widening."[16]

Gandhi had some interesting meetings. It was his contact with British Theosophists which primed again his interest in reading Hindu scriptures and who in fact introduced him to reading the *Bhagavad-Gita*. Gandhi became curious about the Theosophists and even met the movement's founder, Helena Blavatsky. It appears that the lasting effect of the Theosophists would be to invigorate Gandhi's interest in religion in general, as Gandhi would himself identify with the Gita in particular.[17] Gandhi would later say about the Gita: "The book struck me as one of priceless worth. The impression has ever since been growing on me with the result that I regard it today as the book *par excellence* for the knowledge of Truth."[18]

Gandhi had already had a strong sense of conscience and moral bearing, but he had yet to fully comprehend his own Hindu faith. Gandhi's visit to England and his emerging awareness set his religious journey in motion and would prepare him well for his latter campaigns of non-violent resistance.

Gandhi dressed as an Englishman and entertained English customs, but eventually his habits incurred expenses, and he adopted a very frugal, disciplined approach to his studies. On November 6, 1888, Gandhi was admitted as a law student in London and studied his law books in preparation for his exams. Gandhi's own records and those of his biographers show a subtle but significant shift from a man preoccupied with trying to play the English gentleman to the economizing, earnest student. He became a scrupulous accountant of his own finances, a skill that would serve him well in his later endeavors. Gandhi received funds from home to carry out his studies, and he managed to cut his expenses significantly.[19]

One problem had faced Gandhi as a vegetarian, and that was where to find a decent meal. He remained earnest about keeping the vows that he had taken for his mother. Gandhi soon found a vegetarian restaurant and also a book called the *Plea for Vegetarianism*. He was so impressed with the book that he would become a vegetarian by personal choice and from that moment he became active in local vegetarian societies.[20] It is significant that his vegetarianism began with a religious (and also pragmatic) vow to appease his mother and became further reinforced by secular forces as well as Gandhi's own emerging religious consciousness. The *Gita* and its lessons of renunciation, of Hindu *Brahmacharya*, would further reinforce what he thought was right and true.

Gandhi believed in no final, authoritative work that could not be questioned: "scriptures cannot transcend Reason and Truth. They are intended to purify Reason and illuminate Truth."[21] All his life Gandhi was searching for truth, which he increasingly identified as religious: "Often in my progress I have had faint glimpses of the Absolute Truth, God, and the daily conviction is growing upon me that He alone is real, and all else is unreal."[22] Gandhi came to his decisions by both religious and rational pursuits. He could in no way partition one from the other, and if he met a writer who supported a religious principle that made sense to him, his convictions deepened. During the continuum of this process, the rascally youth who experimented with smoking and stealing would later experiment with non-violence and risking his life for his beliefs. The childish adolescent matured gradually into a spiritual titan.

In England, Gandhi made some friends and acquaintances. He paid a visit to the newly built Eiffel Tower but thought it attracted men much like children to trinkets. He was more impressed by cathedrals such as Notre Dame. Gandhi's overall purpose was, however, to get a law degree, and he wasted no time once he completed his studies. Gandhi passed his exams, was called to the bar on June 10, 1891, admitted to High Court on June 11, and on June 12, he was on a ship bound for India.[23]

When Gandhi came back to India, he was told that his mother had passed away while he was in England. He had been spared the news to prevent shock while abroad, and now took it heavily. Gandhi returned to his wife and his growing son Harilal (then age four) and was faced with the prospect of making some money for the family. The problem was that he was not very skilled, and not at all confident as a lawyer. The education in England had told him about the trade, but he had no practical experience. The first small claims case that he took resulted in a terrible embarrassment. Gandhi found that he was too timid to speak out in court during the law proceeding and dismissed himself from the case. His family, and in particular his brother, Laxmidas, were not pleased that Mohandas was reaping little reward from his education. Embarrassment turned to further humiliation when Gandhi's brother Laxmidas asked him to intercede in a case set before a British political agent with whom Gandhi was acquainted. Gandhi went, reluctantly, but the British agent would hear nothing of Gandhi's appeals and had him forcibly removed from his office.[24]

Gandhi was no doubt frustrated with himself. He obtained some work drafting documents for other lawyers but remained somewhat of an embarrassment to himself and his family. Showing resolve to persevere, Gandhi was finally rewarded with an offer from a Muslim law firm to take a court case for one year in South Africa. The sum involved in the suit was £40,000, and Gandhi's annual pay would be £105. The terms seemed very reasonable and a great boon given his struggles in the law field. Gandhi accepted the offer and prepared to set sail for South Africa in 1893. Gandhi landed in May of 1893 planning to spend one year on the case. He would end up staying for 22 years and giving birth to the movement of non-violent *satyagraha*. Up to that point, Gandhi was merely a conscientious lawyer with a deepening moral sense and an obligation to provide for his family. The racial insults he would soon endure would force him into a chrysalis stage.[25] Gandhi had come to South Africa to be a supportive husband, but he would leave South Africa with revolutionary ideas.

Transformation in South Africa

Before South Africa, Gandhi had not personally experienced real racist treatment. He had been accustomed to trying to imitate British custom and dress and had at least received no direct condemnation on account of his nationality or skin color. South Africa was not London, and almost immediately, Gandhi began feeling the effects of the apartheid system in place. After disembarking in South Africa, Gandhi purchased a first class train ticket to Pretoria where his legal work awaited. It was not long before a racist white man noticed Gandhi traveling first class and called upon the train officials to remove Gandhi to third class, where the colored folk belonged, in his opinion. Gandhi protested strenuously, but to no avail. His objections only made matters worse, and his refusal to remove himself to third class seating resulted in him being forcibly removed from the train. Gandhi was thrust onto the lonely train-station platform at Maritzburg.

He was humiliated and angry. It was evening, and the increasing cold began to chill his bones. But it could not put out the outrage that burned within his heart or soothe the boiling anger of his mind. What was he going to do? He had come to South Africa to secure work, to try to better himself as a lawyer and to support his family. Now he was being told by the South African color bar that doing so would be very difficult. He considered retreat, backing out of the contract altogether, and going home to India. But he had come here to do a job, and his sense of honor and pride refused that. Sitting in the cold, and trying to cool his burning frustration, Gandhi concluded that the only possible thing he could do was to stay and resist. His resistance must be legitimate and must not be violent. As yet Gandhi had no clear understanding of *satyagraha*, the religious and philosophical pillar of nonviolence that would guide the rest of his life. He did, however, have an intuitive acceptance of that approach, and he would protest at first by all legitimate channels — newspapers, government, and public meetings. The night on the train station was a creative moment for Gandhi and became a solid milestone on his path towards embracing *satyagraha*.[26]

When Gandhi reached his destination, his employers conveyed to him how they were used to suffering the insults of the racial apartheid system. Looking the other way allowed them to focus on what business they could acquire in spite of it. Gandhi related: "They had therefore made it a principle to pocket insults as they might pocket cash."[27] Gandhi was a new face, however, not inured to the treatment and not inclined to become so. He therefore brought a fresh perspective and a fresh sense of moral outrage that would be invaluable to challenging the discrimination against dark-skinned residents of South Africa.

Indians of Muslim, Hindu, or Parsi background had been coming to South Africa for years as indentured laborers. After working off their debt of service as indentured workers, they could become free residents of South Africa. Yet South Africans were not willing or eager to tolerate free, colored residents and considered them some economic threat. Hence, there was put in place a number of laws to assure the supremacy of the tiny white minority amongst a much larger sea of darker skinned Africans, Indians, Asians and other non-European races.

Some have posited that economics is at root the cause or core of most problems. This is at least partially true, because economics in *some way* is related to all problems we as humans face. But it is false to say that all problems are reducible to economics. The apartheid that colored South Africans faced in Gandhi's day was partially due to economic threats, true, but then the apartheid was only directed at colored South Africans. If color hadn't mattered to them, there was no reason to introduce a color barrier. The economic reason is only partial, or at best an excuse to cover a grosser and all too-human problem: the human tendency to treat our own species as alien, as inferior, because they do not match up to an arbitrarily preferred subset of race, religion, ideals, or national character. It was simple prejudice, which fails to see the self in the human other and uses arbitrary means or justification to set up walls and put on shackles instead of breaking them down or taking them off.[28]

Consequently, the discrimination leveled against colored South Africans was clearly prejudiced on any rational analysis. It was intended to thwart free Indians from wanting to live in South Africa and to allow for only indentured labor to come and render cheap service to the whites and then leave. The £3 poll tax was a prime example. Every colored South African wishing to reside in South Africa was required to pay a tax of £3 per year per member of their household. Hence a family of four could be asked to pay a £12 poll tax. The sum of £3 at that time was roughly equivalent to six months of labor for an indentured laborer. Clearly the tax was written to impose a crippling burden on recently freed ex-indentured Indians or other Asians.

Gandhi helped to win the law case for Dada Abdalla, the client responsible for summoning his presence to South Africa. As he was prepared to leave South Africa in 1894, however, he read in the news of a new wave of repressive measures to be instituted against Indians and Asians. He agreed to stay in South Africa and help fight these repressive measures, provided that he was given some legal work to make a living. He accepted no pay for public work, as he called it, but insisted on carrying his own weight. This would be the first of many episodes in which Gandhi would be on the verge of leaving for India once again, only to have further injustice call him back to fight in South Africa.

Further measures were put forward to harass and further discourage Asians or Indians as permanent residents. In 1894, measures were put forward to disenfranchise colored Africans, and to force their registration and fingerprinting. It was clear to Gandhi that he would be in South Africa for a while, and in 1896, he returned to India to bring his family back with him. This must have been hard on Gandhi's children, having their father absent for so long. The oldest was ten and the youngest four, and Gandhi's attention was pulled away to politics and religion at this point. He later confessed that it was the chief grievance of his sons — his duty to justice and his people conflicted with and often overrode the duty to his immediate family. This burden weighed most heavily on Gandhi's oldest son, Harilal, and the two became estranged later in life. Gandhi said of Harilal, "His grievance against me has always been that I sacrificed him and his brothers on the altar of what I wrongly believed to be the public good."[29]

When Gandhi returned from India in 1896, he had written the "green pamphlet" (describing oppression in South Africa) on behalf of his cause, and it was by pure chance that a large group of several hundred free Indians were coming back with him. White South Africans perceived it as a threat and as an insult to their country. They awaited his return with vengeance planned. When Gandhi's ship arrived, the excuse of an outbreak of plague was used for quarantining his ship at port for some 23 days. Hostile crowds were gathering, and Gandhi was advised by Natal Attorney General Henry Escombe to disembark with caution and stealth and to send his family separately. Gandhi agreed to have his family disembark separately for their safety. A friendly white companion, Mr. F.A. Laughton, recommended against Gandhi's personal stealthy departure and volunteered to accompany him. Encouraged, Gandhi disembarked (on Jan. 13, 1897) with Mr. Laughton, but the two were soon assaulted by a small mob which grew steadily in size. Laughton and Gandhi were separated, and Gandhi received quite severe blows from the crowd. Thanks to the presence of the police superintendent's wife, Gandhi was escorted to safety under her protective status. The crowd did not readily depart, however, and Gandhi had to escape in the disguise of a police constable to ensure his safety.

Gandhi displayed pragmatic, good judgment here. While Gandhi often boasted that non-violence was better than cowardice, to present himself to the mob rage at that time might have spelled his death. Having arrived with a wife and children, he had them to think of also. What is most remarkable about the event is that despite the brutal severity of the attack, Gandhi refused to press charges against his assailants. He believed that a truly non-violent approach necessitated forgiveness.[30]

Gandhi was still referring to his cause as non-violent resistance, or passive resistance — words he didn't quite like. "Satyagraha", had not yet emerged. It is not clear at what point these ideas became explicitly religious in commitment, though they did clearly become so. Responding to the need of political reform, Gandhi reacted against the racism of his time because it was an affront to his moral conscience, his thoroughgoing honesty and pursuit of truth. His growing movement of resistance took on a force which would become at once political and religious.

The Boer War of 1899-1902 interrupted Gandhi's campaign of nonviolence. This was the first time Gandhi would volunteer to establish an ambulance corps. Unable to participate in fighting because of a vow of non-violence, Gandhi nonetheless refused to use wartime as an opportunity to take advantage of the British or any of their imperial holdings. To prove the case that he and his fellow Indians were worthy of full and equal rights, he thought that they had to behave as exemplary citizens themselves. It was a noble gesture not to take advantage of a political opponent when he was down, and it was one that frustrated many of his later allies. Nonetheless, it does seem to ring true to his religious and moral conscience.

At the end of the war, it appears Gandhi thought the repressive measures against Indians would be repealed, for he went home to India and began to prepare to open a law practice. It was not long, however, when news of new repressive measures resulted in yet another plea for him to return to South Africa. Gandhi was experiencing a pull from both sides of the Indian Ocean. Back home in India, his growing celebrity was increasing alliances and friends who needed him for reforms back home. Gandhi again traversed the Indian Ocean responding to his friends in need. It would be the next chapter of the evolving Mahatma.

The discriminatory measures taken by the Transvaal government under Jan Smuts only became worse. The Asiatic or so-called "Black Act" of 1906 would require all non-Europeans to come to register themselves, giving their fingerprints and taking out identity cards that they would be required to carry. It was a slap in the face, a measure that treated all Asians as if they were criminals, guilty before they had committed a crime. It gave birth to a whole new surge of outrage, and Gandhi led the opposition movement. The act would technically give police the right to enter homes in search of such passes for their wives, and one protestor violently declared: "If any one came forward to demand a certificate from my wife, I would shoot him on that spot and take the consequences."[31] It proved difficult, but possible, to tame such hot tempers that often flared up.

Gandhi negotiated. He often did so before he launched any movement of civil disobedience. Presenting his opponent (usually the government in question) with his problem in respectful but forceful language, he offered them a way to escape the coming campaign of resistance. Jan Smuts agreed to negotiate with Gandhi and offered to repeal the so-called "Black Act", if in fact the Indians and other Asians registered voluntarily. It was an odd compromise, but in the spirit of pushing forward, Gandhi agreed.

The Richard Attenborough film *Gandhi* vividly portrays a scene in which Gandhi is beaten for burning registration passes. While the film is accurate about many aspects of Gandhi's life and is overall a commendable work, this part is clearly fictionalized for dramatic purposes. It appears Gandhi was never beaten for burning registration certificates. In fact, what happened is that Gandhi volunteered to register himself and all other Asians if the government would voluntarily repeal the repressive "Black Act" requiring them to do so. Gandhi was actually beaten quite severely by a Pathan man and a few others for voluntarily registering himself. The Pathans had momentarily lost faith in Gandhi as a representative for their cause and thought he had sold them out to the government. The Pathan man, Mir Alam, later expressed his apology for beating Gandhi, and his confidence was restored. It is in fact an even more powerful testament to Gandhi's power as a non-violent leader, for Mir Alam had previously threatened Gandhi with death if he registered himself. Gandhi did so anyway because he was fulfilling his end of the bargain with the government.[32]

The Government, however, did not fulfill its end. After Gandhi had done his best to register all Indians and Asians, Jan Smuts breached his agreement with Gandhi and in fact introduced new repressive legislation. It was a bitter lesson in political betrayal for Gandhi; nonetheless, he remained true to his remarkable doctrine of trusting his political opponent. Gandhi had the difficult task of improving the morale of those who had put their trust in him but was effective in doing so. Gandhi had strong allies — some of them Muslims. He singled out Ahmad Muhammad Kachhalia as a powerful spokesman and an essential leader of their movement. This is important to note, that Gandhi had Muslim allies at the beginning of his non-violent resistance, and even at the end. Gandhi was able to transcend barriers of religion. Those who point to Bin Laden as cheap evidence of Islam's alleged deficiency should also remember the invaluable support of Muslims in Gandhi's movement from its outset.

September the 11th marks a day both of infamy and fame, though Americans may not know it. Of course we know that September the 11th, 2001 was the date of the infamous attacks upon the World Trade Centers and the Pentagon (a fourth plane, due to passenger heroics, having never reached its target). This is a date of sore injuries and painful memories for many. But is the reader also aware that ninety-five years earlier, on September the 11th, 1906, Gandhi and his followers helped give birth to non-violence (satyagraha)? For it was on September the 11th 1906 that Gandhi organized a massive group of followers in a South African theater, and at that meeting, Gandhi and others made a vow of non-violent resistance not to comply with the oppressive legislation. History is full of lessons and ironies, and it would appear that this date marks a significant milestone both in ultra-violent *jihad* and in non-violent *satyagraha*.

At the September 11th meeting, a man named Sheth Haji Habib stood up and took a vow to God not to submit to the law and encouraged others also. The vow to God was a solemn oath and also an opportunity that had not quite been made evident to Gandhi. Gandhi seized the moment and made a passionate speech that they all should seriously consider this vow, but they must also vow to respond non-violently. This would be a tough ordeal, and Gandhi spelled out the financial woes, the brutality, the jailing, deportation, even the possibility of death that might await them. They must all, however, insist that they not break the vow and commit no act of violence. There were members of many faiths there, most prominently Hindus and Muslims. Gandhi pulled them together with an appeal to a common faith, and a common vow:

> We all believe in the same God, the differences of nomenclature in Hinduism and Islam notwithstanding. To pledge ourselves to take an oath in the name of that God or with him as witness is not something to be trifled with. If having taken such an oath we violate our pledge we are guilty before God and man. Personally I hold that a man, who deliberately and intelligently takes a pledge and then breaks it, forfeits his manhood.[33]

Gandhi made a stirring call and secured a leading role in the movement to come. Arrests would follow, and more negotiations, but Gandhi would not give up his pledge to resist and change the law. Whether by odd coincidence or arson, the theater he and his Indians held their meeting in burned down the next day. It did not matter; the movement went on.

Soon Gandhi held a contest in his journal *Indian Opinion*. He needed a name for their movement, for terms like "passive resistance" did not fit. There was nothing passive about such an active and courageous movement. A relative of his, Maganlal Gandhi, suggested calling it "Sadagraha", or "firmness in good cause." Gandhi liked the word, but altered it to *satyagraha,* a combination of the Sanskrit *satya*, for truth or love, and *agraha*, showing the firmness and discipline. "I thus began to call the Indian movement 'Satyagraha', that is to say, the Force which is born of Truth and Love or non-violence, and gave up the use of the phrase *passive resistance*", Gandhi wrote.[34]

It would still be another six years that Gandhi would fight for his ideals in South Africa. During that time, he began to shed his European dress, and to adopt an increasingly simple life-style. A few influences are worthy of note. On a train ride Gandhi had read Ruskin's *Unto This Last*, a work that made a tremendous impact upon him. He speaks of it prominently in his autobiography and relates the key message he took from the book. The primary lessons he learned were three:

1. That the good of the individual is contained in the good of all.
2. That a lawyer's work has the same value as the barber's inasmuch as all have the same right of earning their livelihood from their work.
3. That the life of labor, i.e. the life of the tiller of the soil and the handicraftsman is the life worth living.

Gandhi further interpreted: "The first of these I knew. The second I had dimly realized. The third had never occurred to me. *Unto This Last* made it as clear as daylight for me that the second and third were contained in the first. I arose with the dawn, ready to reduce these principles to practice."[35]

Gandhi increasingly adopted this life of simplicity. He formed communal based ashrams, or farms, first the Phoenix and then the Tolstoy Farm, on which he could publish his newspaper and live out his religious creed. There was to be complete equality on the farm, and even the untouchables were to be accorded fair treatment. Gandhi's wife Kasturbai was at once revolted by these ideas, that she should have to clean the latrine and welcome the presence of untouchables. Reacting in righteous rage, Gandhi threatened to throw her off of the ashram. He soon came to his senses, and Kasturbai did her best to accommodate his wild ideas. This event was reported as early as 1898, and in later years, Gandhi's religious discipline and demands would increase.[36] The patience of Kasturbai to his stubborn ways was also a lesson to him in non-violence.

Gandhi was also influenced by Leo Tolstoy's *The Kingdom of God is Within You*. Tolstoy was old and ailing but had reacted favorably to Gandhi's works in South Africa, as Gandhi had been impressed with Tolstoy's interpretation of Christianity. Tolstoy had written: "A Christian enters into no dispute with his neighbor, he neither attacks nor uses violence; on the contrary, he suffers himself, without resistance, and by his very attitude toward evil not only sets himself free, but helps to free the world at large from all outward authority."[37] Gandhi saw Tolstoy approaching the essence of non-violence from Christianity in much the same way that Gandhi was approaching it with the *Bhagavad-Gita*. Increasingly he affirmed a common message in world religions, and that message was at heart non-violence. Much of Europe had not lived up to the Christianity it espoused, in Gandhi's view, but Tolstoy had interpreted it correctly. Gandhi affirmed, "Jesus lived and died in vain if He did not teach us to regulate the whole of life by the eternal law of love."[38] And that law of love was for Gandhi *ahimsa*, non-violence. Hence, to Gandhi, Jesus was really a *satyagrahi*; an advocate of non-violent truth-force: "Jesus Christ indeed has been acclaimed as the prince of passive resisters but I submit in that case passive resistance must mean Satyagraha and Satyagraha alone."[39]

Tolstoy and Gandhi never met but shared many common ideals. Both wanted to put into effect what he preached and issued a radical challenge to the political order of the status quo. Gandhi named the second, larger ashram after

Tolstoy, the farm that been purchased by his friend Herman Kallenbach and donated to their cause.[40]

Gandhi befriended the Christian clergyman C.F. Andrews. They met towards the end of his stay in South Africa. C.F. Andrews played an important role in Gandhi's life; he was a supporter and long-lasting friend. Andrews apparently donated almost everything he had to their cause and was an important mediator at the end of the South African days. That end would soon come.[41]

Not every one of Gandhi's campaigns need be recorded here, as my purpose is to summarize and offer some interpretive remarks. One of the last campaigns that Gandhi launched was the border crossing into the state of Transvaal. The Transvaal and the Orange Fee State were two regions heavily populated by Boers, and Transvaal in particular was a target of Gandhi's *satyagraha* campaign. A Supreme Court case ruling then denied the legitimacy of Hindu or Muslim marriages. This provoked great outrage, and the inevitable consequence was that many women now joined the campaign of *satyagraha*; Gandhi's ranks swelled.[42]

Gandhi had developed a close friendship with Gopal Krishna Gokhale, who had become his political advisor and who requested him urgently to return to fight in Indian politics. Gokhale came to South Africa to visit Gandhi and his ashram, as well as make a tour to support Gandhi in 1912. Gokhale assured Gandhi that the South Africans told him that the repressive £3 Tax and the Black Act would soon be repealed. Gandhi's movement welcomed Gokhale's support, but when he left, the measures were not repealed. This became interpreted as such a deep insult to India that their Viceroy became involved.[43]

Gandhi led a group of some 2000 striking miners to the Transvaal to test its racially impregnable border laws. Europeans had threatened to shoot at Gandhi's marching demonstrators, but the supportive speech of Herman Kallenbach may have shamed them out of it. The arrests and the pressure had their cumulative effect on the authorities. During the march Gandhi was arrested 3 times in 4 days.[44] At last, Jan Smuts appeared willing to strike up real negotiations. C.F. Andrews was present, and an important assistant to Gandhi here. Smuts had betrayed his confidence, and Gandhi wanted assurance that Smuts would keep his word.

The negotiated settlement became the Indian Relief Bill, which repealed the £3 poll tax, recognized Hindu and Muslim marriages, and backed off of many of the repressive measures that had been created by the government. It was a great victory of Gandhi's *satyagraha* and the first twentieth century proof that non-violent movements could be put into effect for real political change. It was not the end of oppressive measures in that country, but it was a milestone victory after a prolonged effort. Gandhi had the satisfaction of resolving the conflict, and at last set sail (for good this time) to England (and from there to India) on July 18, 1914.[45]

Gandhi unfortunately had bad timing to avoid conflicts. They kept falling upon his shoulder, whether he wanted them or not. As he set sail, ultimately to return home, World War I broke out. Gandhi again would offer to support the British Empire, as he had done in the Boer and Zulu Wars, but his help was not required this time. Gandhi returned to India, where he was greeted by his (soon to be) long-time rival M.A. Jinnah, amongst others. His political advisor Gokhale told him to become re-acquainted with India after his long absence, and so it was that Gandhi began to turn his attention and his newfound methods to his native India. By now his religious and political ideas had developed, and he had written many of them out in his book *Hind Swaraj*, written on an earlier sea voyage in 1909. Gandhi's determination to throw off British rule and to end discrimination against his native India was reflected in the book and its ideals for post-colonial rule. Gandhi's *satyagraha* was now a method and an evolving movement, but it would now face its greatest ever challenge.

Swaraj for India

Gandhi returned to India with a growing interest and attachment to the independence movement, but he followed Gokhale's advice and spent some time learning about the political situation in India. It was not long before more social work found Gandhi — quite literally. From the northern region of Champaran, below the heights of the Himalayas, a determined man by the name of Rajkumar Shukla came searching for Gandhi. He found him in Calcutta and urged him to come north to address the situation in Champaran. Gandhi was not acquainted with the region but promised to come and see what the problem was. He was in for quite a shock.

The tenant farmers there had long been required to pay a 15% tax on the lands. The British landlords collected the rent by taking the harvest of indigo crop that the peasant farmers planted each year. Land was set aside specially to plant this indigo and pay this rent. The problem was that synthetic dyes from Germany had made their crop almost worthless, yet the landlords were still demanding their share of the rent. Gandhi was called in to study the problem and recommend a solution.

Upon entering Champaran, Gandhi was immediately ordered to leave by British authorities, but he refused to go. He would not be ordered about in the country of his birth. Gandhi meant no intentional disrespect to the British, but he heard the "voice of conscience", which was higher than that of the British authorities. Gandhi was brought to trial, but the charges were dropped against him and he was allowed to resume his investigations.

Ultimately, Gandhi would negotiate with the British landlords and get them to return a quarter of the rents they had already collected. It was perhaps a conservative figure, but it was in the nature of Gandhi to compromise when he saw the need. There were other issues, of course, where he could not compromise and committed himself to a "fast unto death" until the issue would be resolved. In Champaran, Gandhi stayed and opened schools, seeing a need for basic education which was absent from the region.[46]

Gandhi would soon embark on his first "fast unto death." The issue involved a labor strike over wages in the city of Ahmedabad. Gandhi in this case knew one of the Ahmedabad mill owners quite well, and commanded his respect. Leading the mill workers in their demand for higher wages, he asked them to promise not to abandon their strike until their demands were met. This was his next project in *satyagraha*, and the psychologist Erik Erikson, in his book *Gandhi's Truth*, maintains that this was a decisive moment in Gandhi's life because it was the first time he ever chose to "fast unto death." Erikson's book is rich in detail and still a recommended read to anyone interested in the history and the details of the strike. Nonetheless, it seems his thesis is not entirely on the mark. Ahmedabad was an important victory for Gandhi, but it was not necessarily the decisive moment in his life. One might look at the death of his father, his humiliation and ejection from the train at Maritzburg, or his later involvement in South African non-violence as equally important moments.[47]

When Gandhi sensed the resolve of the Ahmedabad strikers waning, he announced that he would not touch food until they had fulfilled their promise and realized their demands. It was a move that shocked everyone, but it was successful. Three days into his fast, the strike was settled and the workers received higher compensation. Gandhi was pleased and had chalked up two small, quick victories for *satyagraha* in India. His method would become ever more popular, and crowds would come to catch a sight (or *darshan*) of the person that Rabindranath Tagore had dubbed the "Mahatma — Great Soul."[48]

When the end of the war came, India expected a relaxation of the wartime censorship and austerities that had been put into place. Instead, a committee led by Sir Sidney Rowlatt investigated the situation and recommended a continuation of austerities and censorship. In March of 1919 the Rowlatt Bill became law, as the government kept the privilege to exercise its wartime powers. In response to the measure, Gandhi proposed a national work stoppage, or *hartal*. It would be called a day of prayer and fasting, but no work would be done, and consequently, essential services and parts of the British Empire would be paralyzed or isolated. The hartal was observed in Delhi on March 30 and in Bombay on April 6 (due to some miscommunication). It proved initially to be a success, but soon violent riots would break out in Delhi, Bombay and Ahmedabad. Although pledges had been made to respect non-violence, the population had not been well enough prepared for it.[49]

Then tragedy struck. In response to the Indian non-cooperation movement and the occasional outbursts of violence that ensued, the British military began to clamp down on security. There were attempts to try to prevent mass meetings, and to make announcements to that effect. In the city of Amritsar, India, Brigadier General Reginald Edward Harry Dyer arrived to clamp down on all further meetings and disobedience. His methods were unusually brutal. Arriving in the city on April 11th, he ordered all meetings of Indians banned on the 12th, but it is by no means clear that his warning reached all parts of the city. On April 13th, Dyer and his troops arrived at the scene of a mass meeting in Jallianwalla Bagh, a large courtyard in the city of Amritsar. There was a large gathering of unarmed Sikhs and Hindus present. Without subsequent warning, he ordered his soldiers to open fire into the thickest part of the crowd, it being his intention to "teach a lesson" to those who disobeyed British authority. Reports indicate that of the 1650 rounds discharged by his men, there were 1516 casualties, including

379 dead, and 1137 wounded. Scarcely a shot missed its target, so there was no intention to warn, but to shoot to kill. Dyer had declared "I had made up my mind . . . .I would do all men to death" and that his use of force would "Do a jolly lot of good." Under examination and in testimony afterwards, Dyer was unapologetic.[50]

Dyer then issued a "crawling decree" that all Indians must crawl past a school where Miss Sherwood had been assaulted days earlier. But when Dyer arrived in the city the violence had subsided, and he clearly had overreacted. It was not a measure of enforcing British law at Amritsar, it was a massacre pure and simple. Gandhi, and all of India were shocked.

Gandhi soon announced the end to his first national *satyagraha* campaign in India. The people had been insufficiently prepared for disobedience on a mass scale, and the violence that had broken out deeply disturbed him. He announced a fast of penitence for their actions, but he did not ask for punishment of General Dyer.[51] Declaring that it has been a "Himalayan miscalculation" that the people of India were ready for non-violence, Gandhi declared that the *hartal* should end. It was not a universally popular decision. Many questioned Gandhi about whether any movement for independence could be completely non-violent. Defending his actions, Gandhi asserted that a true movement of *satyagraha* had to be non-violent in its intent and action.[52]

Mass movements are undoubtedly harder to manage in many ways than smaller movements. In South Africa, Gandhi's numbers were small, while his Indian numbers were much larger. The task of keeping that many tempers in line was consequently exponentially more difficult. There was dramatic success, however, as well as some failure. Sometimes the consequences were unexpected. When a non-violent campaign was started in Bardoli, violence erupted in Chauri Chaura several hundred miles away, resulting in the killing of twenty-two police officers. Gandhi's expectations were high for Indians and their civilization — he strenuously tried to teach them non-violence, and with a profound (but mixed) measure of success.[53]

Gandhi continued to agitate against British occupation. He supported Muslims in the Khilafat Movement (responding to the demise of the office of caliph), and joined the India Home-Rule League. He traveled widely and wrote against the evils of British rule, and it got their attention. It was not long before he would be arrested again and brought up on charges of sedition. It was called the "Great Trial." Gandhi plead guilty to the charges, saying that British rule was corrupt and evil. He challenged the judge to either give him the full punishment of law or to resign his office. The judge was clearly reluctant and said that it was "impossible to ignore the fact that you are in a different category from any person I have ever tried or am likely to try." Sentencing Gandhi to six years imprisonment, the judge added that if anyone higher above sought to reverse the judgment "no one would be better pleased than I." Gandhi seemed to accept the verdict cheerfully.[54]

Gandhi did not spend the whole six years in prison. He spent only 22 months in jail, and when he developed appendicitis the British released him from prison on Feb. 5, 1924 for his health and safety. Truth was he was so enormously popular that his demise in prison would not look good at all; the British had little other choice. Gandhi could be a menace to them in or outside of jail. In jail, Gandhi could employ a fast against them, or his many allies outside could keep campaigns going against the British. Outside of jail Gandhi was of course free to organize *satyagraha* himself. Crowds came to him in droves. The "half-naked fakir", as Churchill described him, had all kinds of tools to his advantage: steely determination matched by a fiery religious resolve, and a British education in law teamed up with a spiritual law of non-violence. It was a rare combination of gifts and talents that was difficult to deal with. A small band, a militia of armed rebels might be crushed, but all of India could not be cowed. And though Gandhi came unarmed, his appeal increasingly spread all over India; he was becoming a true Mahatma, whether he liked the title or not.

In the 1920s, Gandhi devoted himself to a "Constructive Program" consisting of three primary goals: 1) Spreading the use of homespun cloth or "Khadi", 2) the removal of the blight of untouchabilty, and 3) the unity of Hindus and Muslims. Sponsoring all three were a means of furthering India's readiness for *Swaraj* or independence from Great Britain, and some explanation is required for each.

Gandhi was very critical of the machine age, of the exploitation that often resulted in the use of machines, and in particular the dependency of India on foreign cloth. Although he was a close ally with Nehru, he was willing to dissent from Nehru's views: "Pandit Nehru wants industrialization because he thinks that if it (India) is socialized, it would be free from the evils of capitalism. My own view is that the evils are inherent in industrialism, and no amount of socialization can eradicate them." Gandhi saw grave problems with industrialism because "Today machinery merely helps a few to ride the backs of millions." [55] Gandhi traveled extensively, and in his travels he found a profound degree of unemployment; people sat idle for large part of the year. Gandhi had hopes that by stirring the people to work and action, by publicly burning foreign cloth and restoring domestic village industry with the spinning wheel, that India could cut her dependent connections to British textiles and increase their own readiness for *Swaraj*. For India, he said "Machinery is a grand yet awful invention."[56] Machinery was a laborsaving device, and India didn't need a laborsaving device, it needed employment. He even suggested there be penalties on machinery or labor-saving devices in India, and his mantra of homespun, while alien to many, was for him an essential way of restoring Indian rigorous activity, employment, and autonomy.[57]

The unemployment of India, the poverty and lack of purpose and aim amongst the destitute really troubled Gandhi. Yet he did not want to just give free handouts. He wanted to teach the people to provide for themselves to uplift them and give them hope. While it was a duty for the State to take care of the poor, Gandhi also saw it as a responsibility of the poor to work for themselves too. At one point he said that the motto should be: "No labor, no meal . . . . I know it is easier to fling free meals in the faces of idlers, but much more difficult to organize an institution where honest work has to be done."[58] More machinery, more laborsaving to Gandhi meant more idleness:

> What I object to is the *craze* for machinery, not machinery as such. The craze is for what they call laborsaving machinery. Men go on 'saving labor' till thousands are without work and thrown on the open streets to die of starvation. I want to save time and labor, not for a fraction of mankind, but for all. I want the concentration of wealth, not in the hands of a few, but in the hands of all. Today machinery merely helps a few to ride the back of millions. The impetus behind it all is not the philanthropy to save labor, but greed.[59]

The motives for Gandhi's passion for homespun become very clear. It was the best thing he perceived that simple Indian villagers could do, and at the same time resist and reject dependence on Great Britain. The economic relations with their colonial master were exploitative and oppressive in Gandhi's view, and weaving on spinning wheels would be a means for independence. Of course the symbol of the spinning wheel would outlive Gandhi and be emblazoned on the Indian national flag.

That was part of his economic program, but there was a necessary social, political and religious program that accompanied it. Gandhi abhorred the doctrine of untouchability. Denying caste distinction and untouchability, he said:

> Caste distinction is not observed in the Ashram because caste has nothing to do with religion in general and Hinduism in particular. It is a sin to believe anyone else is inferior or superior to ourselves. We are all equal. It is the touch of sin that pollutes us and never that of a human being. None are high and none are low for one who would devote his life to service. The distinction between high and low is a blot on Hinduism which we must obliterate.[60]

Gandhi had of course not seen the point of spurning the untouchables since his childhood. His innate attitudes were only later reinforced by his religious and philosophical interpretations. He added: "Untouchabilty is not a sanction of religion . . . . scriptures cannot transcend Reason and Truth. They are intended to purify Reason and illuminate Truth . . . . It is the spirit that giveth the light. And the spirit of the Vedas is purity, truth, innocence, chastity, simplicity, forgiveness, godliness, and all that makes a man or woman noble and brave."[61]

If India wanted independence, it had to be with justice and equality. Gandhi wanted to separate the perceived evils of Western civilization from that of Eastern (or more exactly Indian) civilization. If India were to retain *swaraj* and still harbor the economic motives of the West and the prejudice against the Untouchables (whom he renamed the "Harijan" or "Children of God"), then it would not be an independence worth having. At times, he grossly overstated the difference between the East and West: "The British Government in India constitutes a struggle between modern civilization, which is the Kingdom of Satan, and the ancient civilization, which is the Kingdom of God. The one is the God of War, the other is the God of Love."[62]

One finds Gandhi clearly exaggerating here — as the tenor of the statement has some uncanny similarities to those of Bin Laden, who supports the idea of a "clash of civilizations." Yet Gandhi clearly did not harbor any racist or superior views, as evidenced from an overall study of his life and statements and his long-lasting friendships with people of all colors, nationalities, and religious creeds. Gandhi affirmed, "In my opinion, there is no place on earth and no race, which is not capable of producing the finest types of humanity, given suitable opportunities and education."[63]

This was why untouchability was such an affront to Gandhi. It appealed neither to his intuitive moral reasoning, nor his interpretation of the Hindu religion. As illumined earlier, no religious scripture could transcend a morality that was rational anyhow. Hence, wherever scripture advocated slavery or intolerance to Gandhi, it was not really scripture. It was simply human error. As we shall soon see, the desire to have the untouchables embraced by all of Hindu society was in Gandhi's eyes worth a fast unto death.

Lastly, Gandhi insisted upon Hindu and Muslim unity. Gandhi did find Muslim allies — most strongly in the Pathan leader Abdul Ghaffar Khan. He courted the Ali brothers' friendship in the Khalifat movement, and tried throughout his career to transcend Hindu and Muslim divisions:

> Should we not remember that many Hindus and Mahometans own the same ancestors and the same blood runs through their veins? Do people become enemies because they change their religion? Is the God of the Mohametan different from the God of the Hindu? Religions are different roads converging to the same point. What does it matter that we take different roads so long as we reach the same goal? Wherein is the cause for quarreling?[64]

Gandhi passionately strove for Hindu and Muslim unity, though he found it very difficult to achieve. Ultimately, of course, independence would be realized without unity, and the "vivisection of India" was to Gandhi also a rending of his heart. He was so strongly committed to the goal and concept of religious unity that he may have in part misunderstood how difficult it was to achieve. One cannot fault him for not trying to attain this unity, however. It was an essential aspect of his being to see all religions as inherently equal. Hindu and Muslim unity was essential to him pragmatically to keep the independence movement together, but it was more important religiously because he believed in its truth and in the truth of *ahimsa* or non-violence overcoming any dissent and division. He resisted partition to the very last.

Perhaps Gandhi's most famous movement was the 1930 Salt March. The British had a monopoly on salt production, and the imposed tax upon it became the next target and stepping stone for Gandhi's stride towards independence. In accord with his own principles, Gandhi wrote to the British Viceroy Lord Irwin to advise him of the intended plan for salt *satyagraha* in advance. It was quite a remarkable letter. Gandhi intended to march with his ashram companions to the sea, and there make his own salt, breaking the British monopoly on the process. Lord Irwin seemed unimpressed with the intended plan and took no immediate action against Gandhi.

Gandhi proceeded. On March 12, 1930, Gandhi left from his ashram with seventy-eight companions. As he marched, the movement grew, more members joined, and attention was increasingly drawn to his demonstration. The choice to march such a long way was a strategic success, for it galvanized much more support and attention than a quick train-ride could have mustered. Gandhi reached the sea at Dandi on April 5, 1930 and proceeded to make his own salt. Thousands of Indians followed suit, and soon the Viceroy's government could not ignore such a widespread surge of disobedience to the law. Arrests began to increase. Gandhi was arrested, Nehru was arrested, and one of Gandhi's sons was arrested. The jails began to fill with reports of between 60,000 and 100,000 prisoners all locked up for the trifling crime of making salt. What had formerly seemed an inconsequential act now became a monumental defiance of authority. Irwin was forced to negotiate, to back off and make concessions to Gandhi and India.

During the Salt Campaign, there was an organized non-violent "raid" on the Dharasana Salt Works. Gandhi's own son Manilal and Mrs. Naidu were amongst the leaders of the march (Gandhi was in jail — an example of how his *satyagraha* could be conducted without his physical presence). The march was non-violent but was met forcibly by authorities. Three hundred and twenty injured, and two dead (all Indians) were reported in the non-violent protest. It was a vivid demonstration of the Indian capacity to endure suffering under the British baton. Much like Martin Luther King Jr.'s later campaign (May of 1963), when Bull Connor unleashed fire hoses on non-violent American blacks, the event threw into sharp relief the ugly features of injustice in the oppressive system that was being protested. This is in part what *satyagraha* depended upon to show to the oppressor the brutality of his own methods and to appeal to the better conscience in him to reform.[65]

This may be a fine point, but what if the system doesn't have sufficient moral conscience? What if it is a brutal dictatorship that *satyagraha* is poised against? Can non-violence be effective in tyrannies, or against terrorists? That will be part of our question to explore once we have pinned down the story and roots of *satyagraha* itself.

Following the movement, Gandhi was summoned to meet with the Viceroy and received an invitation to the Second Round Table Conference to negotiate in the interests of India. He was sent as the Indian National Congress representative. He set sail on August 29, arrived in England and remained there until December 5. Gandhi chose to stay in simple accommodations and to dress in his homespun, or *khadi*. Gone were the days of trying to imitate a British gentleman. A newly transformed Gandhi arrived in London this time, and instead of being a widely ignored law student, he was a widely celebrated personality. Meeting with the King of England, jokes were made about Gandhi's lack of attire, and he simply replied that the King had on enough for both of them. While the meetings at the Round Table Conference proved ultimately fruitless, Gandhi's determination to pursue *Swaraj* remained undaunted.[66] Disappointed and empty-handed, he returned to India, but continued his resistance and was rearrested.

Gandhi's next dramatic political statement was another "fast unto death" against separate electorates for the untouchables. A very highly educated and important reformer for the untouchables (or "Dalits", as he preferred to call them), Dr. Bhimrao Ramji Ambedkar was fighting to secure political rights and privileges for his people. Ambedkar himself had grown up as an untouchable and had many painful experiences of untouchability.[67] Ambedkar and Gandhi did not see eye-to-eye. Ambedkar (who later contributed significantly to writing the Indian Constitution that abolished untouchability in India) was seeking political rights and guarantees. Gandhi was trying to smooth over social and religious tensions while engaged in real uplift and fundraising for the Untouchables. Their agendas were dissimilar and their ideas different, though their end goals may have been similar.

The issue that cropped up and which further divided Gandhi and Ambedkar was over separate electorates for the untouchables. It was thought by proponents of the system (Ambedkar and the Viceroy amongst them) that the system would allow the untouchables to vote separately for their own electors, giving them enhanced and special control to steer their future political destiny. It was all part of the process in sketching out what a future independent India might look like and how it might operate. Gandhi opposed separate electorates emphatically, so much so that he was willing to go on a fast unto death if the issue was not resolved *against* the idea of separate electorates. Gandhi was troubled; he sought Rabindranath Tagore's blessing for the fast, and received it. His Yeravda (or Poona) fast began from his jail cell on September 20, 1932.[68]

Many have criticized Gandhi for this fast. The Viceroy thought Gandhi was under some great misconceptions, that the separate electorates were intended to help, not hurt, the cause of the untouchables. As a supporter of the Harijan, surely he would be in favor of it. Nehru also expressed his consternation about the fast. He was angry and somewhat irritated, but also distraught that Gandhi should choose this issue above all others to fast against. He did not always identify with Gandhi's religious approach.[69] Gandhi had wanted to insist that the untouchables be a part of the Hindu fold, that they not be rejected. Ambedkar no longer wanted to have anything to do with Hinduism and had made clear his intention to renounce the religion altogether. The crisis became severe, and it seemed as if Gandhi might lose his life as the negotiations stalled.[70]

So why did Gandhi fast? Gandhi fasted for the principle of unity with the untouchables. One might better understand it (as an American) if the example were to be transferred to this country. Suppose Martin Luther King Jr. had accepted the notion that, for a temporary period at least, only black voters could vote for black legislators to represent them. The measure might be temporarily empowering (in Gandhi's India, the separate electorates were also scheduled to be phased out), but it would run against the grain of color-blindness, of indifference to skin color. Gandhi advocated passionately that Hinduism was "caste-blind" and could not accept the separation of untouchables from the Hindu fold. It ran completely against his principles. In the end a compromise was struck with Ambedkar, and Gandhi ended his fast. His health had deteriorated precipitously, his life had been in real danger. But the effect of the fast was momentous. Across India there was renewed emphasis to accept untouchables, to open the doors of Hindu temples to them, which had been closed for so long. Perhaps nether Gandhi nor Nehru understood the significance of his fast until it was over. It was not his last fast, or his longest, but it did produce dramatic results.[71]

Nehru was pleased that the fast proved effective but thought the fast for the Harijan had distracted attention from the cause of independence.[72] Gandhi may have also unconsciously been thinking very strategically. If the Harijan could be separated from the Hindus, why not the Muslims, and then the Sikhs or the Pathans? The British could use the disunity of India as a trump card to stall negotiations. India was so internally divided, to whom should they return Indian political power? Gandhi's actions seem calculated to unify rather than divide.

Gandhi was not entirely successful, at least not as successful as he would have liked. Independence came, but with a bitter partition of India. Gandhi did not want this, but it came anyway. He had been formerly allied with Muhammad Ali Jinnah in the independence movement, but Jinnah and the Muslim League increasingly pulled away from the Indian National Congress as they feared its (real or perceived) domineering Hindu influence. This was not Gandhi's intent, but unfortunately, Gandhi and Jinnah had very little in common as men and as leaders. Jinnah was by birth a Shia Muslim, but he was not religiously observant, and in dress he looked very much like an English gentleman. Gandhi had repudiated English dress and championed homespun. Jinnah did not support Gandhi's program of civil disobedience, and ultimately, Gandhi and Congress were not able to convince Jinnah and the Muslim League that they could have their fair place in the sun in a united Indian rule. Some historians have faulted Jinnah very much as an obstinate leader of separatism, while others have blamed Gandhi or Congress. Perhaps there is enough blame to go around and little use in pointing fingers. Confidence was lost between Hindu, Muslim and Sikh, and by 1946 religious violence and militant militias were widespread and beyond Gandhi's control. Clearly Gandhi was very stricken with grief when it happened.[73]

Gandhi did not always see eye-to-eye with members of Congress either. When World War Two broke out he and Abdul Ghaffar Khan broke with the Congress over the issue of non-violence and their commitment to it. Gandhi and Khan saw their devotion to non-violence as a matter of principle, while they assessed that many in Congress only regarded it as a policy, giving lip-service to a creed that was expedient as long as it had a powerful leader to guide it. The breach was not permanent — as in 1942, Gandhi would be out sponsoring the Quit India Campaign. It did reflect a diversity of thought and opinion about emerging Indian politics that was not easy to marshal and set in one consistent direction. Some on the extremes advocated violence.[74]

In his last decade, Gandhi suffered some more emotional blows. His lifelong friend and secretary, Mahadev Desai, passed away in 1942, and then in 1943, his wife Kasturbai became ill and died. Harilal, the eldest, was summoned, but Gandhi never fully reconciled with his son, who had turned against him and apparently even converted to Islam.[75] A theatrical play *Gandhi vs. the Mahatma* has been made that probes the sensitive issue of the father and his great demands and expectations of his sons.[76] Harilal was not a totally rebellious son. At least once Gandhi records his son's name as amongst those involved in his *satyagraha* campaigns in South Africa.[77] The division within Gandhi's family would only reflect a greater coming division in India, however.

Gandhi tried his best to resist that violent division. When the partition of India came, and violence between Hindu and Muslim exploded, Gandhi traveled to Calcutta to try and stem the tide of bloodshed. On September 1 1947, he announced another "fast unto death" unless the violence in Calcutta were to be stopped. Remarkably, Gandhi never fasted unto death, as the power of his personality was enough to get so many in India to respond. The violence stopped in Calcutta, at least during that moment, and Gandhi requested a solemn pledge that all Hindus and Muslims abstain from violence against one another.[78] Gandhi soon made his last fast to appeal to Hindu-Muslim unity from January 13 to 18, 1948. During that time, he convinced the government of India to give a reparations package of 550 million rupees in payment to the nascent government of Pakistan, a payment that had been much delayed. Ironically, the very country Gandhi had so much opposed in its very existence, Gandhi was then pragmatically supportive with his fast for unity.

Would independence have come without Gandhi? Did he really speed it along? Many have seen him as the "father of India", Nehru using those words to describe him after his death.[79] Certainly the end of World War Two and Great Britain's exhausted status as an empire greatly accelerated Indian independence, as did the departure of Winston Churchill from leadership. Churchill had been vehemently opposed to Gandhi and to any dismantling of the British Empire: "I have not become the King's First Minister in order to preside at the liquidation of the British Empire." Years earlier he had said, "Gandhism and all that it stands for must ultimately be grappled with and finally crushed."[80] With the war over, Churchill out of power, and Nehru, Gandhi and Jinnah still pulling for independence, Great Britain realized it was no longer in a position to keep the empire it once had. Gandhi had once said during the war, "whether Britain wins or loses, imperialism has to die. It is certainly no use now to the British people, whatever it may have been in the past."[81]

Gandhi by now had more than just Muslim opponents. The militant Hindu Mahasabha and the Rashtriya Sevak Sangha had emerged in strong opposition to Islamic forces and culture and had a separate agenda from the Mahatma. From the ranks of this opposition would emerge Nathuram Vinayak Godse, who was beginning to think that the Mahatma had too much influence in Indian society.[82] Godse proceeded with plans to assassinate Mahatma Gandhi, ironically seeing in him forces too pro-Muslim.

On January 30, 1948, Gandhi held his last prayer meeting. Godse was there, waiting for Gandhi with a concealed pistol. Gandhi was greeted by Godse, who made a gesture to Gandhi and then pulled out the pistol and shot him three times. Gandhi collapsed, shouting "Hey-Rama" (Oh God!), and death soon overtook him. India was struck with horror and grief. Nehru shed tears, as did all India: "The light has gone out of our lives and there is darkness everywhere and I do not quite know what to tell you and how to say it. Our beloved leader, Bapu, as we call him, the father of our nation, is no more", but then Nehru corrected himself, for this was no ordinary light, but a light that "will illumine this country for many more years, and a thousand years later that light will still be seen in this country."[83] General George C. Marshall would say "Mahatma Gandhi was the spokesman for the conscience of all mankind."[84] Albert Einstein perhaps said it best: "Generations to come, it may be, will scarce believe that such a one as this ever in flesh and blood walked upon this earth."[85]

For Gandhi's part, he just saw himself as one striving after truth: "I see that in the midst of death life persists, and in the midst of untruth truth persists, in the midst of darkness light persists. Hence I gather that God is Life, Truth, Light. He is Love. He is the supreme good."[86] Gandhi's legacy has left a brilliant light and inspiration for us all to follow, yet there is a troubling darkness, a religious belief almost diametrically opposed to Gandhi which we are now confronting. Would Gandhi's tactics and beliefs be able to respond to the terror threat of an Osama bin Laden? Gandhi asserted that truth would outlive untruth: "The law of love governs the world. Life persists in the face of death. The universe continues in spite of destruction incessantly going on. Truth triumphs over untruth. Love conquers hate."[87]

Legacy: Martin Luther King Jr. and Abdul Ghaffar Khan

Gandhi's legacy has lived on, in the form of Martin Luther King Jr., and Abdul Ghaffar Khan (to name just two!). The current Dalai Lama and his opposition movement in Tibet have also employed non-violent techniques. Dr. King was the celebrated Nobel-Prize winning Protestant Christian from the West, and the other a Pathan Muslim from what is now Pakistan. It is fortunate that Martin Luther King Jr. is so well remembered, but sad that Abdul Ghaffar Khan is not. Both men have very important legacies to teach us as those who followed in the footsteps of Gandhi.

King made non-violence work in the United States, proving that what Gandhi did was not just a fluke and was not isolated to one circumstance. King made non-violence work from an explicitly Christian perspective, and of course paid some of the credit to Gandhi who had gone before him. King had said "Nonviolent resistance had emerged as the technique of the movement, while love stood as the regulating ideal. In other words, Christ furnished the spirit and motivation while Gandhi furnished the method."[88] We recall of course that Gandhi had said "Jesus Christ indeed has been acclaimed as the prince of passive resisters but I submit in that case passive resistance must mean Satyagraha and Satyagraha alone."[89] Gandhi's interpretation of the New Testament overlapped with his understanding of the *Gita*. Both he and King could tap into their respective religious heritage for their non-violent discipline.

Christopher Hitchens has charged that King's dedication was highly secular, or rooted in a humanist approach. This is not only misleading, it is in fact wrong.[90] King made explicit appeal to religious themes and ideas in all his speeches; it was a part of his essential self as a Christian minister. King trained the members of his movement in non-violence using religious ideas, songs, and a "10 commandments" of non-violence:

> I HEREBY PLEDGE MYSELF — MY PERSON AND BODY — TO THE NON-VIOLENT MOVEMENT. THEREFORE I WILL KEEP THE FOLLOWING TEN COMMANDMENTS:
> 1. MEDITATE daily on the teachings and life of Jesus.
> 2. REMEMBER always that the nonviolent movement in Birmingham seeks justice and reconciliation — not victory.
> 3. WALK and TALK in the manner of love, for God is love.
> 4. PRAY daily to be used by God in order that all men might be free.
> 5. SACRIFICE personal wishes in order that all men might be free.
> 6. OBSERVE with both friend and foe the ordinary rules of courtesy.
> 7. SEEK to perform regular service for others and for the world.
> 8. REFRAIN from the violence of fist, tongue, or heart.
> 9. STRIVE to be in good spiritual and bodily health.
> 10. FOLLOW the directions of the movement and of the captain of a demonstration.[91]

King's ministry of non-violence would not make much sense without his Christian background. This is not to say that non-violence cannot work in a secular context but to assert more broadly that non-violence can obviously work within multiple religious contexts — Christian, Hindu, and even Muslim.

Yes, even Muslim. In this age that idea may not be well received by many people, but in fact, there are plenty of Muslims who take a non-violent approach to their religion. One of the most celebrated was a peer of Gandhi, a Pathan of the Frontier Region (on the border of Afghanistan and Pakistan). This was a people not known for their pacifism. On the contrary, they were known for their belligerent temper. Violence had been more the way of the Pathan, and so it was an incredible feat that Abdul Ghaffar Khan could transform a substantial portion of the population there to the ways of non-violence.

Gandhi himself observed how surreal it was for a Pathan (recall that he had received a beating from Pathans in South Africa) to be non-violent: "That such men who would have killed a human being with no more thought than they would kill a sheep or a hen should at the bidding of one man have laid down their arms and accepted nonviolence as the superior weapon sounds almost like a fairy tale."[92] It was no fairy-tale, it was reality. This Muslim Pathan man had become convinced that non-violence was the way of the Prophet of Islam. He joined Gandhi and recruited some 80,000 to 100,000 Muslim Pathans to his cause of non-violence. They were known as the *Khudai Khidmatgars*, or the servants of God. They took this pledge:

> I am a Khudai Khidmatgar, as God needs no service, but serving his creation is serving him, I promise to serve humanity in the name of God.
> I promise to refrain from violence and from taking revenge. I promise to forgive those who oppress me or treat me with cruelty.

> I promise to refrain from taking part in feuds and quarrels and from creating enmity.
> I promise to treat every Pathan as my brother and friend.
> I promise to refrain from antisocial customs and practices.
> I promise to live a simple life, to practice virtue and to refrain from evil.
> I promise to practice good manners and good behavior and not to lead a life of idleness.
> I promise to devote at least two hours a day to social work.[93]

More will be said about "Badshah Khan", as he was known to those who loved and admired him, in our last chapter. For now, one very interesting historical irony should be pointed out: as a Pathan, he came from the same ethnic stock that would later contribute heavily to the ranks of the Taliban. In the scope of one century, we have had from that culture two radically different interpretations of Islam — one non-violent, universal, and inclusive, and the other violent, oppressive, and exclusive. It must be said that if the spirit of Islam can be interpreted in such radically divergent ways, then this bears some further scrutiny and understanding. We should not be quick to condemn Islam, or indeed Muslims, as having a belligerent character simply because of Osama bin Laden. We will bear witness to the fact that Muslims can have the completely opposite understanding of their religion than Bin Laden, an understanding very much more akin to Gandhi. Islam too can mean peace, if the heart wills it also to be so.

It seems clear then — that Gandhi's legacy remains open to us all, if we are ready to learn from it.

Notes

1. Louis Fischer, editor, *The Essential Gandhi: An Anthology of His Life, Works, and Ideas* (New York, Vintage Books, 1983), 151.

2. Bruce Lawrence, editor, *Messages to the World: the Statements of Osama bin Laden* (New York, Verso / New Left Books, 2005), 120.

3. Louis Fischer, *The Life of Mahatma Gandhi,* (New York, Collier Books, 1962), 20-22.

4. Gandhi read the Laws of Manu and was not impressed, confessing they made him "incline towards atheism"; he also described himself as a "mediocre student" Mohandas K. Gandhi, *Gandhi, An Autobiography: The Story of My Experiments With Truth*, translated from Gujarati by Mahadev Desai (Beacon Press, Boston, 1993), xxviii, 6; Einstein's praise of Gandhi is in fact notable — see Albert Einstein, *Ideas and Opinions,* edited by Carl Selig, translated by Sonja Bargmann (Random House, New York, 1954), 34, 78.

5. Louis Fischer, *The Essential Gandhi*, 135.

6. Gandhi, *Autobiography*, 19-26.

7. Gandhi, *Autobiography*, 12; Fischer, *Mahatma Gandhi*, chapters 1-9; Fischer, *Essential Gandhi*, 245-246.

8. Gandhi, *Autobiography*, Chapter 9.

9. Louis Fischer, *The Essential Gandhi*, 69, 179-183, 318.

10. Louis Fischer, *The Essential Gandhi*, 243.

11. Mohandas Gandhi, *The Bhagavad Gita According to Gandhi,* ed. & trans. John Strohmeir (Berkeley, California, Berkeley Hills Books, 2000), 21, 131.

12. Gandhi actually suggested going to England to be trained for the medical profession, instead of law (see Gandhi, *Autobiography*, 36). Later during two wars in South Africa Gandhi organized two ambulance or stretcher corps in which he played a significant role as a male nurse. Nursing and medicine remained a life-long interest of Gandhi's, as did developing herbal and natural cures. See Fischer, *Mahatma Gandhi*, 62-63, 66, 124; also Gandhi, *Autobiography,* 35-36.

13. Gandhi, *Autobiography,* 40; see also Fischer, *The Essential Gandhi*, 19-20.

14. Louis Fischer, *Mahatma Gandhi*, 31.

15. Patricia Cronin Marcello, *Mohandas K. Gandhi: A Biography* (Westport, Connecticut, Greenwood Press, 2006), 20.

16. Gandhi, *Autobiography,* 34.

17. Gandhi, *Autobiography,* 67-68; Patrician Marcello, *Mohandas K. Gandhi*, 24-25.

18 Gandhi, *Autobiography,* 67.

19. Gandhi, *Autobiography,* Chapters 13-20; Fischer, *The Essential Gandhi*, 29.

20. Gandhi, *Autobiography*, 48.

21. Louis Fischer, *The Essential Gandhi,* 135.

22. Gandhi, *Autobiography,* xxviii.

23. Gandhi, *Autobiography,*77-78; Fischer, *The Essential Gandhi*, 29.

24. Gandhi, *Autobiography*, 97-99; Fischer, *The Essential Gandhi*, 31-33; Fischer, *Mahatma Gandhi*, 46-47.

25. Gandhi, *Autobiography*, 101-102; Fischer, *Mahatma Gandhi*, 47-48.

26. Gandhi, *Autobiography*, 109-112; Fischer, *Mahatma Gandhi,* 48-49.

27. Gandhi, M.K., *Satyagraha in South Africa,* translated from the Gujarati by Valji Govindji Desai (Ahmedabad, Navajivan Publishing House, 6th edition, 2001), 39.

28. Gandhi himself noted the economic motive behind the discrimination, but it is clear the discrimination would not exist if the Indians were not a perceived "other" or alien threat that needed to be exploited or relegated to service. See Gandhi, *Satyagraha in South Africa,* 19-24.

29. Louis Fischer, *The Essential Gandhi*, 182.

30. Louis Fischer, *The Essential Gandhi*, 49-59; Gandhi, *Satyagraha in South Africa*, 49-59; Gandhi, *Autobiography*, 169-198.

31. Gandhi, *Satyagraha in South Africa,* 94.

32. It appears Gandhi may never have been struck by a South African government official, though he was assaulted by a South African mob. See Gandhi, *Satyagraha in South Africa*, 142-154.

33. Gandhi, *Satyagraha in South Africa,* 97.

34. Gandhi, *Satyagraha in South Africa,* 102.

35. Gandhi, *Autobiography*, 299.

36. Gandhi, *Autobiography,* 277-278.

37. Louis Fischer, *Mahatma Gandhi,* 103.

38. Thomas Merton, editor, *Gandhi on Non-Violence* (USA, New Directions Paperback, 2007), 38.

39. Gandhi, *Satyagraha in South Africa,* 106.

40. Gandhi, *Satyagraha in South Africa,* 214.

41. Gandhi, *Satyagraha in South Africa,* Chapter 23 omits Andrew's name, but he becomes quite prominent in Chapter 47. Apparently Gandhi's friendship with Andrews emerged comparatively much later to that of Kallenbach or Polak, some of his other European friends.

42. Gandhi, *Satyagraha in South Africa*, 251-256.
43. Gandhi, *Satyagraha in South Africa*, 238-247.
44. Gandhi, *Satyagraha in South Africa*, 279.
45. Louis Fischer, *Mahatma Gandhi*, 125-129; Gandhi, *Satyagraha in South Africa*, 299-304.
46. Gandhi, *Autobiography*, 414; Fischer 154-158.
47. Erik Erikson, *Gandhi's Truth: On The Origins of Militant Non-Violence* (New York: W.W. Norton & Company, Inc., 1969).
48. Gandhi, *Autobiography*, 242; Fischer, *Mahatma Gandhi*, 134, 160-162.
49. Fischer, *Mahatma Gandhi*, 178-181.
50. Fischer, *Mahatma Gandhi*, 185-188; quote on 188.
51. Fischer, *Mahatma Gandhi*, 189.
52. Gandhi, *Autobiography*, 469-471.
53. Erikson, *Gandhi's Truth*, 387; Louis Fischer, *Gandhi, His Life and Message for the World* (New York, Mentor Books/ New American Library, 1982), 71.
54. Fischer, *Mahatma Gandhi*, 207-209; quotes on 209.
55. Fischer, *The Essential Gandhi*, 292.
56. Mohandas K. Gandhi, *Hind Swaraj and Other Writings*, Edited by Anthony J. Parel (New York, Cambridge University Press, 2003), 167.
57. Gandhi, *Hind Swaraj*, 165.
58. Fischer, *The Essential Gandhi*, 230.
59. Gandhi, *Hind Swaraj*, 166.
60. Fischer, *The Essential Gandhi*, 134.
61. Fischer, *The Essential Gandhi*, 135.
62. Gandhi, *The Selected Works*, vol. 6, 282-283.
63. Gandhi, *Satyagraha in South Africa*, 33.
64. Fischer, *The Essential Gandhi*, 12.
65. Fischer, *Mahatma Gandhi*, 273-283; James A Colaiaco, *Martin Luther King, Jr.: Apostle of Militant Non-Violence* (New York St. Martin's Press, 1993), 64-66.
66. Fischer, *Mahatma Gandhi*, 284-291.
67. A short, compelling read of Ambedkar's life is available in Sangharakshita's, *Amebedkar and Buddhism* (Glasgow, Windhorse Publications, 1986).
68. Fischer, *Mahatma Gandhi*, 307-315.
69. Jawaharlal Nehru, *An Autobiography* (New York, Oxford University Press, 1989; Centenary Edition), 370.
70. M.S Gore, *The Social Context of an Ideology: Ambedkar's Political and Social Thought* (New Delhi Sage Publications, 1993), 133-139; Dhananjay Keer, *Dr. Ambedkar, His Life and Mission*, (Bombay: Popular Prakashan Press, 1990), 173-227.
71. Fischer, *Mahatma Gandhi*, 316-324.
72. Nehru, *An Autobiography*, 372.
73. Louis Fischer in *The Life of Mahatma Gandhi* portrays Jinnah in a very negative light, as the chief obstacle to unity and the main driving force for an independent Pakistan. By contrast, M.S. Korejo in *The Frontier Gandhi* lays the blame more squarely on the shoulders of Congress or Gandhi. See M.S. Korejo, *The Frontier Gandhi: His Place in History* (New York, Oxford University Press, 1993). Another source sees the violence as beyond the control of any party by 1946, and due to a number of tragic miscalculations about the partition process — see Yasmin Khan, *The Great Partition: The Making of India and Pakistan* (New Haven, Yale University Press, 2007), Chapter 4.
74. Fischer, *Mahatma Gandhi*, 354-357.
75. Fischer, *Mahatma Gandhi*, 394-395.

76. Michael J. Nojeim, *Gandhi and King: The Power of Nonviolent Resistance* (Westport, Connecticut, Praeger 2004), 87.
77. Gandhi, *Satyagraha in South Africa*, 197.
78. Fischer, *Mahatma Gandhi*, 466-467, 475-476.
79. Fischer, *The Essential Gandhi*, 368-369.
80. Fischer, *Mahatma Gandhi*, 357, 364.
81. Fischer, *The Essential Gandhi*, 347.
82. Fischer, *Mahatma Gandhi*, 479, 491-501.
83. Fischer, *The Essential Gandhi*, 368-369.
84. Fischer, *Mahatma Gandhi*, 17-18.
85. Einstein, *Ideas and Opinions*, 78.
86. Fischer, *The Essential Gandhi*, 228.
87. Fischer, *The Essential Gandhi*, 190.
88. King, *The Essential Writings*, 17.
89. Gandhi, *Satyagraha in South Africa*, 106.
90. Christopher Hitchens, *God is not Great: How Religion Poisons Everything* (New York, Twelve/Warner Books, 2007), 174-177.
91. King, *The Essential Writings*, 573.
92. Eknath Easwaran, *A Man to Match His Mountains: Badshah Khan: Non-Violent Soldier of Islam* (Berkley, California, Nilgiri Press — division of Random House, 1984), 20.
93. Easwaran, *A Man to Match His Mountains*, 111.

Chapter 3: Gandhi — His Beliefs

Gandhi's Ahimsa, Satyagraha

Let us return to the boxing ring. Bin Laden breaks free of the audience members who have come to restrain him. He strikes at Gandhi again, and the Mahatma goes down. Another two men, Islamist-Jihadists, jump up from the audience and attack the men trying to apprehend Bin Laden. They strike, and soon a brawl breaks out. A dozen more people enter the fray to land some good, satisfying and vengeful punches. Screams, grunts, shouts and insults fill the air until the combat reaches its frenzied height. But then soon, as always happens, the brawl settles down (as all brawls and fights invariably do with time), and the belligerent energies dissipate. Afterwards, Bin Laden is again restrained, the Mahatma is standing in the opposite corner, and smiles as he wipes blood from his face carefully. He speaks in a weak and frail voice, but somehow its power resounds in the after-brawl silence. "What have we now accomplished?" he asks. And the power of his message begins to sink in. At some point we have to put down our fists, and start using our heads, for both cannot be effectively used at the same time. This is the long-lasting power, the patient moment of quiet sanity for which non-violence yearns.

Are the forces of Gandhism and Islamist-Jihadism really dueling in the world? No. They have no immediate fight, but they are competing religious ideologies that are available to be believed or rejected. And the historical grounds where they found a home are not far off. Gandhi was born in Gujarat, India, and Bin laden took his Jihad to Afghanistan. The Pathan people of the frontier may be the most immediate and real historical battleground for these opposing ideas — for Pathans have followed Gandhi (in Abdul Ghaffar Khan), and later Pathans have also joined the Taliban. The choices and temptations that they face are not so rare, however. We may all be at times tempted by extremes. And of course the world is still filled with no shortage of pummeling brawls.

Without question, Mohandas Gandhi believed that non-violence was the highest principle to espouse. He ends his *Autobiography*: "My uniform experience has convinced me that there is no other God than Truth. And if every page of these chapters does not proclaim to the reader that the only means for the realization of Truth is Ahimsa, I shall deem all my labor in writing these pages to have been in vain."[1] When India seemed to have rejected that belief at partition, Gandhi's heart was rendered in two. It was as if the life-long teaching he had hoped to impart had fallen on deaf ears. Yet we must recall that he maintained faith in the method itself and refused to give up on non-violence: "*Ahimsa is always infallible. When, therefore, it appears to have failed, the failure is due to the inaptitude of the votary.*"[2] Gandhi believed non-violence was a religious creed incumbent upon all human beings.

Non-violent disobedience became dubbed *satyagraha*, and it was of course *satyagraha* that pursued the highest truth of non-violence. If we recall that *satya*, means "truth" and *agraha* is "firmness" or "the pursuit of", it becomes clear why Gandhi thought that non-violence itself may be infallible, but humans are imperfect advocates for it. Our ideals in any system are always held slightly higher than our natural capacity to realize them, otherwise they would cease to inspire and motivate us. Gandhi insisted that "Satyagraha is soul force pure and simple, and whenever and to whatever extent there is room for the use of arms or physical force or brute force, there and to that extent is there so much less possibility of soul force." In his mind you could not compromise the method. You could not threaten your opponent with the force of arms and the force of truth simultaneously, as the increased use of one diminished reciprocally the use of the other. Gandhi further reiterated this distinction: "Passive resistance may be offered side by side with the use of arms. Satyagraha and brute force, being each a negation of the other, can never go together."[3]

The key to *satyagraha* and *ahimsa* involves Gandhi's understanding of the Gita and renunciation. Those who forsake their passions selflessly are the best masters of their person and most able to fulfill their duty, truthfully, non-violently, and without attachment. In interpreting the *Bhagavad-Gita*, Gandhi wrote: "Only with the body, mind and intellect, and also with the senses, do the *yogis* perform action without attachment for the sake of self-purification."[4] The oath of celibacy, or *brahmacharya*, which Gandhi took was in his view essential for the pursuit of truth. Previously we observed Gandhi positing "A man or woman completely practicing Brahmacharya [Chastity] is absolutely free from passion. Such a one therefore lives nigh unto God, is Godlike."[5] The truth of one's life could then be measured by the fullness of one's devotion to *ahimsa* or nonviolence, and the consequent willingness to abandon every attachment or passion, which might interfere with that goal. It was a goal Gandhi believed any man could pursue whether basing it on the Bible, the Qur'an or the Gita.

The goal was an enormously high hurdle, and Gandhi appreciated that it could not be fully accomplished. "There will never be an army of perfectly non-violent people. It will be formed of those who will honestly endeavor to observe non-violence." Gandhi understood that not everyone (even the Indian National Congress, his closet allies) could fully attain this goal. He did not mandate that others must follow him, but he encouraged them as gently and firmly as he could. Living faith and the belief in God made the raising of an army of *satyagrahis* possible: "The positively necessary training for a non-violent army is an immovable faith in God, willing and perfect obedience to the chief of the non-violent army, and perfect inward and outward cooperation between the units of the army."[6] Faith, nonviolence, truth, all operated in one pursuit — *satyagraha*. The ideals Gandhi held above him were quite far above the norms we might expect of ourselves.

Gandhi knew this. He knew that the ways of the world were not always welcoming to non-violence. For much of history, the laws of savage brutality, of "might makes right", had operated as a kind of law unto itself: "Brute force has been the ruling factor in the world for thousands of years, and mankind has been reaping its bitter harvest all along . . . . There is little hope of anything good coming out of it in the future." Human beings, however, also have a choice: "Man is superior to the brute in as much as he is capable of self-restraint and sacrifice, of which the brute is incapable." According to Gandhi, this choice of good is the stronger choice. Behind the villains and the evil that mars so much of human existence, which tore down the twin towers on September 11 or possessed Hitler to push forward with his "Final Solution", there is a stronger force of love and justice. He believed "the law of love governs the world. Life persists in the face of death. The universe continues in spite of destruction incessantly going on. Truth triumphs over untruth. Love conquers hate." While love cannot tear down buildings, move armies into war, or produce any of the more provocative or Earth-rending forces that violence can, Gandhi believed "the more efficient a force is, the more silent and the more subtle it is. Love is the subtlest force in the world."[7]

Gandhi has given us a preliminary answer to how the *satyagrahi* responds to the *jihadist:* with love, patience, and forgiveness! Yes, this does seem absurd and outrageous answer on the surface. A suicide bomber could make short work of a battalion of non-violent *satyagrahis*. A ruthless man, such as Brigadier General Dyer at Amritsar in India, can kill a lot of innocent people and not even receive the fully justified punishment. How far, and in what contexts *satyagraha* may be plausible, is a question we will discuss further. Gandhi would suggest, however, that the forces of truth and non-violence simply have a greater and more lasting niche in the human spirit. While we are willing and tempted to loan our energies to violence with incessant regularity, there is also a higher calling in us that responds to non-violence. It is the deeper, more lasting truth that endures, as we know we wish to live our daily lives free of violence or its threat. Gandhi bet on the odds that human beings would recognize this, and ultimately that moral conscience would at some point weigh more heavily than savage brutality.

If Gandhi did not expect that all people would be able to commit themselves to non-violence, he at least hoped, prayed, and preached that they should. This dedication that he asked for has implications in the extreme: the willingness to die for one's cause and the truth was a mark of total dedication to *satyagraha*. The language Gandhi uses to describe this is sometimes startling: "The art of dying for a *satyagrahi* consists in facing death cheerfully in the performance of one's duty." This "art" was a serious affair to Gandhi and must be learned: "Just as one must learn the art of killing in the training for violence, so one must learn the art of dying in the training for non-violence." If one had not "learned the art" or mastered the will to do so, one could not be a perfect *satyagrahi:* "So long as we have not cultivated the strength to die with courage and love in our hearts, we cannot hope to develop the *ahimsa* of the strong." It would appear that Gandhi's *satyagrahi* has in common with some violent *jihadists* a complete willingness to die for a cause, but there the similarity would end, for Gandhi called upon one to endure suffering while inflicting none. Indeed, "to die in the act of killing is in essence to die defeated."[8]

This kind of dedication is extreme, and we must ask can Gandhi realistically expect everyone to fulfill it? Gandhi's immediate answer was of course "no." He was remarkably pragmatic as well as dedicated to non-violence. In his own words, Gandhi affirmed, "My resistance to war does not carry me to the point of thwarting those who wish to take part in it. I reason with them. I put before them the better way and leave them to make their choice." Not all could share his level of dedication and Gandhi admitted he could "conceive of occasions when it would be my duty to vote for the military training of those who wish to take it. For I know [everyone] does not believe in non-violence to the extent that I do. It is not possible to make a person or a society non-violent by compulsion." His ideals for himself and for humanity were high, but he also had a flexible approach in trying to realize them. Appreciating the essence of human nature, Gandhi knew that what he was calling for was by no means easy.[9]

While being clear that he abhorred war and violence, Gandhi conceded that *himsa* was a part of life, and *ahimsa* the spiritual hurtle that was so hard to leap. For those who were not able to receive this doctrine, Gandhi allowed for them to follow another. Mohandas explained:

> If we want to learn the use of arms with the greatest possible dispatch, it is our duty to enlist in the Army .... When two nations are fighting, the duty of a votary of Ahimsa is to stop the war. He who is not equal to that duty, he who has no power of resisting war, he who is not qualified to resist war may take part in war and yet wholeheartedly try to free himself, his nation and the world from war.[10]

Of course it is often noted that Gandhi qualified "I do believe that, where there is only a choice between cowardice and violence, I would advise violence. . . . But I believe that non-violence is infinitely superior to violence, forgiveness is more manly than punishment."[11] In his own life, Gandhi experienced personally the alternatives of war and peace, having lived through two world wars, as well as the Boer and Zulu Wars. In three of those wars in which he participated, he offered help in an ambulance corps. He did not absolve himself of responsibility to his nation completely. And during World War One he even helped recruit for Great Britain in defense of war.

This drew quite a bit of negative criticism. How could Gandhi have it both ways? He advocated non-violence, he conceded violence was allowable in extreme circumstances, but would have nothing to do with it himself. Some criticized the line he tried to walk and were disappointed that he did not have as pure a dedication to *ahimsa* as he might have claimed. In reality, however, one finds Gandhi's position quite defensible. He realistically understood he could not wave a magic wand and do away with the violent impulses in human nature. He knew also he could not stop and had no wish to forcibly stop others from participating in self-defense. But as an exemplar to *ahimsa* himself and an inspiration to those of us unable to hold his high ideals, Gandhi knew his own life had to be free of violence. He practiced personally what he preached, but he did not impose an inflexible absolutism upon others, and conceded that such high-minded principles had to be negotiated in a low-principled world. But as he himself stated and understood, he believed nonviolence to be the superior moral ground, and the path we all should choose when we are able. While the point in human history during which violence is absent seems imaginary, we regularly imagine and fantasize about a day when violence is minimized. Gandhi helped push us forward as best he as knew how.

Gandhi as Believer: His Universal Faith

Gandhi seemed innately geared towards a perspective that was inclusive, and universal. We observed before how he asserted: "Is the God of the Mohammedan different from the God of the Hindu? Religions are different roads converging to the same point. What does it matter that we take different roads so long as we reach the same goal? Wherein is the cause for quarreling?"[12] Remember also that Gandhi had predicted: "The time has now passed when the followers of one religion can stand and say, ours is the only true religion and all others are false. The growing spirit of toleration towards all religions is a happy augury of the future."[13]

He was not interested in conversion, because he believed that a sound moral heritage was the common gift of all religions. Gandhi observed:

> I came to the conclusion long ago, after prayerful search and study and discussion with as many people as I could meet, that all religions were true, and also that all had some error in them, and whilst I hold my own, I should hold others as dear as Hinduism. . . .So we can only pray, if we are Hindus, that not a Christian should become a Hindu, or if we are Moslems that not a Hindu or a Christian should become Moslem, nor should we even secretly pray that anyone should be converted, but our inmost prayer should be that a Hindu should be a better Hindu, a Moslem a better Moslem, and a Christian a better Christian . . . . I broaden my Hinduism by loving other religions as my own.[14]

Conversion was not necessary, but it was necessary to make a person a better practitioner of his or her own faith. We know that Gandhi saw the same nonviolent truths preached in the Gospel as in the Gita, so he sincerely did not believe that one religion necessarily had an advantage over another. He did frequently note, however, that religion could be corrupted, that Western Christianity had not lived up to the Gospel, and that Muslims had not realized the essence of their religion, which to Gandhi was a religion of peace.

Regarding Islam, Gandhi observed:

> The sword is the emblem of Islam. But Islam was born in an environment where the sword was and still remains the supreme law. The message of Jesus has proved ineffective because the environment was unready to receive it. So with the message of the Prophet. The sword is too much in evidence among Muslims. It must be sheathed if Islam is to be what it means — peace.[15]

If Gandhi could talk to Bin Laden he would tell Bin Laden that he had misinterpreted the Qur'an. He would say that Bin Laden had extracted all that was belligerent in the tradition of Islam and that he had forgotten everything that was essential to Islam: peace, justice, mercy. Gandhi would remind Bin Laden of an Islamic friend of his own time, Abdul Ghaffar Khan, who had raised an army of nonviolent Muslims. Would Bin Laden listen? Perhaps that is impossible to expect, but perhaps it is possible to hope that the wisdom of Gandhi and Khan can turn future Muslims away from Bin Laden's ideas and to the principles of nonviolence that Gandhi and Khan found in the religion of Islam. Gandhi read the Qur'an from his prayer meetings, and was convinced that its central message was peace.

Gandhi also of course had affirmed that Jesus was the first *satyagrahi*, a discovery later observed by Martin Luther King, Jr. Gandhi loved the message of the Gospel and celebrated its spirit of nonviolence. He did also, however, observe times when the Christian religion (or rather, members of it) had gone astray. He loved the works and thoughts of Tolstoy so much because he believed that Tolstoy had concretely put the message of Christ into practice. Much of Europe had, in Gandhi's view, forgotten the essential truth of Christian principles and of the Gospel itself. The Mahatma did not think that Christianity was bad, or that Christians were lesser, but that they had (much like many Muslims and Hindus) not lived up to the full potential in their religion. He was sorry to say that "as a matter of fact Europe does not believe in it (the New Testament); in Europe, however they do claim to respect it, although a few know and observe Christ's religion of peace."[16]

No person and no religion was perfect. In his *Autobiography*, he reflects upon flaws in Hinduism and Christianity: "if I could not accept Christianity either as a perfect, or the greatest religion, neither was I then convinced of Hinduism being such. Hindu defects were pressingly visible to me."[17]

While critical of all religions and their observers, Gandhi affirmed them all. Louis Fischer once asked Gandhi about a portrait of Christ he kept on his wall, and Gandhi replied, "I am a Christian, and a Hindu, a Moslem, and a Jew." There was truth and beauty in all religions and their followers.[18] Elsewhere Gandhi identified morality as the common link: "it is seen that the rules of morality laid down in the world's great religions, are largely the same. The founders of religion have also explained that morality is the basis of religion."[19]

No religion was perfect. All had problems, but all had the promise of pointing human beings towards an essential moral and spiritual truth. Imagine a telegraph machine, and the telegraph is not perfectly functioning. Some of the words come through on the opposite end clear, but some letters are not clear, or incorrect. The telegraph does not make complete sense, and it is up to the interpreter on the other end to fill in the blanks and make corrections where they occur. There is of course the risk of misinterpretation, yet there is enough integrity to the message (be it any world religion, in Gandhi's view) to be able to make sense of a moral truth that is binding, inspirational, and universal.

The Jains have another analogy. They consider a parable in which a number of blind men are groping with an elephant. One blind man grabs a hold of the elephant's tail and concludes that "elephant" feels somewhat like a snake. Another blind man grips the elephant's leg and thinks that elephant is like a tree trunk, because it is large and round and a little bit course. Then a third blind man touches the long trunk of the elephant and says that it feels like the branch of a tree. Yet a fourth blind mind puts his hand on the side of the elephant's belly and thinks that its nature is like a wide, curved wall. None of the blind men have observed the elephant in its real state, and so all are only clinging to partial, but real truths. So we are all blind to the ultimate and final nature of the Divine (God) in this sense, but we all have at least enough information to make some sense of it; enough sense for our purposes.

Whether one prefers the Jain parable of the elephant or the analogy of the imperfect telegraph, the point is the same: that there is an essential truth contained in religion, but that it operates from a different perspective and set of assumptions from other religions. Ultimately, in Gandhi's view, these all became pathways up the same mountain. He explains this in his own words:

> Religion of our conception, being thus imperfect, is always subject to a process of evolution and re-interpretation. Progress towards Truth, towards God, is possible only because of such evolution. And if all faiths outlined by men are imperfect, the question of comparative merit does not arise. All faiths constitute a revelation of Truth, but all are imperfect and liable to error. Reverence for other faiths need not blind us to their faults.[20]

Finding faults in religion, sometimes in their adherents, sometimes in their texts, Gandhi rejected the exclusive mode of thinking: "I do not believe in the exclusive divinity of the Vedas. I believe in the Bible [and the] Koran to be as much divinely inspired as the Vedas."[21] This did not mean that religion should be dismissed, on the contrary, it deepened the necessity of the religious pursuit. For Gandhi, by studying all religions, one might compensate for the errors that had crept into any given religion. Religion, though imperfect, was essential: "For me all the principle religions are equal in the sense that they are true. They are supplying a felt want in the spiritual progress of humanity."[22]

It became imperative to study *world religion* in as comprehensive a measure possible. Gandhi often had time to read scriptures when he was jailed for his social activism. He maintained: "I hold that it is the duty of every cultured man or woman to read sympathetically the scriptures of the world. If we are to respect others' religions as we would have them respect our own, a friendly study of the world's religions is a sacred duty."[23] It is impossible to imagine Bin Laden saying or suggesting anything of this nature. As we shall see, his theological exclusivism is at the radical extreme from Gandhi's, and therein may be the great advantage of Gandhism over Islamism.

Radical Islamists tend not to recognize diversity in religion or in the opinions about religion. By contrast, Gandhi conjectured, "In theory, since there is one God, there can be only one religion. But in practice, no two persons I have known have had the same and identical conception of God."[24] The idea of going beyond toleration, appreciating that no two people have the exact same religious conception, and a willingness to commit himself to the study of all religions demonstrates a profound religious humility in Gandhi. He did not think he had a monopoly on religious understanding, nor did he think that Hinduism had such a monopoly. Instead, all faiths to him made vital (if partial) contributions to the overarching understanding of religious truth.

One might point to real difficulties within this model of thinking. The universal, inclusive model of thought that Gandhi championed is not without inherent flaws or difficulties. Religions *do not* all share an exactly identical moral evaluation, nor do religions all agree on the essential truth of God. There are glaring contradictions in religious beliefs and dogmas, and there are distinct differences about the nature of the divine truth.

Is there a single God, for example? Christianity, Judaism, and Islam would agree that there is and even share Abraham as a major figure in their faith. Each religion, however, has its own distinctive religious texts, and the moral tenor and tone of them vary. Islam asserts that Jesus was a Prophet, but Muslims reject the idea of the Divinity of Christ that so many Christians hold dear. Gandhi would have believed that if Christ could have been an incarnation of the Divine, then why not Buddha, or Muhammad, or Krishna? Yet the idea that there was *any* incarnation of the Divine would be repulsive to Muslims, and the idea of multiple incarnations (commonly attributed to Vishnu) would be unacceptable to many Christians.

Does in fact the Divine exist at all? Buddhism asserts that the self reincarnates, but with no eternal Soul, and no God. Jainism also challenges the idea of an overarching God, but has 24 leading "Tirthankaras", or "Ford-Makers", who are something like Prophets in their religion. Some religions believe in reincarnation and *karma*, while others indicate an eternal soul that faces an eternal judgment. Religions do not all agree, and one cannot easily sweep the disagreement under the rug merely by declaring that all religions are flawed. How can Gandhism reconcile these problems?

Perhaps it can't, and perhaps it doesn't need to. Gandhi was not a systematic theologian. He never sat down with the intent of rendering a philosophical account of all the religions and the contradictions amongst them. Instead, he was a social activist, a campaigner, letter-writer, and editor of several journals. His writings were toward effecting immediate moral and political change. Louis Fischer describes Gandhi's method as eclectic: "Gandhi took from a person, a book, a religion, and a situation that which was congenial to him and discarded the rest."[25]

The contradictions amongst religions do suggest a profound weakness with the inclusive, universal lens that Gandhi adopted. Nonetheless, that lens offers many comparative advantages. It goes beyond the ideas of tolerance and promotes an inquisitive and healthy sense of learning about other cultures and other religions. In the absence of any final proofs about God, Truth, or Religion, it makes the assumption that all of us have a flawed perception and an incomplete understanding, and that these same flaws may be found in our various religious traditions. Yet, as Gandhi affirmed the importance of all races, he also affirmed that all religions had this shared possibility, as if each had grasped a different spark of the divine, and that by further attending to the spark of that truth, one can ignite the imagination to grasp a higher divine reality. Gandhi thought he might have had glimpses of that reality in his life, but he never claimed to have any special revelation and always asserted a humble attitude towards the highest truths a mind can hope to know. Religion lives in such a domain, as it reaches up into the metaphysical realm where there are our highest hopes and darkest fears. Some measure of that humility is good for us all.

Gandhi suggested, "[All] religions are more or less true. All proceed from the same God but are all imperfect because they come down to us through imperfect human instrumentality." Gandhi believed that since all bore flaws, none should be unduly stigmatized: "[No] propaganda can be allowed which reviles other religions . . . . The best way of dealing with such propaganda is to publicly condemn it."[26] Gandhi considered it an act of *himsa* or violence to view another religion in a pejorative light, as all religions were potential paths to God. The God of Gandhi's mind was a God who allowed for free will, free choice, and freedom to pursue the Divine in differing ways: "To me God is Truth, and Love, God is ethics and morality, God is fearlessness. . . . He is all things to all men . . . . He is ever forgiving for He always gives us the chance to repent. He is the greatest democrat the world knows for He leaves us 'unfettered' to make our own choice between evil and good."[27]

Trying to emphasize what we have in common in terms of a shared morality, and setting aside our differences as best he could, Gandhi said, "I believe in the absolute oneness of God and therefore of humanity."[28] Islam also believes in the oneness of God, that God is indivisible, and that it is a crime of *shirk* or idolatry to think of anything secular as linked to the Divine God. But the Islamist has come to interpret this in a radically different way than Gandhi. Idolatry, or false worship, to Gandhi was commitment to a false set of ethics, a deviation from the true morality he saw in *ahimsa*. So for Gandhi (and, ironically for the Islamists as well), there was little point in separating religion in politics. Indeed, religion and politics for Gandhi have an essential and indivisible unity.

Gandhi's Religion & Politics

Gandhi believed in the *karma yoga* approach to spiritual freedom of *moksha*. In this Hindu scheme, the soul finally exits the state of reincarnation and attains a state of peace and spiritual bliss. It is the Hindu counterpart to going to heaven. The *karma yoga* approach to this is simply that by one's actions one sets the self free. Hence Gandhi was very preoccupied not only with making an impact in political life, but also with his personal appetites, drives, and motivations. As we observed before, the highest degree of spiritual purity made one most fit for *satyagraha*, the realization of *ahimsa* and of truth here on Earth. Gandhi had therefore insisted that there was an inextricable connection with religion, morality, and politics. We observed him saying:

> True religion and true morality are inseparably bound up with each other. Religion is to morality what water is to the seed that is sown in the soil.[29]

> For me, there is no politics without religion — not the religion of the superstitious and the blind, religion that hates and fights, but the universal Religion of Toleration. Politics without morality is a thing to be avoided.[30]

> Religion which takes no account of practical affairs and does not help solve them is not religion.[31]

Gandhi's idea that religion should be about political activism and change is in some ways akin to the conception of the *jihadists*. "Jihad" after all means "struggle", and in particular to realize Islamic values in society. The specific moral values that Gandhi and some *jihadists* have advocated could not be further apart, but the sole fact that their religious outlook is equally politicized is the same. They also see their battle in part as a fight against dominant, Western civilization. To some observers, it might be inferred that these ideas are a threat to the notion of the separation of Church and State, and this seems a problem for those who cherish that notion.

But here we see an essential and very important difference between Gandhi's political religion and that of the *jihadists*. Gandhi never sought to make India a *Hindu* state. He was an ally of the Indian National Congress, of Nehru and Patel, and it was the stated goal of Congress (in contradistinction to Jinnah, who advocated strenuously for a separate Muslim Pakistan) that India should be a secular state that would accommodate both Hindus and Muslims. Gandhi fought hard for the cause of unity and was terribly distraught when Hindu and Muslim violence escalated beyond his control. At the moment of independence he sat separately, incapable of savoring the long-sought-after moment because it was tainted by blood and violence. Although it was Gandhi's intent to unify India, the critical measure of mutual trust was lacking. Agreements failed between Congress and the Muslim League, just as Gandhi was unable to be reconciled with Jinnah.

The creation of Pakistan as a Muslim state also by some default created the image and fears of India as a Hindu State. Although this was not intended, tremendous fears and rioting of a tragic scope erupted. Too few were clear about what the rights, privileges and freedoms in the independent nations would be. There were too many cries of fear and division, which in critical moments and in backwater villages and urban cities, led to drowning out Gandhi's pleas for a tolerant, inclusive State.[32] Gandhi had once said, "the spirit of democracy is not a mechanical thing to be adjusted by abolition of forms. It requires change of the heart. . . . The spirit of democracy requires the inculcation of the spirit of brotherhood."[33] Sadly, this spirit of brotherhood did not exist in sufficient measure, though Gandhi made efforts to put it together. Militant Hindus feared Gandhi had made too many compromises with Muslims, while some Muslims feared Gandhism would be at the champion of *Bharat Mata*, the deified Goddess of Mother India.[34]

These fears are notable and a reflection of a possible problem with secular democratic politics. The simple non-establishment clause of our own Constitution protects against Congress establishing any form of "State Religion." The clause, "separation of church and state", does not appear in the Constitution of course, but in the letters of Thomas Jefferson.[35] Yet this cannot and should not prohibit persons with religious convictions from entering politics, or from formulating moral and ethical views.[36] They must, however, walk a very fine line between expressing views and ideas, with some basis and reason, and actually establishing religious practices in government. This is of course why issues such as abortion and euthanasia become so politically charged, because they walk that fine line and boundary in which it is perceived that religious views might be imposed upon a secular society. It must be appreciated that the difficulties that Gandhi experienced are by no means unique. The dramas and tensions of religion and politics also play out here, but with a different stage and different actors.

To fully reconcile how politically explosive the matter of partition was for Gandhi to handle, imagine the following scenario: that the U.S. recently battled to redeem a lost independence, but unity was not a possible compromise, so the United States is to be partitioned, somewhere along the 36th to 40th degree of latitude. The states of Virginia, Indiana, Illinois, Utah, Nevada and California are amongst those that will be divided between the North United States, and the South United States. Add to this that the North will be declared a Catholic entity, and that the South will be Protestant. Which will you choose? And you have less than a year to decide.

If you are Protestant in the North, do you stay amongst a Catholic majority? Will your freedoms of religion be protected? Will the Northern Catholic States be under the authority of the Pope? If you were a Catholic in the South, you would face similar questions. And Protestants anywhere might ask — will the Southern States be Baptist, Methodist, or Lutheran? And what of Mormons? You can see what a frightening nightmare it would become and how the pain of India's partition was so burdensome to Gandhi. His lifelong plans of preaching unity had dissolved into Hindustan and Pakistan.

Gandhi would have advocated religious unity and a secular state, but there are many *Islamists* now who want the opposite. Can a democracy still function if it is based upon explicitly religious principles? It may not be what Americans or Gandhi would want, but it is an option that appeals to many who are discontent with their status quo.

Gandhi and Equality

By now a consistent principle of equality should be evident in Gandhi's life and thought. Rejecting racism, inequality and oppression by economic classes, and also "caste-ism", or discrimination against the untouchables of India, Gandhi developed a thorough dedication to the idea that all men and women are created equal, regardless of religious creed, racial, social, or economic background. To erect barriers between people, to give benefits to one while simultaneously depriving them of another, was *himsa*, or violence against humanity. Hence Gandhi would be sympathetic to radical thinkers who challenged inequality on any level, whether it was based upon gender, caste, or class.

In addition to his "crusade" against untouchability, Gandhi believed that women should be free and equal in India.[37] He opposed arranged child marriages. One of his "five virtues" was in fact equality for women.[38] Women came to play a prominent role for Gandhi, as his followers, friends, contributing funds for his campaigns, and even being arrested in the cause of *satyagraha*. Gandhi's language about women could be very complimentary: "I have suggested. . . .that woman is the incarnation of *Ahimsa*. *Ahimsa*, which again means infinite capacity for suffering." This might not sound complimentary until one remembers that *Ahimsa* was his highest principle. Elsewhere Gandhi's words about women reinforced some traditional stereotypes of females as passive and males as active. "It is a woman's right to rule the home. Man is the master outside it. Man is the earner, woman saves and spends. Woman looks after the feeding of the child. She shapes its future. She is responsible for building its character." Mohandas admitted that "Man has regarded woman as his tool", and insisted that women "should labor under no legal disability suffered by a man." Hence his concept and expression of women's rights were still very conservative. While Gandhi may therefore have been a positive force for women's rights, his conception hardly falls in line with that of many progressive feminist voices.[39]

Gandhi was not the first to observe the desire for the essential equality of women. The Hindu reformer Rammohun Roy, known as the "Father of Modern India", had been an advocate for women's education and equality. Roy had insisted it was unfair to be biased against women's intellect without having given them the opportunity of education. He cited examples of very intelligent women he had known and believed that the character of women could be very courageous and much more trustworthy than that of men.[40] Gandhi did not much refer to Roy in his more popular writings, but in many ways, he was continuing the unfinished work of the latter.

"Caste-ism" was also unacceptable to Gandhi. He became a passionate advocate of the cause of the untouchables and an opponent to all discrimination that they suffered. It must be made clear that Gandhi was not always consistent about caste, and many have criticized him for this. Many look to his opponent B.R. Ambedkar as a more consistent and effective advocate for the untouchables.[41] At an earlier point (1921), Gandhi had insisted that caste barriers should be observed in social and dining matters, but later (1932), he refuted that idea and abandoned distinctions of caste altogether.[42] Gandhi confessed, "I have never made a fetish of consistency. I am a votary of Truth and I must say what I feel and think at a given moment on the question without regard to what I may have said before on it."[43]

Gandhi had, however, opposed the idea of untouchability from childhood. As previously stated, Gandhi confronted his mother about this, and was known to play with untouchables from his youth.[44] This sense of fair play he claims from an early age:

> I was hardly yet twelve when this idea had dawned on me. A scavenger named Uka, an untouchable, used to attend our house for cleaning latrines. Often I would ask my mother why it was forbidden to touch him .... I was a very dutiful and obedient child and so far as it was consistent with respect for parents I often had tussles with them on this matter. I told my mother that she was entirely wrong in considering physical contact with Uka as sinful.[45]

Gandhi later came to call the untouchables *Harijan*, or "Children of God." He insisted that in fact untouchability had nothing to do with Hinduism, that it was an affront to the Hindu religion.[46] Recall that Gandhi said:

> Caste distinction is not observed in the Ashram because caste has nothing to do with religion in general and Hinduism in particular. It is a sin to believe anyone else is inferior or superior to ourselves. We are all equal. It is the touch of sin that pollutes us and never that of a human being. None are high and none are low for one who would devote his life to service. The distinction between high and low is a blot on Hinduism which we must obliterate.[47]

Gandhi in fact came to be very open and even insistent upon inter-caste marriage. He took it upon himself in his *ashram* to obliterate the social and religious barriers that existed in the world outside. If it could not be done under his roof, it could not be done at all. If Gandhi had been able to confine his social reforms to simply a few hundred people, his dedication to *ahimsa*, *satyagraha*, Hindu-Muslim unity, and the abolition of untouchability might have been more successful. In India at the time, however, he had to wrestle with three hundred million people, and he traveled by third-class train ticket or on foot, for the most part. He was only one man amongst millions to spread a difficult message.[48]

Some have credited B.R. Ambedkar as a more effective advocate of the untouchables than Mohandas Gandhi. Ambedkar was after all from the untouchables himself, and his remarkable story of how he attained an education, abolished discrimination against the untouchables in the Constitution, and finally converted to Buddhism is one that should be more broadly told. Ambedkar was focused on the political and economic problems of untouchability, as he had no confidence that the Dalits (his term for the untouchables) could be bettered by Hinduism (his life story demonstrably speaks to that legitimate fear). Gandhi still had hopes that Hinduism could be reformed and untouchables welcomed within the fold. That hope had long died in Ambedkar's heart.

Ambedkar had not rebelled wholly against religion itself. Marxism or atheism was no answer for him. He replied to critics, "some people think that religion is not essential to society. I do not hold this view. I consider the foundations of religion to be essential to life and practices of society." He further added "What good things I have in me, or whatever have been the benefits of my education to society, I owe them to the religious feelings in me. I want religion but I do not want hypocrisy in the name of religion."[49] Finally Ambedkar decided that Buddhism was the only religion that would be appropriate for the untouchables. In a mass conversion ceremony, he converted up to a half million untouchables to Buddhism, indicating his proper stature and importance in Indian religious history.[50]

Gandhi and Ambedkar had other differences than merely over how to emancipate the untouchables, but we will not go into them here. If Gandhi was not always consistent in his life about caste, it is thought that he ended up on the right side of the issue. His efforts to free the oppressed straddled categories of race, caste, class, and nation. Few people have fought for social justice on two continents as he has.

Tolstoy and Ruskin reflected Gandhi's principles of equality and equal living. We saw above how Ruskin taught him that all labor had equal worth, or at least inherent value. Gandhi could not reconcile a system of complete equality, but the religious zeal he found in Tolstoy for better, fairer, more equal living was one he permanently took to heart.

Gandhi had rejected wealth and opulence. Leaving behind the proper dress of an English gentleman, Gandhi came to live with the poorest of the poor alongside the untouchables of India, even inviting them into his *ashram*. He disliked any in-egalitarian boundary, whether it was against women, the untouchables, or simply the impoverished. He was as critical of the diamonds and jewelry on display by Hindu Maharajas as he was of Western materialism.

While Gandhi believed "the rich and the poor will always be with us"[51], he emphatically opposed capitalist inequality:

> [Economic equality] is the master key to non-violent Independence. Working for economic equality means abolishing the eternal conflict between capital and labor. It means leveling down the few rich in whose hands is concentrated the bulk of the nation's wealth . . . . and the leveling up of the semi-starved millions . . . . A non-violent system of government is clearly an impossibility so long as the wide gulf between the rich and the hungry millions persists. The contrast between the palaces of New Delhi and the miserable hovels of the poor laboring classes nearby cannot last one day in a free India, in which the poor will enjoy the same power as the richest in the land. A violent and bloody revolution is a certainty one day unless there is a voluntary abdication of riches and the power that riches give, and a sharing of them for the common good.[52]

These are strong words, so the question must be asked, was Gandhi a Communist or sympathetic with Communism? The answer to this question must be no. Gandhi opposed the violence he saw in the Communist system of thinking. Violence was not the cure for the workingman's woes: "[Destruction] of the capitalist must mean destruction in the end of the worker, and no human being is so bad as to be beyond redemption, no human being is so perfect as to warrant his destroying him who he wrongly considers to be wholly evil."[53] Capitalists and labor could possibly work out their differences:

> Capital. . . . and labor should supplement each other. They should be a great family living in unity and harmony, capital not only looking to the material welfare of the laborers but their moral welfare also, capitalists being trustees for the welfare of the laboring classes under them.[54]

Further he reiterated:

> I do not fight shy of capital. I fight capitalism. The [example of the] West teaches one to avoid concentration of capital, to avoid a racial war in another and deadlier form. Capital and labor need not be antagonistic to each other. I cannot picture to myself a time when no man shall be richer than another. But I do picture to myself a time when the rich will spurn to enrich themselves at the expense of the poor and the poor will cease to envy the rich. Even in a most perfect world, we shall fail to avoid inequalities, but we can and must avoid strife and bitterness."[55]

There were aspects to socialism which Gandhi admired. Indeed, Gandhi went so far as to state that he believed, "truth and *Ahimsa* must incarnate in socialism. In order that they can, the votary must have a living faith in God. Mere mechanical adherence to truth and *Ahimsa* is likely to break down at the critical moment. Hence have I said that truth is God. This God is a living Force. Our life is of that Force. That force resides in, but is not the body."[56] Further, Gandhi said, "Socialism is a beautiful word and so far as I am aware in Socialism all the members of society are equal — none low, none high. In the individual's body the head is not high because it is [at] the top. . . . nor are the soles of the feet low because they touch the earth. Even as members of the individual's body are equal so are the members of society."[57]

The egalitarian aspects of a Socialist way of thinking were acceptable to Gandhi, but he rejected Socialism and Communism on the grounds of their materialism and atheism. He had had the opportunity to read some of the works of Marx while in prison, and he rejected the idea of violent revolution (even if he forewarned elsewhere that it might be a possibility if society did not reform itself). Gandhi's use of Socialism and Communism was probably much like Martin Luther King, Jr.'s — King rejected it as a materialist, atheist creed, but accepted the message of equality that was consonant with Christian ethics. King critically observed both systems:

> Capitalism may lead to practical materialism that is as pernicious as the theoretical materialism taught by communism. We must honestly recognize that truth is not to be found either in traditional capitalism or in Marxism.
>
> My reading of Marx also convinced me that truth is found neither in Marxism nor in the traditional capitalism. Each represents a partial truth. Historically, capitalism failed to see the truth in collective enterprise and Marxism failed to see the truth in individual enterprise.[58]

King and Gandhi appropriated from Marxism the political emphasis on remedying the inequality which capitalism tends to exacerbate. It is, in this author's opinion, foolish to assert that this makes either one a Communist or a Socialist. They were both religious progressives with a strong sense of social and economic justice. It must be conceded that at some point, radical political and religious ends do meet, but it would be nonsensical to assert then that Marx was (truly) religious or Gandhi was a Marxist. They shared some radical ideas, but explicitly rejected the ideological vehicle (be it religious or atheistic) that got the other person there. Despite the irreconcilable nature of some of their ideas, it is hoped that their idealism about a better, more equal and just economic world can yet make positive impact in the world.

Gandhi's View of Civilization

The modern day Islamists such as Bin Laden have accepted an idea of a "Clash of Civilizations." Bernard Lewis was one of the first to suggest the notion, and Samuel Huntington has famously described the concept that in the modern day we are witnessing the clash of civilizations and their values. Huntington has written: "The underlying problem for the West is not Islamic fundamentalism. It is Islam, a different civilization whose people are convinced of the superiority of their culture and are obsessed with the inferiority of their power."[59] Actually this statement is really incorrect. The clash seems to be with radical Islamism, and not with the religion of Islam itself. Most Muslims categorically reject the radical attacks of the Jihadist-Islamists. In fact, the idea that we are at war with Islam seems to be one of the bad overreactions that Bernard Lewis has warned us about.[60] Nonetheless, as we shall soon see, it is the idea of a Clash of Civilizations which Bin Laden himself accepts and wishes others to accept as well.

Did Gandhi entertain any such views? He was a leader of a colonized nation resisting the reign and hegemony of the British Empire. Gandhi did not always look charitably upon the idea of "Western Civilization." When one person asked him what he thought of "Western Civilization", Gandhi once impishly answered, "it would be a good idea." If taken out of context, some of Gandhi's words can seem quite harsh, as we previously saw: "The British Government in India constitutes a struggle between modern civilization, which is the Kingdom of Satan, and the ancient civilization, which is the Kingdom of God. The one is the God of War, the other is the God of Love."[61] Gandhi had romanticized the moral potential of Indian Civilization and no doubt scorned the greed and oppressive brutality that he witnessed in the British Colonial Empire. There was a very real contest going on, and Churchill loathed the "half-naked fakir" and his values of simplicity and apparent poverty. There did seem to be some basis for the idea that there was a clash of values of opposing civilizations, and all one has to do is read Gandhi's *Hind Swaraj* and other works to see evidence of this.

There is, of course, a critical difference that must be made clear in the battle that Gandhi was fighting and the battle which the Islamist-Jihadists have waged. That of course is over the issues of violence and forgiveness. Those are two critical components. Gandhi rejected categorically the use of violence in this "clash of civilizations", and believed in forgiving one's opponent, and converting the conscience. It is also important to emphasize that Gandhi believed there was essential religious equality between Christianity and Hinduism. Gandhi did not think that Western Christians were "Kaffirs" or "Infidels", or in any way inferior. In his view, many European Christians had not properly understood the essence of their own religion, but this was also true for Hindus, and Gandhi made this clear. It must be reiterated that Gandhi was not in any way making this a war of cultural supremacy. The abuse of power and the choice of service to the laws of brutality instead of to the laws of love was part of the basic problem. That choice belonged to all cultures. Gandhi thought the West had made some wrong choices and was trying to avoid those same mistakes in India.

Gandhi did think there was a clash of civilizations, but those were largely in value choices which the West had made, and which it could unmake. Gandhi believed those value choices were to the service of greed and power and that the "craze for machinery" had alienated Westerners from true values. Marx had believed that capitalism alienated oneself from the control in one's own labor, in his *species being*.[62] Gandhi believed that capitalism really alienated ourselves from our morality in that it forced us to make the expedient choice of the profit of a few and the misery of the many. His critique was not quite Marxist, but it did share some striking similarities. While Gandhi expressed some potential for capitalists and workers to reconcile their difference, he had suggested (as we noted) "today machinery merely helps a few to ride the backs of millions."[63] It was *industrial civilization*, with its dependency on the machine and its ranks of lower class workers serving upper class interests, that troubled Gandhi: "Industrialism is, I am afraid, going to be the curse of mankind. Exploitation of one nation by another cannot go on for all time. Industrialism depends entirely on your capacity to exploit, on foreign markets being open to you and on the absence of competition."[64] That is why Gandhi broke with his friend saying, "Pandit Nehru wants industrialization because he thinks that if it is socialized, it would be free from the evils of capitalism. My own view is that the evils are inherent in industrialism, and no amount of socialization can eradicate them."[65] In some ways Gandhi actually rejects modernity more explicitly than Bin Laden.

Gandhi really did not want India to mimic the West when it attained independence. He believed that inequality was inherent to industrialism, and severe inequalities were tantamount to *himsa* or violence against the people. He wrote, "Machinery is the chief symbol of modern civilization; it represents a great sin."[66] Favoring the autonomous village, which wove its own clothes and was not dependent upon machines or any aspect of modern civilization, Gandhi at times appears to be very anti-modern in his thinking. Nehru and some others refused to take the ideas of *Hind Swaraj* seriously, seeing them as out of place in a modern world, and in many ways they were. But Gandhi wanted as much as possible to do away with the evils and inequality of modern civilization, and if that meant insisting upon simple living and homespun, it was fine by him. Pragmatically he realized there was little chance that the rest of India would follow the ideals of his ashram. As he displayed a willingness to compromise on violence and allow those to defend themselves who chose, he sometimes showed some flexibility on machines. His answers were religious, and rooted in his reading of the Gita, the Bible, of Tolstoy and Ruskin.

Gandhi was definitely not a Communist. He opposed maximizing the powers of the State: "I look upon an increase of the power of the State with the greatest fear, because, although while apparently doing good by minimizing exploitation, it does the greatest harm to mankind by destroying individuality which lies at the root of all progress."[67] In some places Gandhi almost sounds downright conservative, touting the (Federalist) maxim "[A] Government that is ideal governs the least." Though he did insist the Government had a responsibility to take care of poor citizens, Gandhi time and again rejected the Communist model and asserted that a progressive democracy had a duty to help its own but also to keep its government in check.[68]

The "Clash of Civilizations" which Gandhi viewed is that he did not want to exchange British masters for Hindu masters. He did not care for the unequal, oppressive fabric of Western Civilization, and if *Hind Swaraj* could be styled on an alternative set of values, he sought it. Gandhi even once said, "I hold that economic progress. . . . is antagonistic to real progress."[69] What Gandhi meant is that the pursuit of material gain and greed had blinded Western Civilization to its own best values. Hindu Civilization would suffer the same fate if it made the same choices. The great "Clash of Civilizations" thus amounted to an existential moral choice, to be attached to the fruits of ones actions (the greedy oppressive way), or to renounce those fruits. It was much the same choice which Gandhi had read in the Gita or the Gospel. This basic moral choice would, for Gandhi, have political repercussions in all institutions of modernity.

Gandhi's Ideas — Strengths and Weaknesses

We must remember that Gandhi was a human being. He has been much revered and even mythologized as a hero of our age, and rightly so. There is some use to mythology. To elevate some heroes above ourselves and wrap them in some measure of myth and legend helps them serve as an inspiring example to the rest of us. To be true to historical fact, however, we must remember that "de-mythologizing" and reconstructing the human identity of revered figures such as Gandhi is also important. Gandhi often voiced his displeasure with the title of "Mahatma", and acknowledged his faults. He invited criticism: "Let those who will, therefore, denounce me if I am the impostor they imagine me to be though they may not say so in so many words. It might disillusion the millions who persist in regarding me as a Mahatma. I must confess the prospect of being so debunked greatly pleases me."[70] We must take some time to criticize the weaknesses of Gandhi's thoughts and spiritual program as well as to find the strengths. Once we complete our review of Bin Laden, we will be able to extend and revise these remarks in our conclusion.

Most people would not take the oath of *Brahmacharya* (celibacy), which Gandhi did. Of course Gandhi took this oath as a part of his total program of moral reform to be the best Mahatma he could be, whether he welcomed the title or not. He wrote once, "Those who want to perform national service or those who want a glimpse of real religious life, must lead a celibate life, no matter married or unmarried."[71] Most would not make that sacrifice to be an Olympian moralist. "What is *Brahmacharya*?" he continued, "It is the way of life which leads us to *Brahma* (God). It includes full-control over the process of reproduction."[72] Gandhi's views on sexuality are very conservative. In some respects his views are compatible with Catholic views over human sexuality and a challenge to modern, secular attitudes.

Gandhi believed, following in line with his dedication to *Brahmacharya*, that self-control was the best method of birth control. He resisted the idea of contraceptives, thinking them to be a poor substitute for the discipline of the self and its appetites.[73] It was consistent with his ideas of renunciation, but it would be difficult to expect this iron discipline from the rest of civilization. His words might easily be comparable to any number of Catholic edicts on the subject. Gandhi wrote:

> This sex urge has been isolated from the desire for progeny and it is said by the protagonists of the use of contraceptives that conception is an accident to be prevented except when the parties desire to have children. I venture to suggest this is a most dangerous doctrine to preach anywhere, much more so in a country like India . . . . Marriage loses its sanctity when its purpose and highest use is conceived to be the satisfaction of the animal passion without contemplating the natural result of such satisfaction.[74]

Gandhi remained determined to uphold the highest sexual ideals himself but at times had an almost lurid fascination with doing so. In his waning years, there were reports of him sleeping nude alongside young girls just to prove his strength against temptation. Some of his followers and opponents have criticized him severely for this.[75] It was a most odd thing for an old man to do. Fischer writes that Gandhi had "deliberately surrounded himself with women to prove that his mastery over lust was not achieved by avoiding women."[76] Had Gandhi been able to conquer his feelings? Gandhi admitted to moments of temptation.[77] He wrestled with sexuality over his lifetime. The legacy of these thoughts about sex seem undoubtedly linked to the guilt surrounding his sexual activity at the time of his father's death.[78] Gandhi seemed ever after to want to stamp out the demon that he perceived possessed him at that moment. Most today, I suspect, would consider this zeal for celibate purity to be excessive.

A critical question must also be leveled at Gandhi's ideal of Home Rule, or *Hind Swaraj*. The accepted mantra of today is free trade and bringing down any import or export barriers that lie in the way to making the production and sale of goods as efficient and cheap as possible. It is not a new dogma and finds its roots back to Adam Smith's *Wealth of Nations*. Smith believed that nations should produce and sell what goods they can at the greatest absolute advantage; Ricardo and others have elaborated upon and continued this doctrine as comparative advantage. Intuitively it makes some great sense: why force consumers to buy goods at more expensive rates if they can get them more cheaply from another source that manufactures them just as well? Free markets may not always be fair markets, in that they can result in labor disruption and loss of employment in a competitive playing field that is not always evenly stacked. Yet free markets (and a comparative lack of government controls) enjoy an obvious current advantage to the command economies of Communism that have failed.

All the same, there has been great resistance to the ideal of the free market as well. With dominant monopoly powers, many have argued that the free market isn't so free. A move away from global free markets and towards local, community production has also been put forward. Gandhi would have favored the ideal of small, autonomous markets. His book, *Hind Swaraj*, champions the village economy, as we illustrated before. Many have discarded *Hind Swaraj* as an unworkable economic model for India. There is crass oversimplification that can be found in *Hind Swaraj*; it is from an earlier point in time when Gandhi was prone to make sharp and simplistic dichotomies. He once wrote there that he thought "The tendency of Indian civilization is to elevate the moral being, that of Western civilization is to propagate immorality. The latter is godless, the former is based upon a belief in God."[79] Such syllogism would seem to spring more readily from the mouth of Bin Laden than of Gandhi, and I think if his attention was drawn towards it he would have repented of making it. Elsewhere statements contradict this idea and Gandhi admits to learning considerably from the West. What he probably meant, however, was that copying the mode of industrial civilization, with its greed and inequality, would be a bad paradigm for India. It would exchange Eastern problems for Western. That Gandhi's own economic model was workable seems very doubtful to me.

Gandhi also seemed naïvely overconfident in *ahimsa* and *satyagraha*. Let me be clear that I believe Gandhi's method is one of the most important religious and political contributions of recent times, and that he was correct to always affirm that nonviolence is better than violence. Those priorities are shared here, and Gandhi continues to be an inspiration to all of us. But I am not entirely satisfied that Gandhi's program of non-violence could have positive effects in all places, at all times, or against all types of regimes. There are some political contexts in which *satyagraha* would seem to have very limited effect. One of those would be in trying to overwhelm and persuade persons such as Osama bin Laden. Both men have intractable views and would mix like oil and water.

Without the protection and recourse to the military, it is also hard to imagine nonviolent resisters melting the hearts of some of the most savage persons in our history, taking Hitler as one example.

Yet Gandhi seemed to have confidence that *satyagraha* could in fact be effective against Hitler. He believed that non-violence could be a novel experience for Hitler, for "hitherto he and his likes have built upon their invariable experience that men yield to force." Gandhi assumed that Hitler and the Nazis "have the same soul that I have", which shows his amazing willingness to consider possible good latent in all people.[80] But did Hitler and the Nazis really have the kind of moral conscience to respond to nonviolence? Did Brigadier General Dyer? Or had that conscience already been purged from their souls? It seems Gandhi has underestimated humanity's capacity for inhumanity.

At the outset of World War II, Gandhi did not wish to lend his support to yet another conflict. His appeals to a non-violent response from Great Britain seem badly utopian:

> I appeal to every Briton, wherever he may be now, to accept the method of non-violence instead of that of war. . . . I want you to fight Nazism without arms or, if I am to retain military terminology, with non-violent arms. I would like you to lay down the arms. . . . being useless for saving you or humanity. You will invite Hitler and Mussolini to take what they want. . . . let them take possession of your beautiful island with your beautiful buildings. You will give all these, but neither your souls nor your minds. If these gentlemen want to occupy your houses, you will vacate them. If they do not give you free passage out, you will allow yourselves, man woman and child, to be slaughtered, but you will refuse to owe your allegiance to them.[81]

This was at the outset of war in 1939, so neither Gandhi nor the world had a full appreciation of the brutality of Hitler's Nazis, so these remarks taken in context might ameliorate the unrealism that they convey. No doubt Gandhi was appealing to the highest idealism, and the British chose wisely not to follow Gandhi here. Elsewhere Gandhi displayed a similar naiveté when he asked for the Jews to respond nonviolently to the Nazis. Fischer's extended biography of Gandhi offers some controversial material that is worth reproducing here.

Gandhi had also written earlier in November 1938:

> If I were a Jew born in Germany and earned my livelihood there, I would claim Germany as my home even as the tallest gentile German might, and challenge him to shoot me or cast me in the dungeon. . . . And for doing this I should not wait for the fellow Jews to join me in civil resistance, but would have confidence that in the end the rest were bound to follow my example. If one Jew or all the Jews were to accept the prescription here offered, he or they cannot be worse off than now. . . . The calculated violence of Hitler may even result in a general massacre of the Jews by way of this first answer to the declaration of such hostilities. But if the Jewish mind could be prepared for voluntary sacrifice, even the massacre I have imagined could be

> turned into a day of thanksgiving that Jehovah had wrought deliverance of the race even at the hands of a tyrant. For to the God-fearing, death has no terror.
>
> Gandhi continued: The Jews of Germany can offer Satyagraha under infinitely better auspices than the Indians of South Africa. The Jews are a compact, homogenous community in Germany. They are far more gifted than the Indians of South Africa. And they have organized world opinion behind them.[82]

These remarks coming as early as they did in 1938 and 1939, and the Holocaust not having yet transpired, might be understandable. Yet Fischer interviewed Gandhi again in 1946 and his ideas seem not to have changed. Gandhi said in 1946, "Hitler killed five million Jews. It is the greatest crime of our time. But the Jew should have offered themselves to the butcher's knife. They should have thrown themselves into the sea from the cliffs. . . . It would have aroused the world and the people of Germany. . . . As it is they succumbed anyway in their millions."[83]

I believe these words debunk the Mahatma as one also capable of poor judgment. Gandhi had no immediate experience of what the Jews went through in Europe. It was worse than the most brutal treatment of the untouchables. The untouchables were oppressed, spurned, and set aside, but they were never systematically murdered in the way that Hitler murdered Jews, Gypsies, and other "unwanted persons." A missionary who addressed Gandhi on this issue had said to him, "You do not know Hitler and Mussolini — they are incapable of moral response. They have no conscience, and they have made themselves impervious to world opinion." The missionary said Gandhi's nonviolence would be playing right into the dictator's hands, and Gandhi's response was, "Your argument presupposes that the dictators like Mussolini and Hitler are beyond redemption."[84]

That seems to be precisely the point, however, and it appears here that the missionary knew the "children of light" from the "children of darkness" more squarely than Gandhi did. Gandhi's hope in the inner humanity of man was unconquerable, but so great was his faith in *ahimsa* and in *satyagraha* that it blinded him to the fact that while he had captured the greatness of the human spirit, there may be those who had lost it altogether. It is no easy argument, for religious scholars such as Thomas Merton wisely point out that it is totalitarian ideologies that benefit most from the concept of "irredeemable evil." Because some are thought to be beyond redemption (for the Nazis this was the Jews) it makes them easier to obliterate.[85] One never wishes to commit oneself to the same error of the Nazi ideology, but the extremes of nonviolence that Gandhi recommended here were simply, in this case, wrong.

If Jewish *satyagraha* had been heavily backed by Christian and Socialist support, and even defection from Nazis, then nonviolence against Hitler might have been possible. Barring Christian, Socialist or even defecting Nazi support, it is difficult to imagine a successful Jewish *satyagraha*, even with a man of Gandhi's stature at its head. Given the badly divided politics of the time, that solidarity and the climate for nonviolent success seems absent. Was there a better way?

Reinhold Niebuhr maintained that Gandhi himself was confused about his concept of nonviolence. Niebuhr's critique suggests that Gandhi had over-idealized his concept of *satyagraha*. Persons who resist nonviolently, by strike or boycott, nonetheless do resist and therefore are employing some form of coercion in the physical realm. This physical coercion can potentially become violent, as it sometimes did. A nonviolent strike or boycott still has the real effects of putting others out of work, losing their jobs, and perhaps starving or being compelled to use counterforce. Hence no absolute distinction, in Niebuhr's view, can be made between a force that resists nonviolently and that which resists violently. The potential for one can spill over into the other.[86] Niebuhr's belief that Gandhi was "confused" about what he meant is patronizing and wrong, but the idea that nonviolence is not easily controlled or does not always fit the context seems right.

A simpler critique is really that of the missionary who challenged Gandhi: are all people really capable of redemption (especially via human means)? Can *satyagraha* really penetrate the dark heart of the likes of Hitler, and bring it back to moral light? Realism would assert "no", while idealism would hope "yes." But those forces would have to have a very Godly power, a purity and a strength which is really beyond most human beings to muster, and a willingness to endure suffering that is beyond most anyone's capacity to endure. In my view, there are some persons and political contexts in which *satyagraha* would be ineffective, and that I would have to recommend the use of violent force. I commend Gandhi for his high idealism, but I believe that his intense dedication to those ideals at times blinded him to a courser reality.

Reinhold Niebuhr had once declared himself a pacifist before turning quite forcefully against pacifism. His Christian Realist approach would insist that an evil of the magnitude of Adolf Hitler had to be resisted. Niebuhr wrote in 1942:

> To be in a battle means to defend a cause against its peril, to protect a nation against its enemies, to strive for truth against error, to defend justice against injustice. To be above the battle means that we understand how imperfect the cause is which we defend, that we contritely acknowledge the sins of our own nations, that we recognize the common humanity which binds us to even the most terrible foes, and that we know also of our common need of grace and forgiveness.[87]

Niebuhr did not believe war to be a good thing, but sometimes it was a necessary thing, and "to be above the battle" was to admit one's common need for the redemption of sin while using lethal force to uphold justice and protect the innocent. Strikingly, Gandhi had elsewhere conceded also the possibility to use force. Recall just above that Gandhi said:

> My resistance to war does not carry me to the point of thwarting those who wish to take part in it. I reason with them. I put before them the better way and leave them to make their choice.

That further Gandhi could: conceive of occasions when it would be my duty to vote for the military training of those who wish to take it. For I know [everyone] does not believe in non-violence to the extent that I do. It is not possible to make a person or a society non-violent by compulsion.[88]

If Gandhi would have (more reluctantly than Niebuhr) allowed for the use of force, why did he not simply admit so in the context of the Jews and Hitler? Gandhi had no "fetish for consistency", except in striving to realize every possible measure of *ahimsa*. If he did not understand the full measure of Hitler's brutality, it is probably because he had no immediate experience of it himself. We must bear in mind, Gandhi's concept of *satyagraha's* success against Nazis existed only in his hypothetical imagination. Suffice it to say that nonviolence is a higher ideal than war — we agree with that; but that nonviolence can be applied in any or every circumstance seems a false proposition.

Gandhi was by no means perfect. His thoughts strayed, and sometimes he contradicted himself. He wrote and spoke prodigiously. If anyone were to take bits and slices, sound bytes and excerpts from moments of any of our own lives when we have lost our temper, we could all be made out to be fools or devils. Gandhi was no devil, and mythologizing him as a saint offers us all a hero to emulate, but the reality of course was that he was only a man. He was a man with remarkable ideas and an almost unparalleled commitment to truth and justice. His appeal to *ahimsa*, to an inclusive, universal and tolerant outlook of religion is especially appreciated here. If indeed the best aspects of the Gandhian way were to have more traffic in modern civilization, it would have a huge impact in making this world a more tolerable place.

Notes

1. Gandhi, *Autobiography*, 503-504.
2. Merton, *Gandhi On Nonviolence*, 93.
3. Gandhi, *Satyagraha in South Africa*, 105-106.
4. Gandhi, *The Bhagavad-Gita*, 106.
5. Fischer, *The Essential Gandhi*, 243.
6. Merton, *Gandhi on Nonviolence*, 40, 88.
7. Fischer, *The Essential Gandhi*, 90, 190, 198, 205.
8. Merton, *Gandhi On Nonviolence*, 43, 61, 85, 91.
9. Fischer, *The Essential Gandhi*, 208, 334.
10. Fischer, *The Essential Gandhi*, 125.
11. Narayan, *The Selected Works*, volume 6, 175.
12. Fischer, *The Essential Gandhi*, 12.
13. Gandhi, *The Selected Works*, vol. 6, 272.
14. Fischer, *The Essential Gandhi*, 212.
15. Fischer, *The Essential Gandhi*, 211.
16. Gandhi, *Satyagraha in South Africa*, 15.
17. Gandhi, *Autobiography*, 137.
18. Fischer, *Mahatma Gandhi*, 335.
19. Narayan, *The Selected Works*, volume 4, 22-23.

20. Narayan, *The Selected Works*, volume 4, 241.
21. Fischer, *The Essential Gandhi*, 213.
22. Narayan, *The Selected Works*, volume 6, 266.
23. Narayan, *The Selected Works*, volume 6, 267.
24. Narayan, *The Selected Works*, volume 6, 268.
25. Fischer, *Mahatma Gandhi*, 219.
26. Fischer, *The Essential Gandhi*, 213.
27. Fischer, *The Essential Gandhi*, 228-229.
28. Fischer, *The Essential Gandhi*, 229.
29. Narayan, *The Selected Works*, volume 6, 264.
30. Gandhi, *The Selected Works*, volume 6, 435
31. Gandhi, *My Religion,* 3, 4.
32. Khan, *The Great Partition*, Chapters 2-5.
33. Fischer, *The Essential Gandhi*, 221.
34. Earlier in the 1920s Gandhi had shown a willingness to compromise on cow killing. Muslims could kill and eat beef, but the cow was a sacred animal to Hindus. It shows that he was willing to stretch beyond the orthodox fold. Gandhi also much later had fasted for reparations to be paid to the Muslim nation of Pakistan. It was perhaps for that willingness to bargain with Muslims that he was assassinated by a militant Hindu. See Gandhi, *Autobiography*, 478-479; see also Fischer, *Mahatma Gandhi*, 501-502; and Yasmin Khan, *The Great Partition*, 94-95.
35. Clyde Wilcox and Carlin Larson, *Onward Christian Soldiers*, third edition, (Boulder Colorado, Westview Press, 2006), 16-17.
36. Kent Greenawalt, *Religious Convictions and Political Choice* (New York, Oxford University Press, 1988).
37. Fischer, *The Essential Gandhi*, 196.
38. Fischer, *Mahatma Gandhi*, 251.
39. Narayan, *The Selected Gandhi*, volume 6, 481-486.
40. Sophia Dobson Collet, *The Life and Letters of Raja Rammohun Roy*, (Calcutta, Brahmo Mission Press, 1962), 92-94.
41. D.C. Ahir, *The Legacy of Dr. Ambedkar* (Delhi: B.R. Publishing Corporation, A Division of D.K. Publishers, 1990), 28-30.
42. Fischer, *Mahatma Gandhi*, 338.
43. Fischer, *The Essential Gandhi*, 311.
44. Fischer, *Mahatma Gandhi*, 147-148;
45. Fischer, *The Essential Gandhi*, 135.
46. Fischer, *The Essential Gandhi*, 134-5.
47. Fischer, *The Essential Gandhi*, 134.
48. A fine novel on the lives of the Untouchables, and their experience with Gandhi is here recommended: Mulk Raj Anand, *Untouchable* (New York, Penguin Books, 1940).
49. Dhananjay Keer, *Dr. Ambedkar, His Life and Mission* (Bombay: Popular Prakashan Press, 1990), 259, 305.
50. Sangharakshita. *Amebedkar and Buddhism*, 131-142.
51. Fischer, *The Essential Gandhi*, 285.
52. Fischer, *The Essential Gandhi,* 284-5.
53. Fischer, *The Essential Gandhi*, 288.
54. Fischer, *The Essential Gandhi*, 232.
55. Fischer, *The Essential Gandhi*, 288.
56. Narayan, *The Selected Works,* volume 6, 234.
57. Fischer, *The Essential Gandhi,* 308.

58. King Jr., Martin Luther, *Martin Luther King Companion*, selected by Coretta Scott King (New York, St. Martin's Press, 1993), 39.

59. Samuel P. Huntington, *The Clash of Civilization and the Remaking of World Order* (New York, Touchstone Book, Simon & Schuster, 1996), 217.

60. Huntington, *The Clash of Civilizations,* 213.

61. Gandhi, *The Selected Works*, volume. 6, 282-283.

62. Karl Marx, and Frederick Engels, *Economic and Social Manuscripts & Communist Manifesto*, translated by Martin Milligan (Prometheus Books, New York, 1988), 76-78.

63. Fischer, *The Essential Gandhi*, 292.

64. Fischer, *The Essential Gandhi*, 287.

65. Fischer, *The Essential Gandhi,* 292.

66. Gandhi, *Hind Swaraj*, 107.

67. Fischer, *The Essential Gandhi*, 304.

68. Fischer, *The Essential Gandhi,* 196, 231. Whether Gandhi had in fact read the Federalist Papers, or derived this maxim of limited government from a similar source, or whether he derived this preference independently I have not seen documented.

69. Erik Erikson, *Gandhi's Truth,* 281.

70. Fischer, *The Essential Gandhi*, 312.

71. Narayan, *The Selected Gandhi*, volume 6, 131.

72. Narayan, *The Selected Gandhi*, 132.

73. Fischer, *Mahatma Gandhi*, 245-246.

74. Fischer, *The Essential Gandhi*, 241.

75. Marcello, *Mohandas K. Gandhi,* 150.

76. Fischer, *Mahatma Gandhi*, 438.

77. Marcello, *Mohandas K. Gandhi*, 131; Fischer, *The Essential Gandhi*, 318.

78. Erik Erikson, *Gandhi's Truth*, 120.

79. Gandhi, *Hind Swaraj,* 71.

80. Narayan, *The Selected Gandhi*, volume 6, 226.

81. Korejo, *The Frontier Gandhi*, 32.

82. Fischer, *Mahatma Gandhi*, 349.

83. Fischer, *Mahatma Gandhi*, 350.

84. Fischer, *Mahatma Gandhi*, 349.

85. Merton, *Gandhi on Nonviolence,* 21-22.

86. Reinhold Niebuhr, *Moral Man & Immoral Society: A Study in Ethics and Politics*, (Louisville, Westminster John-Knox Press, 2001), 242-243.

87. Charles C Brown, *Niebuhr and His Age* (Philadelphia, Trinity Press International 1992), 107.

88. Fischer, *The Essential Gandhi*, 208, 334.

Chapter 4: Bio of a Jihadist

Mohammed bin Laden

Osama bin Laden represents the antithesis of what we have discovered in Gandhi so far. Gandhi insisted upon nonviolence as the highest ideal, while Bin Laden insists upon violence as a religious duty. Believing that all religions were essentially pathways up the same mountain, Gandhi represented religious universalism. The absolute opposite is the exclusive view of Bin Laden, who accepts only a limited view of Islam. Both men have emphasized and declared a willingness to die for their cause, but in a radically different manner. How the infamy of Bin Laden will compare and measure next to the fame of Gandhi's legacy is something yet to be decided. We must ask first, where did Bin Laden come from? Whom does he represent?

Peter Bergen visited the ancestral home of Osama bin Laden, from which his father and family had originated. It is the Hadramawt region of Yemen, a place known for its builders and also it migrant laborers. Visiting the town of al-Rubat, Bergen found Sufism (a strand of Islam not generally accepted in Bin Laden's Islamist thinking) and a rejection of Bin Laden's ideology. A local Mullah reported, "We are against this holy war. The *Cole* [the U.S. warship attacked by Al-Qaeda agents] attack does more harm to Yemen's reputation than America's reputation. We feel sorry for the American boys and girls. They are our guests." Asking a storeowner and cousin of Bin Laden what he thought of Osama's *jihad* (or "struggle"), the man pointed to his three-year old son and said, "This is my jihad."[1]

This must be kept in mind, as Bin Laden's view is *not* the mainstream of Islam. Islam has some 1.3 billion adherents. If only 1% of 1% of that total majority (that would equal 1 in 10,000 persons) accepted violent means, then that would be 130,000 persons. If only 1% of *those* accepted radical ideas such as suicide bombing (that is 1 of 1 million Muslims), it would be 1300 people, or enough for one suicide attack per day for 3.5 years straight, without interruption. It takes only a very small minority to cause a great disturbance, especially when the tactics of terror are concerned and the base population is so large.

The same figures could be applied to any category — Christians, Americans, South Americans, Asians, Hindus, or Atheists. The larger the body of persons of one class, the more possibilities there are that a minority will cause some problems. Because Christianity and Islam together comprise over 3 billion of the world's population, it becomes very important that these religious adherents come to understand one another in order to minimize the potential for conflict that is simply inherent in such a large body of persons. Gandhi would have wanted this tolerance and understanding, and it is important to keep in mind that most Christians and Muslims really have a fairly mainstream, nonviolent view. But then there are exceptions. Bin Laden is one of them.

He once claimed that he is doing the will of his father: "My father was very keen that one of his sons should fight against the enemies of Islam. So I am the one son who is acting according to the wishes of his father."[2] There is mixed and limited evidence to suggest this, however. Mohammed bin Laden, the founder of an enormous construction company, expressed his grievances against Israel and the occupation of Palestinians lands.[3] There is other evidence to suggest that Mohammed bin Laden's agenda was primarily business, and that he knew better than to get deeply involved in politics, especially the politics of the Saudi royal family. Osama's father once said, "We are a construction company. We are business people. We do what we are told to do. This was our upbringing."[4]

Mohammed bin Laden was born in the Hadramawt region of Yemen around 1905, but the exact date is not certain.[5] After some family financial difficulty, the family moved to the town of Rabat. Awadh, his father, would soon pass away, and Mohammed made a trip to work in Ethiopia where he was blinded in one eye. Returning, Mohammed bin Laden and his brother set off again to find their fortune in Saudi Arabia. It was a perilous journey, and upon arrival the Bin Laden brothers took a number of jobs in Jeddah; Mohammed was a porter and grill owner before obtaining work as a dependable bricklayer for Aramco.[6] It was a fortuitous time to arrive in the Saudi state, as the royal family had just consolidated its power after centuries of struggle and would soon come to enjoy a vast oil fortune.

The context of the Saudis ascension to power is important. For centuries the Arabian peninsula had been controlled by various regional Emirs. The Saudi royal family would establish two empires controlling large regions of the peninsula before a third effort resulted in the declaration of the Kingdom of Saudi Arabia in 1932. The final State emerged under Ibn Saud with the help and aid of the British, but also the emerging interest of American oil companies such as SOCAL, which would combine interests with other companies to form Aramco, the Arab American Oil Company.[7] The oil controlled by the Saudi royal family would give them a vast resource of wealth to spend, which would benefit the Bin Laden family.

It was not only oil that would be important, but also religion. The Saudis royal family came to power under an alliance with the followers of the Wahhabi strand of Islam. Wahhabism was a movement founded by Muhammad ibn Abd-al Wahhab (lived circa 1703-1792).[8] Al-Wahhab believed that Islam had become perverted from the original intentions of the founder, that it was practicing the veneration of Sufi saints and other Imams, which was in fact a crime of *shirk*, or loosely put, idolatry. Muhammad al-Wahhab led a religious campaign to purge the Arabian peninsula of these inauthentic Islamic practices, and so he created a militantly exclusive movement dedicated to recapturing what he believed to be the essential practices of Islam. Wanting to restore the peninsula to a religious purity of the days of the Prophet, the emphasis was to do away with these innovations, or *bida.*[9] Eventually the Wahhabis would find supporters in the Saudi lineage, which would create an uneasy alliance that would span generations and hundreds of years.

There are interpretations and schools of Islam that are open to a more pluralistic understanding of the religion, but Wahhabism is not one of them. Insisting upon the purity of religious practice and getting rid of unwanted accretions to the faith, later Wahhabis became participants in murderous attacks upon perceived apostates. One of these was the infamous sack of Karbala in 1802, a sacred site to Shi'a Muslims, but a place where in the Wahhabi view, the unacceptable veneration of Shi'a Imams (*shirk*) was taking place. It was said that those Muslims were actually apostates in *jahiliyyah*, or ignorance of the true Islam. The alliance between the Wahhabi religious school of thinking and the Saudi family would not always be an easy one. The *Ikhwan*, a movement of Wahhabi warriors raised in support of the Saudis, would ultimately have to be challenged and crushed for their extreme agitation.[10] The contest of religion and political violence in establishing political Kingdoms was nothing new, however. In reading the history of Gandhi's India, one finds also a long story of conquest and counter-conquest, and also competition between religious ideologies.[11] What must be understood is that the interplay of oil, religion, and politics play an especially critical role in the development of the nation where the Bin Laden's would find a home.

Mohammed bin Laden soon started his own business and developed a reputation for his construction work. Attending the *majlis* or open court of the Saudi royal family, he soon came to their attention and acquired a contract to build a special palace for them in 1939. The palace was completed with a special automobile ramp that would take Ibn Saud directly to the second floor where he could hold his open court. The project created a lasting bond, and soon Mohammed bin Laden would have a monopoly on the Saudi construction contracts (his brother stayed with him for a while but ultimately would return to his native region of Hadramawt, Yemen).[12]

Mohammed would pull off a nifty "hat trick" of construction projects. In addition to a number of palaces, roads, and other personal projects for the royal family, Mohammed bin Laden would secure renovation projects in all three of the holiest cities of Islam: Mecca, Medina, and Jerusalem. Mecca badly needed space for Muslim pilgrims to go on the *Hajj* (the Muslim duty to visit the Ka'ba, the central shrine of Islam), and this resulted in a lucrative project that would renovate and improve the facilities for Muslims going on their spiritual retreats. In Medina, the Prophet's Mosque would undergo expansion and renovations by the Bin Laden company. Finally, in Jerusalem the company won a competitive bid to restore the Dome of the Rock that had been much in need of repairs. The last project in Jerusalem was supported by the Saudis, and reportedly finished at a net loss. Mohammed wrote off the debt of Jordan, considering it his honorable Islamic duty to complete the job. This prestigious accomplishment elevated the family to quite prominent status in the Kingdom, if not the Muslim world itself. Mohammed bin Laden was not without adversaries in the Kingdom or the Islamic world, but quite remarkably he established one of the largest construction companies in the region with no formal education.[13]

The family also grew exponentially. It was the custom of the Saudi royal family to take multiple wives (attempting to stick to the four wives allowable at one time, by Islamic law), and to marry and divorce serially. Mohammed began to adopt this practice as a wealthy construction magnate who could now afford it. In all, the Bin Laden family would grow to an astounding 54 brothers and sisters, by a variety of different wives. Osama was born in the middle of this pack and initially seems to have been a rather shy figure who did not stand out from the rest. Osama himself would marry multiple wives (no more than four at once), but avoided the serial marriage practice of his father.[14]

The eldest of the Bin Laden boys was Salem bin Laden (born 1944/45), who would take over the construction business upon the untimely death of his father. If one wants a quick education in the diversity of Muslims, one need only look at the Bin Laden family itself. Salem bin Laden was very much the opposite of his younger half-brother Osama. Salem had a very secular attitude and acted very much as the carefree playboy, having girlfriends scattered across the world, and enjoying music, karaoke, practical jokes and parties. Occasionally he would drink. He purchased a property in Orlando, Florida (now sold) that became a frequent stop for Bin Ladens who wished to visit Disney. Salem even had a vision of marrying four international brides and making a kind of "UN Compound" of wives back in Saudi Arabia. Though this plan did not pan out, Salem did marry and had a daughter, and matured into a fairly successful patriarch of the family. His worldliness was in marked contrast to the conservative religious demeanor of Osama. Salem reportedly would bring foreign girlfriends into the country and into Mecca against the law and Islamic tradition there. Before he died (also an untimely death), he had traveled quite extensively in the U.S., Europe and Asia. He was not particularly concerned about religion, nor marked by any discernable opposition to Zionism.[15]

Both Mohammed bin Laden and his eldest son Salem perished in plane accidents. Both had private jets and propeller planes, and enjoyed flying themselves or with copilots. Mohammed bin Laden died when his pilot landed at an irregular airstrip at one of Bin Laden's construction sites on September 3rd, 1967. Twenty-one years later, on May 29, 1988 Salem bin Laden died flying a lightweight aircraft after taking off from a runway in Texas. Death and plane violence have certainly traumatized the family greatly, and the savage irony is that plane violence is also what would make Osama infamous (though it was not his idea, the 9/11 plot was reportedly masterminded by Khaled Sheik Mohammed).[16]

The Saudi bin Laden Group, one of the main legacies of the Bin Laden family, certainly had a wealth of assets at its command. Contracts had been formed with a variety of companies ranging from Caterpillar to Disney to Snapple, but there are exaggerations about how much of the wealth Bin Laden retained. By Islamic law, Bin Laden was entitled to a share in the company equal to that of his brothers, or in his case, about 2.27%. Annual salaries which Bin Laden collected range in estimates, some putting them at $150,000 to $200,000 annually, with reports of a lump-sum inheritance of perhaps $8-9.9 million, depending on how the family's finances are traced and interpreted. Over a lifetime, the amount he inherited as his share in the company may have been $27 million. This is quite a haul, but far short of the mythic CIA reports of 1998 that Osama had inherited $300 million.[17] Bin Laden did not inherit that sum, and other lower estimates concur that the amount of cash salary he drew from the company did not exceed $20 to $30 million.[18] The current patriarch of the family and head of the company has consistently claimed that the family has broken off all ties with Osama, and made public denunciation of his acts.[19]

Osama bin Laden's Education

Birthdays are not the cause for celebration in Saudi Arabia that they are in the United States, a distinction of religion and culture being the cause; hence the birthdates for many of the Bin Laden family tend to be inexact. Most accounts report that Osama bin Laden was born in 1957 (or possibly January 1958) as one of the middle-group of Bin Laden's children. His mother, Ali al-Ghanem, was of Syrian birth, and recalls her son as "a shy kid, very nice, very considerate. He has always been helpful. I tried to instill in him the fear and love of God, the respect and love for his family, neighbors and teachers." She was later divorced from Mohammed Bin Laden. Steve Coll reports that despite this, it appears that Osama was well cared and provided for, but the contact with his father was probably limited. He likely visited with his father and other sons in a kind of open court, and he could have been present at any one of the various demolition and reconstruction projects which the family company had contracted. From youth, Osama (meaning "young Lion") displayed an affection for horseback riding which he has maintained in his elder years.

Pictures of the Bin Laden family on vacation reveal a very secular, westernized influence in their dress. One popular picture shows the Bin Laden family on vacation in Scandinavia in 1971, but the accounts of Osama being present in the picture are apparently false. Bin Laden may have made a few trips to the West, London included, but it is likely he has never been to America and certainly never traveled as freely as his half-brother Salem.[20]

Bin Laden was a quiet, unobtrusive youth by all accounts. He briefly received an education in a private school in Beirut, which did not seem to work out. The primary basis of his education was the Al-Thaghr Model School in Jeddah, Saudi Arabia.[21] Osama was reported to be a solid but not exceptional student. He apparently loved Westerns like *Fury*, *Bonanza*, and karate movies such as Bruce Lee. These tastes he would later outgrow.[22] He became a conservative youth, disinclined to party and eager to become a pious Muslim. Accounts of Bin Laden as a Beirut party youth appear to be fictionalized or false.[23]

During his time at Al Thaghr, a hybrid club that offered both soccer and Islamic study appealed to Osama, and he joined. The movement appears to have been more about Islamic indoctrination and could have been a front for the Muslim Brotherhood, an Islamist organization that traces its roots back to Egypt. Originally, as an Islamist organization, members advocated maximizing Muslim *sharia* or Qur'anic law in society. The organization became increasingly militarized with time, however, especially by the life, writings and deeds of Sayyid Qutb. By the time of Osama's youth, it was a recruitment agency for possible later radical involvement. Bin Laden seems to have accepted it and its radical agenda. He would read Qutb's works, and be influenced by them.[24]

Osama was ten years old when his father died, and when the Jews won the 6-days war that gave them the West Bank and the Sinai Peninsula. Both events would make a major impression on Bin Laden's mind. Feeling the loss of his father, likely he wanted to follow in his footsteps, and become the pious defender of the faith. In 1967, Osama bore not only the loss of his father, but also the city of Jerusalem. There the Mosque his father had renovated fell into the hands of his perceive enemy, the Jewish State. Bin Laden later declared "Every Muslim, from the moment they realize the distinction in their hearts, hates Americans, hates Jews, and hates Christians. This is a part of our belief and our religion. For as long as I can remember, I have felt tormented and at war, and have felt hatred and animosity for Americans."[25] Whether this was truly heart-felt reaction from 1967, or mere retroactive projection is open to argument.

Elsewhere Osama echoed this resolve "Unless we, the new generation, change and become stronger and more educated and more dedicated we will never reclaim Palestine."[26] The nonviolent, inclusive response became alien to Bin Laden's fiber and his interpretation of Islam. Seeing the Jewish victory and feeling the radical influence of the Muslim Brotherhood, Osama's conservatism may have developed a darker undercurrent long before he became fully radicalized in Afghanistan.

Graduating from the Al Thaghr School, Bin Laden went on to study at King Abdul Aziz University in Jeddah. Another student, Jamal Khalifa, who befriended Bin Laden, there reported that Osama was already religiously conservative about dress, women, and music.[27] Osama was majoring in the field of business administration, economics and management, and became exposed to some very radical influences there. The writings of the Qutb brothers — Mohammed and Sayyid — also apparently influenced Osama greatly at this time.[28] Mohammed Qutb apparently even lectured at Abdul Aziz University.

More significantly, Osama met and was influenced by the radical Islamist authority Abdullah Azzam. Azzam had a long history of fighting and advocating *jihad*, and it was at the university in Jeddah that a fateful mentorship would begin.[29] From reviewing his history, Osama was not radicalized from day one anymore than Mohandas was born a Mahatma. They grew into their respective roles. Azzam would be a powerful mentor for Osama in the next few years, so it will be necessary to tell a little of his story soon.

The year 1979 was almost as good for breeding Islamists as 1776 was good for breeding American patriots. In the year of 1979, Bin Laden was twenty-two.

It was one of the most tumultuous years for Muslims of the twentieth century. In Iran, the Shiite revolution occurred, and with it the beginning of the hostage crisis. In Saudi Arabia, a group of radical Muslims seized the holiest site of the Grand Mosque in Mecca. The group that took charge denounced the Saudi royal family as corrupt, and claimed to have the *Mahdi*, an awaited Islamic savior, in their midst. Bin Laden's oldest brother Salem was called out with the blueprints of the mosque his father had designed to expose weaknesses and points of attack to get to the insurgents. Osama himself may have been arrested along with a brother on the mistaken idea that he had been involved in the plot. The year 1979 also marked the Soviet Invasion of Afghanistan. It was a good year for producing radicals.[30]

Afghanistan

Before introducing the very important influence of Abdullah Azzam on Bin Laden, we must review Bin Laden's religious and psychological growth. There appears to have been no unusual element of radicalism or anti-Zionism that was introduced into his family life (anti-Zionism is not uncommon there, however). His father mostly stuck to business, voicing some sentiment against Israel, and his mother introduced no Islamist teachings to him. His family was wealthy, but that allowed many of his brothers greater contact with the West, and in Salem bin Laden we see a very secularized, Westernized person. The idea that Bin Laden was reared for radicalism should be dismissed, as I have found no evidence of it in prominent literature on the matter. Indeed, the fact that Bin Laden liked American Westerns as a youth indicates a fairly regular, curious childhood.

The religious culture of Saudi Arabia may well have been a significant factor, however. The Sunni Wahhabi view is strongly exclusive. Exclusive religious views tend to be conservative, to emphasize also that they are the one and only redemptive religious message present in the world, and to view alternative interpretations of their own religion as well as other religions as unwanted or even threatening. It is very much a zero sum mentality, where one party can be right, and all other parties less right or merely wrong. It is a mentality distinctively opposite from the one Gandhi cherished,

In addition to this, the writings of Sayyid and Mohammed Qutb would have reinforced this view, that there is one and only one true interpretation of Islam, and that alternative views such as Sufism or Shiism are not properly Islamic. Fellow Muslims (to all outside observers) may therefore be labeled in *jahiliyyah* (ignorance of Islam). The struggle of the Islamist — which is to establish and realize an Islamic State, where all law is based upon *sharia* or Islamic law — is one that naturally pits competing understandings of Islam against one another. Hence the Islamist may be as unwelcome from a Muslim point of view (which asserts the truth of the Qur'an, but allows for some diversity about the understanding or approach to it) as he or she is from the Western point of view. By his adolescence and early adulthood, however, it appears Bin Laden's mindset was receptive to the Islamist point of view. His exposure to Abdullah Azzam at university and in Afghanistan further increased his drift into the radical fold.

Who was Abdullah Azzam? Azzam was born in Palestine in 1941 and participated in the 1967 war against Israel. He had immediate experience of the Jewish occupation of the West Bank, and this battleground became a clarion call for appeal to Islamist causes. It is not exactly clear why, but he became disenchanted with the Palestinian cause there or felt compelled to leave. He later went to Al-Azhar University in Cairo where he received a PhD in Islamic jurisprudence in 1973. Azzam became a leading intellectual and active participant in the *jihad* to revive the strength and vitality of Islam. Wright reports that Osama "revered" Azzam, and other sources confirm the towering importance of Azzam in mentoring Bin Laden to Islamist causes. He would not only come to the battlefront, but he authored works such as *In Defense of Muslim Lands* to popularize his cause.[31]

Clearly Azzam was a militant. The most famous quote that is attributed to him is that Muslims should fight "Jihad and the rifle alone; no negotiations, no conferences, no dialogues."[32] Azzam would be instrumental in the effort to fight the Soviets, a cause which he also drew Bin Laden into. While Azzam was militant in his pursuit of *jihad*, there are some indications that he was less militant than the most extreme of Islamist-Jihadists. Lawrence Wright writes that Azzam was opposed to *takfiri* Islamic ideology, or in other words, an ultra-exclusivist approach in which some Muslims were right interpreters and all other Muslims or non-Muslims who did not share their view were wrong. Azzam suggested that the problem was not within the Muslim community itself, so while exclusive in his views, he was not automatically belligerent to other Muslims who had theological disagreements with him. Reportedly, he even wrote *fatwas* opposing terrorism and violence against civilians as un-Islamic.[33]

Azzam and Bin Laden would ultimately by their united efforts form the organization that would morph into Al-Qaeda. When the Soviets invaded Afghanistan in December of 1979, it became an encroachment of the *infidel* upon the *dar-al-Islam*, the territory of Islam, and hence an international appeal was sent out to enlist Muslims in the cause. The atheists had to be driven from Muslim lands by force, and Azzam was one of the leaders to issue the call. His journal *Jihad Magazine* had an international subscription and appealed to the causes of radical Islamists throughout the world. Peter Bergen relates this excerpt from *Jihad Magazine:*

> 1. That Jihad is a religious duty for the Umma [Muslims around the world], so as to free the people and give them Islamic justice and protection of the religion.
> 2. That the religion of God and the blessed religion is that of all humanity, and we want to spread it all over four corners of the world.
> 3. Jihad in God's will means killing the infidels in the name of God and raising the banner of His name. And we do not want to make this great Jihad only words to be said on podiums, or articles to be published in newspapers. Jihad is done in the will of God only if you fight the infidel with the sword until he submits to Islam.[34]

The militant rhetoric is clear, but it seems also clear that Azzam insisted that only enemy combatants should be targeted in combat. Azzam would be better identified as an Islamist Guerilla fighter than a terrorist. His powerful belief and rhetoric magnetized Bin Laden, who began to support and bankroll the causes of the Afghans fighting against the Soviets. It appears Osama may have made a transformation from a "weekend warrior" who would visit Afghan-Pakistan region periodically and then return to his home in Saudi Arabia. Eventually the weekend warrior became the career *jihadist*, and Bin Laden drifted deeper into the folds of radicalism. At the beginning there was certainly a warm relationship between Osama and Azzam as they worked in common cause against the Soviets. While Azzam initially had been sent as a teacher to Pakistan, his role in supporting the conflict went beyond writing and academics.

Azzam and Bin Laden formed the *Mektab al-Khidmat*, or Service Offices, in Pakistan. The organization was kind of a halfway house for supporting the jihad in neighboring Afghanistan. Islamic recruits, many from Saudi Arabia, would volunteer for the war effort to help the *mujahedeen* of Afghanistan who were battling the Red Army. In the aftermath of the war when the Soviets withdrew, the remaining bones and apparatus of this organization would be morphed into the organization known as *Al-Qaeda* in August of 1988. By that time, however, a growing rift was emerging between Bin Laden and Azzam, as they had differing directions in which they wanted to take their *jihad*.[35]

The strange irony is that during the period of the Soviet war in Afghanistan, from 1979 to 1989, the United States and Saudi Arabia were funding the same side that Bin Laden was also supporting. The *mujahedeen*, or holy warriors, of Afghanistan were being given weapons and material from international sources, much of it funneled through the supportive network of Pakistani intelligence or ISI. There exists no evidence of any receipts or connection between the United States and Osama bin Laden. Bin Laden himself denied the link and has at times praised and belittled U.S. support of the *mujahedeen*. Again, no evidence connects him with the CIA or any other U.S. organization. Osama's role was through the organization he established with Azzam.[36]

Steve Coll relates an account of the eldest Bin laden brother, Salem, flying into Afghanistan and visiting a refugee camp that Osama was involved with; orphans were prominently visible. Salem made several trips and possibly some deliveries to help his brother.[37] No doubt Osama's role there was initially as supporter, fund-raiser, and assistant in a number of different dimensions. Initially, however, Osama did not have a combat role, and his role and that of other Saudis in the conflict seems to be very marginal compared with that of the native Afghans who were defending their own turf. There were reported tensions between those Afghans who fought for their home country, and the supporting Arabs who were fighting for religious duty. This should be understood, as there is a gross misperception risked in conceiving of Islamist, Jihadists, Freedom-Fighters and Terrorist as all one undifferentiated mass. In fact the West's inability to perceive the gradations and causes of our opponents may inadvertently contribute to the transformation of freedom fighters into future terrorists.

The war years dramatically transformed Bin Laden. He had been mentally prepared for radicalism before; the stage was set, but there were no actors upon it. Yes he had some grievances with Israel, and with America, but no great and belligerent animosity had yet emerged. It soon would. War transforms people, and it transformed Bin Laden: "I have benefited so greatly from the *jihad* in Afghanistan that it would have been impossible for me gain such a benefit from any other opportunity, and this cannot be measured by tens of years but rather more than that."[38] During the course of the war in Afghanistan, Israel would open up the invasion of Lebanon in 1982. Already prone to anti-Zionist sentiment, his ongoing support of war in Afghanistan, his exposure to Azzam's ideas and leadership, and this 1982 invasion seemed to send him towards a tipping point. Bin Laden relates of the 1982 Israeli invasions into Lebanon:

> I still remember those distressing scenes: blood, torn limbs, women and children massacred. All over the place, houses were being destroyed and tower blocks were collapsing, crushing their residents. . . In those critical moments, many ideas raged inside me, ideas difficult to describe, but they unleashed a powerful urge to reject injustice and a strong determination to punish the oppressors. As I looked at those destroyed towers in Lebanon, it occurred to me to punish the oppressor in kind by destroying towers in America, so that it would have a taste of its own medicine. . . . On that day I became sure that the oppression and intentional murder of innocent women and children is a deliberate American policy.[39]

By 1986, Bin Laden's ire against the United States and Israel was becoming clearer. He saw the former as puppets of the latter: "Americans take our money and give it to the Jews, so they can kill our children with it in Palestine."[40] There were other influences as well. Bin Laden met Ayman al-Zawahiri in Afghanistan. Zawahiri had been involved in Islamist insurgency against the government of Egypt. Arrested shortly after the assassination of Sadat, he had been detained and tortured. Video footage of Zawahiri's fiery pride in Islamic identity exists from that period in prison:

> Now we want to speak to the whole world! Who are we? Why do they bring us here, and what [do] we want to say? About the first question, we are Muslims! We are Muslims who believe in their religion! We are Muslims who believe their religion, both in ideology and practice, and hence we tried our best to establish an Islamic state and an Islamic society![41]

Eventually Zawahiri was set free (perhaps having been forced to report on some companions). Zawahiri found his way to Bin Laden and encouraged him to support the cause of *jihad* internationally — in Egypt, and elsewhere. This is a direction that had been opposed by Azzam, who apparently wanted to keep the funds of their organization contained to the Afghan region. Some suggest that it was Zawahiri who pushed Bin Laden to the final extremes, but perhaps the more accurate assessment is that the two personalities radicalized each other.[42]

Zawahiri had membership and connections to Islamic Jihad, the branch of radical jihadists in Egypt, and one of those was the Blind Sheikh Omar Abdel Rahman. The Sheikh (indicted and sentenced for supporting terror plots against the United States) has been listed as one of the possible influences that radicalized Bin Laden. The connection does not seem unlikely, given Rahman's involvement in Egyptian causes with Zawahiri, but the lines of direct influence are less prominent than those of Abdullah Azzam. Whatever the influence, the embittered agenda of the Blind Sheikh is very much at the far extremes, where Bin Laden would ultimately follow. One letter later attributed to the Sheikh in prison read:

> America is in the process of eliminating the *ulema* (clergy) who are speaking the truth. And America has suggested to its clients in Saudi to imprison Sheik Safar al Hawali and Sheik Salman al Awdah, and all the others who speak the truth, just as Egypt had done. . . .
> And the Koran has made a decree upon these Jews and Christians which we have forgotten or allowed to be forgotten:
> Allah said "If they could, they will continue to kill you until they make you turn away from your religion."
> And so all Muslims everywhere:
> Cut off all relations with [the Americans, Christians, and Jews], tear them to pieces, destroy their economies, burn their corporations, destroy their peace, sink their ships, shoot down their planes and kill them on air, sea, and land. And kill them wherever you may find them, ambush them, take them hostage, and destroy their observatories. Kill these Infidels. Until they witness your harshness. Fight them, and God will torture them through your hands, and he will disgrace them and make you victorious over them, and the nation of the believers is on the verge of creation, and the rage will go from them.
> Your brother Omar Abdel Rahman from inside American prisons.[43]

Exposed to these extreme ideas, Bin Laden also changed as a leader of *jihad*. Instead of becoming the quiet assistant and bankroller of Azzam's activities, Bin Laden began to have increasingly independent influence. His ideas and his vision of leadership began to move in ways that departed from Azzam. He had his own funds which had been collected in support of the *mujahedeen*. Bin Laden began to agitate to form a separate battalion of Arabs who would engage in active combat in Afghanistan. For much of the time, he had remained as a supporter and financier in Pakistan with only limited incursions into the Afghan conflict. Now he wanted a more direct role, and Azzam did not see the merits of this idea. Bin Laden formed the Arab combat unit in spite of their differences and prepared for conflict.[44]

The siege at Jaji marks Bin Laden's entrance into the conflict against the Soviets. Taking on some of the toughest *Spetsnaz* troops the Red Army had to offer, the Arab Muslims held their own for some time but suffered a great loss of life, so much that Jamal Khalifa (a former friend of Bin Laden) saw it as an appalling waste. Bin Laden did not demonstrate excellence as a military commander, but perhaps foolhardiness in face of superior Soviet forces. Win, lose, or draw it appeared to elevate his stature as proponent of *jihad*. When Bin Laden finally came home to Saudi Arabia, he had some welcome press as an Afghan war hero.[45]

Bin Laden did not win the war for the Afghans, but the Afghans did win the war in 1989. Shortly before the end, in 1988 as stated above, *Al-Qaeda* was created. At this point there was already some growing rift between Bin Laden and Azzam. Should *jihad* be kept to Afghanistan, should it be internationalized? Who were the appropriate targets? Was this to be a guerrilla war against military forces, or a clandestine cell network of terrorist violence? At this point these questions seemed unresolved.

Another saga would end in 1989, and that was Abdullah Azzam's life. In late November of 1989 a car bomb killed him and two of his sons as they were on their way to the mosque. There are various stories and explanations for the deed, but the identity of the culprits remains a mystery. Some authors have indicated that they thought it was Bin Laden who ordered the hit in a deliberate attempt to take over Al-Qaeda, and so full leadership of the organization. The war, however, was over, and the very reason for the organization to exist at all could be called into question.

Additionally, more than one author has pointed out that Bin Laden appeared sincerely stricken by the death of his friend and find it implausible that he would have lashed out against the man he so revered. An alternative explanation for the murder may have been that Azzam was about to back Ahmad Shah Massoud, the Tajik leader of the Northern Alliance who opposed the Taliban. Since Massoud was a rival of the Afghan war leader Gulbuddin Hekmetyar, Bergen has suggested that Hekmetyar could have done it to stop the endorsement of a rival war leader who had great prominence in post-Soviet Afghanistan. In short, a power struggle of war leaders may have ended Azzam's life. With Azzam dead, Bin Laden was now on his own. He returned to Saudi Arabia with high expectations but instead received the greatest shock of his life.[46]

The Gulf War

Osama returned to Saudi Arabia in 1989, and on August 2, 1990, Saddam Hussein decided to invade the neighboring tiny Arab state of Kuwait. Saddam had payment problems with the Kuwaitis, as well as disputes about the ownership of oil. Bungled diplomatic signals from Washington may have further encouraged him. Whatever the reasons, the implications of Saddam's invasion were clear. He was in possession of a vast quantity of gulf oil and was now considered an unreliable dictator who could get beyond our means to control him. Moreover, his formidable armed forces were now poised on the border with Saudi Arabia. If Saddam ordered his forces to continue, he could soon seize the vast quantity of gulf oil in the region that supplied widespread regions of the world. Saddam, simply put, had a knife poised at the jugular of the world's oil and in one motion could cut it off. It was a strategic and economic threat which the United States was not prepared to let slide. President George Bush Sr. orchestrated a highly successful campaign for world opinion to lead a UN force against Saddam. He had the open ears and cooperation of the Saudis.

Bin Laden had been busy and very interested in supporting the liberation of friendly forces in Yemen, but Saddam's invasion now fully grasped his attention. Immediately he set about devising a plan in which the Saudis could kick Saddam Hussein out of Kuwait without the aid of the United States military or any foreign power. It was reported to be a detailed, 60-page account, using the tactics that he had acquired from the war in Afghanistan to apply to Saddam Hussein's forces in Kuwait. There would be no need to involve the Americans, he claimed. Prince Turki noted of Osama "This shy, retiring and seemingly very reticent person has changed."[47] Osama had not calculated the odds against him, however. By one account Saddam stood at the Saudi border with a million-man force, against the Saudis' standing army of 58,000.[48] Against this million-man army Bin Laden may have been able to muster 5000 *mujahedeen* guerilla-style warriors. Reports vary, some putting the figure at 10,000 or higher.[49] The Saudis did not have the personnel, the tanks, or the training to match Saddam in battle. What was the rational choice, to side with Bin Laden and raise an army of a few thousand ragtag guerilla warriors, or to side with the entire, military industrial might of the United States and its allies? The Saudis made the choice they thought was best, and sided with the Americans. Bin Laden's offer was rejected, and no doubt he was fuming mad.

Let us pause to make an example to try to drive home the effect on Bin Laden's mind. The example will be difficult to make, because the United States is not under the threat of a foreign invasion, nor has it been for decades. Militarily, imperially, the U.S. citizens will find it very difficult to understand the "underdog" effect that afflicts the mentality of much of the Arab Muslim world (which has formerly been under colonial power). Some imagination must be given to this example in order for it to register.

Imagine that a U.S. veteran returning from fighting a perceived Communist threat in Vietnam. The Soviet Union is still a mighty power and a great rival. Now upon returning home there is an economic and political collapse, such that (and here we must rewrite facts and history with imagination) *Mexico invades the United States* and annexes almost all of Texas. The U.S. veteran finds himself in a country once a great power, but now unable to defend itself, and to add insult to injury our government decides to invite *Soviet troops* onto U.S. soil in order to liberate Texas from the Mexican threat. Can you imagine asking the Soviets or the Canadians or the French to help liberate Texas? Far fetched? Only for Americans. For the Arab Muslim world, they knew that they were once a great and mighty power and that a supervening period of colonialism resulted in a vast reduction in their might. Now they have to invite foreign powers to help defend the very territory they call a sacred home. Imagine any veteran, freshly home from war, who finds his own government unable to defend his native soil and who has to call upon an arch rival to defend that territory against an adjacent power. This cannot justify Bin Laden's actions but helps comprehend them.

Bin Laden's pride as a "patriot for *jihad*" was hurt, no doubt. He was humiliated, frustrated with his country, and the puppet strings (whether they existed or not) which he perceived to be connected between the United States and Israel now began to be traced in his mind to the government of Saudi Arabia. His dissent was not loud, or obvious at first, but this event entrenched and embittered his alienation from the Saudi regime and "opened a gulf" (to use a strategic pun) between him and his oil-rich government.

There were other reasons and justifications. Bin Laden began to link up his political frustrations with his religious ideology. He appealed to an ancient *hadith*, or a traditional practice that was ascribed to the Prophet Muhammad himself. Now the *hadith* are very controversial. They do not carry the same weight and authority as the Qur'an itself, and many of the hadith are thought to be false, inaccurate, or misleading.[50] At any rate, Bin Laden believed this hadith was real. It apparently dated back to the deathbed of the Prophet and was enforced by the second Caliph Umar. It stated that there should be "no two religions" in the territory of the *hijaz*, or the holy territory of Mecca and Medina. For Bin Laden, and other Muslims, this meant that there should be no Jews and Christians on the Saudi Arabian peninsula. But the Saudis had just invited the Americans, meaning Christian and Jewish troops, to station themselves on the holy territory in preparation for the defense against Saddam and his forcible removal from Kuwait. For Bin Laden it was a shocking affront to his religious views, as well as a humiliation for him politically and militarily. Bin Laden saw the move as weakness and capitulation of Islamic authority. As Zawahiri believed that Sadat and Mubarak had already sold out their Muslim souls to the West, now Bin Laden was beginning to turn his critique against the Saudi royal family.[51]

Was the hadith authentic? Are Jews and Christians, or any non-Muslims to be restricted from the *hijaz* (Mecca & Medina) or other part of Saudi Arabia? There are restrictions that apply under the current Saudi rule, but the authenticity of this hadith may be criticized as many *hadith* have been. In some ways it does not matter, it could have been partly heartfelt, but partly pretext for his embittered alienation and opposition to the Saudi regime. Bin Laden believed it, and it shows again his faith in the exclusive model of religion and politics.

Osama could not contain his discontent, and an emerging period of strained relations with the Saudi government would force Bin Laden to seek refuge elsewhere. He felt his country had abandoned him and the true religion of Islam (in his view) and came to a point where he simply could not reconcile the Saudi service and cooperation with the United States. Bin Laden came to Sudan in 1991 to establish a home there and was welcomed by Omar al-Bashir and his right-hand man Hasan al-Turabi.[52]

Bashir's Sudanese government had been placed on the terrorist watch list by the United States. They were open proponents of Islamism and culpable for later ethnic massacres that occurred in that country. Bin Laden began to establish various businesses there as his radicalism increased. The Saudis made several attempts to get Osama to recant his criticism of the government and come back to Saudi Arabia. Family members were sent, including his mother and his uncle Abdullah. None of their attempts were successful, as Bin Laden would not be swayed. A friend was even sent with a tape recorder to try to record words of reconciliation with the Saudi government, but Bin Laden didn't give in. His political convictions had become ossified by his religious interpretation that resistance to the Saudis (and increasingly the Americans) was part of a true Muslim's *jihad*.[53]

Bin Laden was not there on his own. He had his four wives and twenty children, some of whom complained about the austerities of Sudan and wanted to go back to Saudi Arabia. His son Abdallah wanted to return to the rich life of the Saudis, and Bin Laden relented, allowing him to do so.[54] Another son became alienated from Bin Laden's cause and also left. Omar would later call the 9/11 attacks "craziness" that accomplished nothing, and blame Zawahiri and Osama's Egyptian allies for radicalizing him. Bin Laden's eldest son took an oath of *jihad* to the cause, however, and Osama retained many loyal supporters.[55] These and a number of stalwart members of Al Qaeda stood by him as the emotional and political distance from his homeland increased.

Ultimately the efforts of reconciliation failed, and in 1994 the Saudis revoked Bin Laden's citizenship. The breach had become permanent. In 1994 there was also an assassination attempt on Bin Laden. The immediate perpetrators seem to have been a rival, radical Islamist group that did not agree with Bin Laden or his tactics. Surviving, he remained undeterred to carry out his jihad. Fighting groups were sent abroad to places nearby like Somalia and as far away as Bosnia. Al-Qaeda was becoming internationalized, possibly in part due to the fact that Bin Laden had no true home anywhere. In 1995, Al-Qaeda would sponsor a failed assassination attempt on the Egyptian leader Hosni Mubarak. In the same year there would also be a deadly bombing of the Saudi Nation Guard headquarters in Riyadh, which killed seven and wounded thirty-four.

The years 1994 and 1995 also produced a financial crisis for Bin Laden as his assets were frozen, and he had to cut pay for Al-Qaeda members. Pressure from the United States and Saudi Arabia to extradite Bin Laden was finally successful. Omar Bashir and Hasan al-Turabi seized Bin Laden's business assets in the country or purchased them at bargain basement prices. At that point, in 1996, Bin Laden was forced to leave Sudan and come back to Khandahar with three wives and eleven sons and daughters.[56]

This may actually have been a mistake, and a grave tipping point for Osama. Some experts have noted that it would have been easier for intelligence to keep an eye on Bin Laden in the deserts and streets of Sudan than in the cold, remote mountains of Afghanistan. Additionally it provided added fuel to the fire of his radicalism. He had (in his mind at least) helped win a war in Afghanistan, had returned to an occupied homeland, and then been estranged, alienated and exiled from that home. Then the Sudan that had welcomed him from that exile also turned around, seized his assets, and exiled him. Bin Laden came back to the Afghan mountains as a man without a country, and so the focus of his program internationalized, and his determination to strike fixed upon the United States. He perceived the U.S. to be pulling the strings behind all the countries that had forced him into exile.

Having returned to Afghanistan, he did not immediately recognize the political landscape. Mullah Omar and the Taliban had taken charge since he was gone, but Bin Laden used the remaining assets he had to help lubricate a friendship with them. They offered him sanctuary to re-establish Al-Qaeda operations, provided that he keep quiet and not make too many political proclamations. He seemed to ignore that order, and in 1996 for the first time Bin Laden officially declared war upon Israel and America. His gripe with the Saudis, the U.S. and the troops stationed in his homeland was still topping his list of grievances:

> I say to our Muslim brothers across the world: your brothers in Saudi Arabia and Palestine are calling for your help and asking you to share with them in the *jihad* against the enemies of God, your enemies the Israelis and Americans. They are asking you to defy them in whatever way you possibly can, so as to expel them in defeat and humiliation from the holy places of Islam.[57]

How profoundly different this is from Gandhi! One cannot conceive of Gandhi labeling and believing any given nationality to be "the enemies of God", despite some of Gandhi's own documented rhetorical extremes.

The current "occupation" (the stationing of U.S. troops on Saudi soil) of Saudi Arabia was only the last straw in Bin Laden's mind. He also claimed to be agitated by the failure of the 1967 war: "I feel still the pain of [the loss of] Al Quds in my internal organs; [Al Quds: Jerusalem, the site of the third holiest place of pilgrimage in Islam, was annexed to Israel in 1967. It was a mosque his father had rebuilt, so in a way it was personal.] That loss is like a burning fire in my intestines."[58]

In terms of its political essence, there are some parallels between the complaints of Bin Laden and those of Gandhi, in that they both faced powers with great hegemonic or imperial might that exerted political and military prowess far beyond their borders and were perceived to be oppressive. Of course personally I sympathize with the struggle of Gandhi and reject the grievance and abhorrent methods of Bin Laden, but their nature as political and religious figures resisting Western might is as fascinating as the radically different solutions they chose. Gandhi hoped *satyagraha* would be bloodless, but it wasn't, while Bin Laden pledged *jihad* to be bloody, and it was. How can *satyagraha* resist Jihad?

It does not seem that Bin Laden's grievances are falsely put on airs, or deceptions for some ulterior motive. Bin Laden really believes them and has "gone ballistic" about the power of the United States and Israel abroad, and his perception that the Saudis have capitulated to those powers. He is a believer in conspiracy theories and exaggerates the powers of Jews in Washington:

> We speak of American government, but it is really an Israeli government, because if we look into the most sensitive departments of the government, whether it is the Pentagon or the State Department or the CIA, you find that it is the Jews who have first word inside the American government. Consequently they use America to execute their plans throughout the world.[59]

To believe that Jews direct American foreign policy is really absurd. It shows the extremes of his radicalism and the degree to which he was conflating the U.S and Israel. Nonetheless, from his point of view and from the point of view of the extremist minority, this is not conspiracy theory, this is a given reality. Reportedly Bin Laden has read and approved of the *Protocols of the Elders of Zion*, the Bible for those paranoid enough to give any credit to Jewish conspiracy theories.[60]

Bin Laden believes the "Crusader-Zionist" alliance has been going on for decades, citing prior U.S. support for Israel:

> It appears to us, from the writing of the Prophet, that we will have to fight the Jews under his name and on his land [Palestine] . . . . and the United States has involved itself and its people again and again . . . . and dispatched a general air supply line in 1973, during the days of Nixon, from America to Tel Aviv, with weapons, aid, and men, which affected the outcome of the battle, so how could we not fight it? . . . . Any nation that joins the Jewish trenches has only itself to blame.[61]

Bin Laden was a sixteen-year old conservative (but not yet fully radicalized) youth in 1973. How politically concerned he was at that time may be in question, but certainly Bin Laden has woven the political history of the Middle East into his conception of conspiracy theories, giving the quality of exaggerated paranoia to many of his statements, but with enough measure of historical truth in them to be compelling to his followers. Even if his claims have some meager measure of fact in them, however, his methods have none. His belief that violence against civilians is justified has no moral merit nor any genuine roots in Islam that I can discern, but his rhetorical skills have convinced many otherwise.

Establishing his new home base in Afghanistan, with his new allies in the Taliban, Bin Laden would set about making his attacks upon his enemies more systematically. Clandestine operations were set in motion to accomplish his ends, which resulted in the most calamitous attack upon the U.S. in a century.

Al-Qaeda

The attempt to understand Bin Laden must never be confused with any justification or excuse for his actions. There is no justification for terrorism, as Gandhi said, "[All] terrorism is bad whether put up in good cause or bad."[62] It must be condemned under any scheme of morality, be it Muslim, Christian, Jewish, Hindu, Buddhist, or secular. The attempt to understand him should be made instead to *defuse* the power of his ideological belief to make it less compelling, and to equip ourselves with some of the knowledge we will need to further *diffuse* the intensity and quantity of people who will agree with and try to fulfill his aims. Al-Qaeda cannot be conquered only with a war of bullets, but also must be challenged with a more forceful war of ideas. That is where Gandhi's alternative can become more compelling.

When Osama bin Laden settled in Afghanistan, a region ravaged by war for decades, his message became compelling there and abroad. His training camps were full, and the number of available persons he had to commit to *jihad* was quite plentiful and their talents quite ranging. Many came to him without his need of soliciting them. Rohan Gunaratna reports that of over ten thousand recruits that passed through the training camps of Afghanistan, Al-Qaeda could pick the top three percent for its organization. It was a heyday for Bin Laden, and Al-Qaeda training manuals reveal a complete rejection of all tactics of nonviolence: "Islamic governments have never been and will never be, established through peaceful solutions and cooperative councils. They are established as they [always] have been by pen and gun by word and bullet by tongue and teeth."[63]

A series of attacks would follow, but the United States and its allies were slow to respond to the growing threat, despite the consternation and efforts of some within the intelligence community. Bin Laden's organization plotted and carried out the bombings upon the U.S. Embassies in Kenya and Tanzania of August 7, 1998. Truck bombs were detonated almost simultaneously at embassies in Nairobi and Dar es Salaam, resulting in the deaths of over 200 people, and the wounding of thousands. Scores of people received disfiguring injuries, and one hundred and fifty were blinded by the flying projectiles of glass shards from shattered windows. It is hard to imagine a more arbitrary and meaningless way to resolve disputes, as most of the injured were not Americans and had nothing to do with Bin Laden's grievances. They happened to be outside vulnerable U.S. targets. Soon after, the Clinton Administration launched controversial cruise missile strikes in retaliation which proved ineffective.[64]

Bin Laden's attacks continued. On October 12, 2000, a small dinghy, laden with high explosives, collided with the *U.S.S. Cole* in the port of Aden, Yemen. The explosion killed 17 sailors and wounded 39 and crippled the U.S. vessel. Bin Laden was pleased and wrote a poem about it afterwards, which he read at his son's wedding, glorifying the event as a great victory. The asymmetrical terror tactics used against the Cole can cause disproportionate injury to an enemy, and in that they have some advantage. In Afghanistan a guerilla insurgency proved to be as much problem for the Soviets as Vietnam was for Americans. A mobile, underground enemy that strikes at random targets cannot easily defeat an enemy army of the scale of the U.S. or the Soviets, but it can harass, erode confidence, and give small victories for propaganda purposes. Unfortunately as the U.S. was in the cycle of electoral politics in a very controversial election, no effective measures were taken against Al-Qaeda by the outgoing or the incoming administration, which may have emboldened Al-Qaeda.[65]

The September 11 attacks were the most infamous but were not the original conception of Osama bin Laden. The World Trade Centers themselves had been the target of violent Islamists since February of 1993 when the first car bomb detonated underneath them and killed six, and injured a thousand others. Ramzi Yousef had engineered the attack and hoped to bring the towers down and kill as many as two hundred and fifty thousand people. It was not an Al-Qaeda sponsored attack, and Yousef was later apprehended in Islamabad in 1995.[66]

Sometimes terror is a family business. It was in fact the uncle of Ramzi Yousef, a man named Khalid Sheikh Mohammed, who masterminded the 9/11 attacks. He may have been inspired or acquired some of the ideas from his nephew. Khalid Sheikh Mohammed was born to Pakistani parents in 1965, his brothers attended Kuwait University, but Khalid became radicalized as an Islamist as early as age sixteen. Ironically he attended school in the Bible Belt of North Carolina, first going to Chowan College (a small Baptist school) and then transferring to North Carolina Agricultural and Technical State University in Greensboro. Even here, there were peer Muslims who would oversee the piety and dedication of fellow Muslims to proper religious ritual. Sheikh Mohammed appears to have turned decidedly against the United States and independently began to pursue his own visions of jihad.[67]

Khalid Sheikh Mohammed originally had a more elaborate plan for the "planes operation", as it would come to be known. He was hoping to strike targets on the east and west coast of the United States, using ten planes and hitting twice as many targets. Khalid had in mind that he would pilot the last of the planes, land it, kill the male passengers aboard, and make a statement to the press denouncing U.S. foreign policy in the Middle East. Khalid Sheikh Mohammed finally came with the idea of the plan to Bin Laden in 1996, but originally Bin Laden took a dim view of it, seeing it as too farfetched. Around 1999 Bin Laden changed his mind and adopted a scaled back version of Khalid Sheik's plan, without the western planes or the final statement to the press. It was this version of the plan which would unfortunately take flight and culminate on September 11, 2001.[68]

There is a differentiated rank and file of Islamic radicals, and it would be useful here to illustrate that and spell out some terms. I have tried to use the word "Muslim" or "Islamic" to refer to mainstream interpretations and accepted practices of those who proffer faith in the Prophet Muhammad and the Qur'an. "Islamist" has meant those who advocate a political state based on the Qur'an, with no Jeffersonian "wall of separation." Sometimes "Islamist" has been used interchangeably with "Islamist-Jihadist", which properly indicates those who are willing to use violent force in order to attain the end of an Islamic State. Why review this here? Beyond the importance of clarification, we must illustrate that there are a variety of Islamists out there, some of them violent, some of them not. Even within the category of those who are violent, there are some who act as coordinators, such as Bin Laden, those who act as strategic planners, such as Khalid Sheikh Mohammed, as well as those who fulfill various other support roles. The most dramatic category is of course the suicide bomber, such as Mohammed Atta.

The "war on terror" is not a duel against an undifferentiated and mindless stream of suicidal zombies, programmed to be such from birth. Some are willing to give their lives, while others do not. The "war on terror" is not against Islam, but it is against those radicals who have claimed Islam for themselves. Whether they have a claim to be proper Muslims many Muslims themselves would deny, while a minority has affirmed. The "war on terror" is also about political situations in the Middle East and the values and principles deemed to be essential to religion. It must never be forgotten that it cannot be won without a war of ideas. Abdullah Azzam was wrong; one cannot assert "Jihad and the rifle alone; no negotiations, no conferences, no compromises."[69] While less responsible persons are fighting this conflict as a terrorist campaign or a war of attrition to chalk up the most bodies, more sober-minded and rational persons must of course engage in dialogue to iron out grievances in as peaceful a manner as possible.

Muhammad Atta did not become one of these peaceful persons. Yet it is also true that Atta did not grow up as a programmed radical. He came from a middle-class Egyptian home where his father had been very strict about his studies. Born in 1968, Atta showed a lifelong propensity for skill in academics and would attend Cairo University for engineering, and later went to school in Hamburg, Germany. Some pictures of Atta as a youth reveal what looks to be a bright smile, but this would soon disappear and be replaced with a brooding, taciturn man who had devoted his life to the idea of radical Islamism. Atta's roommates in college reported him to be an uncommunicative and unfriendly person, very self-absorbed and impossible to reach. He seemed also to have had a prudish attitude towards sex, and no reports of lasting girlfriends have surfaced. One woman in Aleppo caught his attention, but he "couldn't pursue her because she was too forward, and thus not properly Islamic."[70]

Unemployment and economic frustration may be a part of the discontent of the Islamic world. The disgruntled do not always come from the lowest economic strata, however. Atta graduated as an engineer, but in Egypt if one did not have connections, one was seldom employed. Terry McDermott relates that "In one recent year, young Egyptians with graduate degrees were 32 times more likely to be unemployed than illiterate peasants."[71] In understatement, that has to be frustrating. The disillusioned middle class may be as much participants in jihad as the rest, because they have participated in trying to get ahead, and often have gotten nowhere due to the lack of opportunity. Economic want or lack of opportunity is not a sole determining factor in this crisis, but it is possibly an important contributing one.

We cannot posit that these Islamists are prudes in life who await the promise of virgins in the hereafter either. Ziad Jarrah, the pilot of Flight 93 that crashed in Shanksville, Pennsylvania, was on the surface a more jovial person who could easily crack a joke and get along. Perhaps most eerie, throughout his entire involvement in the 9/11 plans he kept his girlfriend Aysel Sengun in the dark about the plot. She sensed there was something amiss, she could read his sometimes troubled demeanor, but she never had any idea of what he was really up to. Jarrah professed his love for her, declaring it in communications to her even up to the day of the attacks. One wonders who is more disturbing as a figure, the obviously brooding and isolated figure of Atta, or the seemingly happy Jarrah. Jarrah came from an affluent Lebanese family, no doubt equally shocked by his involvement.[72]

Atta and Jarrah met in Hamburg, and together with Marwan al-Shehhi and Ramzi bin al-Shibh they became radicalized in Germany and known as the "Hamburg Four." Ramzi bin al-Shibh wanted to participate in the attacks, convincing himself that "the life to come was better." But he was denied a visa three times, and in his place Hani Hanjour would become the fourth pilot. Most of the other "muscle hijackers" (15 of the total 19) were taken from Saudi Arabian recruits.[73]

The Hamburg Four would ultimately come to the attention of Al-Qaeda networking agents and find their way to Afghanistan and into Bin Laden's camps. They were just what he needed. Khalid Sheikh Mohammed's plot called for persons who could pilot commercial aircraft, who therefore had an education and could speak some English. The group came to Bin Laden and trained to become the pilots needed for the operation.

The horror of that day will not be forgotten, but to some it is more tragically personal than others. On September 11, 2001, Mohammed Atta piloted Flight 11 into the face of the North World Trade Center at 8:46 AM. Marwan al-Shehhi struck the South Tower with Flight 175 just seventeen minutes later at 9:03 AM. American horror magnified as we realized then it was a concerted attack. Hani Hanjour smashed into the wall of the Pentagon with Flight 77 at 9:37. Ziad Jarrah, aboard Flight 93, had been delayed, and took over his flight last. Perhaps in part due to the delay, passengers were able to appraise the situation and launch a heroic takeover, which resulted in the tragic crash in Pennsylvania. The World Trade Center South collapsed first at 9:59 AM and the North Tower last at 10:28 AM. Within a few short hours, the most devilish dreams of Khalid Sheikh Mohammed and Osama bin Laden had been realized in congruence with the darkest nightmare for thousands of innocent families. Two thousand nine hundred and seventy-three people had perished for Bin Laden's vengeance.[74] While immediately denying responsibility, Bin Laden later boasted that the damage had been beyond his wildest hopes and dreams and claimed that the net loss from the "blessed attacks" added up to some $1 trillion.[75] Of course that is just assets, not the loss of human life.

It must be remembered that ninety-five years earlier on the same day Mohandas Gandhi and a group of faithful Hindus and Muslims took an oath to God to behave nonviolently, and that was a distinctive moment for the birth of *satyagraha*. It is hoped that the truth in nonviolence of that date is not overshadowed by the devastation and mayhem of violence decades later. Whenever Gandhi launched a nonviolent program, he would often take pains to write a letter of his grievances to the authorities to give them notice of his intent to disobey them. The family members of the 9/11 attacks never received any such letter of warning. Their loved ones showed up for work that day, doing what they did to support their families. Then a huge commercial jet plane crashed through their office windows. Most had probably never heard of Bin Laden and none had any statement of formalized word that he had a complaint. The point is reiterated that Bin Laden's tactics for resolving grievances were completely wrong, and wrong minded. Now we have become embroiled in this conflict where the dead are mounting, and one can imagine the soul of the Mahatma shedding tears for the tragedy. Not only the Mahatma weeps, to be sure.

Why do we so readily and so easily seek recourse to violence when the best callings of human conscience tell us otherwise? What was Osama thinking?

Bin Laden Today

The memory of September 11, 2001 is chilling to many, while the memory of September 11, 1906 is now in history books. It is an unnerving thing to consider that nineteen men plotted their own demise, and that of thousands of others in advance. While we leapt before we really looked in reaction to the WMD situation in Iraq, it nonetheless remains true that men of such grim determination and grisly mindset cannot be allowed to come into possession of such weapons. We can do this by making the weapons hard to possess, but also by challenging the underpinning factors and justifications that produces this belligerent mindset to begin with.

While global polls of Muslim opinion reveal only 7% considered the 9/11 attacks to be justified, another poll indicated that only 7% thought the West had a fair perception of Muslim countries.[76] The 9/11 Commission report indicated extremely low approval ratings of the United States in various parts of the Muslim world. It reported that in Egypt, 15% viewed us favorably, while in Saudi Arabia that was 12%. Approval in Indonesia had plummeted from 61% to 15%, and in Nigeria from 71% to 38%.[77] Yet Muslims do not reject democracy. Polls also indicate that in many countries, 90% of Muslims desire free speech and political rights, and that in other countries support for the right to vote for men and women also rises to 80% or more.[78] While Muslims seem to want democracy, many do not seem to think we are representing democratic values well. Whether Muslim countries can make workable a form of democratic government based on the Qur'an yet remains to be seen, but clearly the United States is fighting an uphill battle in terms of our global popularity with Muslims. Let us hope we can do better.

Meanwhile a "cult of Bin Laden" has emerged in the Islamic world as one who stood up to an unpopular military and economic giant.[79] If only 7% of the Muslim population approved of the 9/11 attacks, paradoxically, regional polls indicate an approval of Bin Laden that was much higher than that. Perhaps this is in part due to the fact that at one point 61% of Arabs had even refused to believe that Arabs had perpetrated the attacks (even in the United States, conspiracy theories still are plentiful).[80]

The most brutal man to pledge allegiance to Bin Laden was Abu Musab al-Zarqawi. Zarqawi had been a troubled Jordanian youth who decorated his body with tattoos, consumed alcohol, and had a reputation for petty crime and violence. Coming into the fold of radical Islam, Zarqawi became a most savage and cold-blooded killer, and a leader of the emerging network of Al-Qaeda in Iraq, subsequent to our invasion. It was Zarqawi who had conducted the grisly beheading of Nicholas Berg, an American businessman he had abducted in Iraq. Zarqawi had pursued a bloody jihad against the Shia Muslims of Iraq, hoping further to destabilize the country and to make the occupation difficult for the United States. His vengeful and bitter campaign was at times almost too much for the Al-Qaeda leadership. Zarqawi's death on June 7, 2006 in a U.S. military operation was a severe blow to Al-Qaeda in Iraq, and after his death, the Iraqis turned against Al-Qaeda as an unwanted force within its borders.[81]

While men like Zarqawi are rare, they are precisely the kind who can be most dangerous. Showing some capacity and skill for organization, while many of Zarqawi's plans were foiled, some were also successful. Zarqawi had grown to hate the government of his home country, Jordan, for making peace with Israel. Links have been drawn to his support of a chemical weapons attack on Amman. The attack was fortunately foiled on April 26, 2004, but had it succeeded, it would have released up to 20 tons of toxic agent upon a defenseless urban people and could have resulted in the deaths of tens of thousands. It could have made the attack of 9/11 look very small in terms of the gross loss of life.[82] Since the ideology which Bin Laden has helped make popular has not been fully defused, continuous attempts must be made to batter it with words no less than it has been battered by bullets, for (as Gandhi understood) only the former can have a more lasting and permanent impact. To be sure, political and economic reforms, greater hope for the Muslim people, many of whom are jobless, frustrated, and marginalized, will also help in that end.

Bin Laden at the moment of this writing is still at large, possibly in the border region of Afghanistan and Pakistan. While Al-Qaeda has thankfully not perpetrated an act of terror on the same scope as 9/11, we cannot take the risk that his name will simply drift into oblivion. He has followers, he has friends, he has loyal adherents to his beliefs, and they must be challenged. Gandhian techniques are not of course effective against subterranean networks of terror; that is where their limits are thrown into sharp relief. It should be very clear however that Gandhian principles, the same principles of nonviolence which many Muslims and Christians have espoused, have the upper hand in the war of religious ideas. There is nothing enduring, sophisticated, or true about the kind of tit-for-tat violent strikes which Bin Laden justifies, and there is everything about Truth in Gandhi's appeals to nonviolence. People in their better minds want to get up in the morning and contribute to something meaningful, lasting, and sustaining. We would all much rather grab our car keys and go to work than grab the AK47 or M16 and go on our respective *jihad* or *crusade*. People, men and women, can survive nonviolent conflict, whenever and wherever it is possible. Conversely, men and women either die, suffer horrible injuries, or post-traumatic stress disorders wherever violence is seen. Nonviolence interrupts the cycle of pain that violence perpetuates. It is the unfortunate conundrum of our political and religious lives that the latter has become far too appealing, while we know it is the former (nonviolent) approach that must ultimately reign in our hearts.

Notes

1. Bergen, *Holy War Inc.*, 193-194.
2. Bergen, *Holy War Inc.*, 52.
3. Peter L Bergen, *The Osama bin Laden I Know: An Oral History of al Qaeda's Leader* (New York, The Free Press, 2006) 8.
4. Steve Coll, *The Bin Ladens*: An Arabian Family in the American Century (New York, The Penguin Press, 2008), 67.

5. Steve Coll, *The Bin Ladens*, 12.
6. Steve Coll, *The Bin Ladens*, 26-31.
7. Alexei Vassiliev, *The History of Saudi Arabia* (London, Saqi Books, 2000), Chapters 3-12, 14, 16.
8. Birth dates for Muhammad Wahhab vary, but tend to agree upon 1703-1979, see Vassiliev, *The History of Saudi Arabia*, 64.
9. Vassiliev, *The History of Saudi Arabia*, 65-74.
10. Vassiliev, *The History of Saudi Arabia*, 96-98, 220-281.
11. John, Keay, *India: A History*, New York, Grove Press, 2000.
12. Steve Coll, *The Bin Ladens*, 39-43.
13. Steve Coll, *The Bin Ladens*, 84-92.
14. Steve Coll, *The Bin Ladens*, xiii, 43-44.
15. Steve Coll, *The Bin Ladens*, 108-318.
16. Steve Coll, *The Bin Ladens*, 119-120, 324-325. Lawrence Wright has written a compelling account of the 9/11 attacks and Khalid Sheik Mohammed's role, see Lawrence Wright, *The Looming Tower: Al Qaeda and the Road to 9/11* (New York Alfred A. Knopf, 2006), 307-309.
17. Steve Coll, *The Bin Ladens*, 230, 348, 488-493.
18. Bergen, *The Osama I Know*, 10; see also Rohan Gunaratna, *Inside Al Qaeda, Global Network of Terror* (Columbia University Press, New York, 2002), 19.
19. Steve Coll, *The Bin Ladens*, 407-408.
20. Steve Coll, *The Bin Ladens*, 73-74, 136-140.
21. Steve Coll, *The Bin Ladens*, 142-144.
22. Bergen, *The Osama I Know*, 4, 5, 14; Steve Coll, *The Bin Ladens*, 151.
23. Reports of Bin Laden in Yossef Bodansky's book *Bin Laden: The Man Who Declare War on America* do not seem to be on track. Some are accurate, others clearly false or fictionalized. Accounts of Bin Laden as a party youth seem inaccurate in Yossef Bodansky, *Bin Laden: The Man Who Declared War On America* (New York Forum Prima / Random House, 2001), 3.
24. Steve Coll, *The Bin Ladens*, 151, 198-207.
25. Steve Coll, *The Bin Ladens*, 204.
26. Bergen, *The Osama I Know*, 15.
27. Bergen, *The Osama I Know*, 16.
28. Bergen, *The Osama I Know*, 18-19; Steve Coll, *The Bin Ladens*, 204.
29. Bergen, *Holy War Inc.*, 47; Bergen, *The Osama I Know*, 24-26; Steve Coll, *The Bin Ladens*, 204, 253-282; Gunaratna, *Inside Al-Qaeda*, 17.
30 Bergen, *The Osama I Know*, 23; Steve Coll, *The Bin Ladens*, 226-232; Vassiliev, *The History of Saudi Arabia*, 396; see also Bernard Lewis, *The Crisis of Islam: Holy War and Unholy Terror*, (New York, The Modern Library, 2003), 82.
31. Wright, *The Looming Tower*, 95-102; Bergen, *The Osama I Know*, 24-29.
32. Wright, *The Looming Tower*, 95.
33. Wright, *The Looming Tower*, 130; Gunaratna, *Inside Al-Qaeda*, 22, 86.
34. Bergen, *The Osama I Know*, 35.
35. Bergen, *The Osama I Know*, 45-48; Steve Coll, *The Bin Ladens*, 256-259, 336-7; Gunaratna, *Inside Al-Qaeda*, 22; Wright, *The Looming Tower*, 130.
36. Bruce Lawrence, *Messages to The World*, 86, 147.
37. Steve Coll, *The Bin Ladens*, 7, 8, 152, 259.
38. Bruce Lawrence, *Messages to the World*, 48.
39. Steve Coll, *The Bin Ladens*, 258.
40. Steve Coll, *The Bin Ladens*, 289.

41. Wright, *The Looming Tower,* 54-55.
42. Wright, *The Looming Tower,* 53-56; Bergen, *The Osama I Know,* 64-69; Esposito, *Unholy War,* 20; Gunaratna, *Inside Al-Qaeda,* 26, 224.
43. Bergen, *The Osama I Know,* 204-205.
44. Bergen, *The Osama I Know,* 47-60; Steve Coll, *The Bin Ladens,* 290-335; Lawrence Wright, *The Looming Tower,* 111-119.
45. Steve Coll, *The Bin Ladens,* 291-304; Peter Bergen, *The Osama I Know,* 52-59; Lawrence Wright, *The Looming Tower,* 145.
46. Bergen, *The Osama I Know,* 87-93; Steve Coll, *The Bin Ladens,* 340-341; Gunaratna, *Inside Al-Qaeda,* 23-25.
47. Steve Coll, *The Bin Ladens,* 376.
48. Lawrence Wright, *The Looming Tower,* 158.
49. Gunaratna, *Inside Al-Qaeda,* 27-28; Bergen, *The Osama I Know,* 108.
50. Reza Aslan, *No God But God: The Origins, Evolution, and Future of Islam* (New York, Random House Trade Paperbacks, 2006), 67-68.
51. Lawrence Wright, *The Looming Tower,* 158; Peter Bergen, *The Osama I Know,* 112-115; Steve Coll, *The Bin Ladens,* 379-380.
52. Bergen, *The Osama I Know,* 121-123; Steve Coll, *The Bin Ladens,* 381-397.
53. Steve Coll, *The Bin Ladens,* 401-407.
54. Bergen, *The Osama I Know,* 168; Steve Coll, *The Bin Ladens,* 414-415.
55. Bergen, *The Osama I Know,* 257, 384.
56. Bergen, *The Osama I Know,* 127-139; Steve Coll, *The Bin Ladens,* 408-9, 461-462.
57. Bruce Lawrence, *Messages to the World,* 30.
58. Bergen, *The Osama I Know,* 165-166.
59. Bergen, *The Osama I Know,* 291.
60. Steve Coll, *The Bin Ladens,* 464.
61. Steve Coll, *The Bin Ladens,* 205.
62. Fischer, *The Essential Gandhi,* 151.
63. Gunaratna, *Inside Al-Qaeda,* 5-8.
64. Oddly accounts of the number killed in the East African Embassy bombing vary between 212 and 225 killed, with thousands injured — see Bergen, *The Osama I Know,* 219-224; Lawrence Wright, *The Looming Tower,* 272; Steve Coll, *The Bin Ladens,* 225; Gunaratna, *Inside Al-Qaeda,* 160. The Al-Qaeda tactics of simultaneous strikes may have been the hallmark of (the now late) Imad Mughniyeh, who masterminded the first simultaneous suicide bombings on U.S. & French barracks in Beirut in 1983 — see Gunaratna, *Inside Al-Qaeda,* 147-148.
65. Bergen, *The Osama I Know,* 251-256; Bruce Lawrence, *Messages to the World,* 193; Clarke, *Against All Enemies,* 223-224.
66. Bergen, *The Osama I Know,* 144-145; Gunaratna, *Inside Al-Qaeda,* 177-179; Wright, *The Looming Tower,* 177-178.
67. Terry McDermott, *Perfect Soldiers, the Hijackers: Who They Were, Why They Did It* (New York HarperCollins Publishers, 2005), 109-118.
68. McDermott, *Perfect Soldiers,* 166-167; Wright, *The Looming Tower,* 307-308.
69. Wright, *The Looming Tower,* 95.
70. McDermott, *Perfect Soldiers,* 20-29.
71. McDermott, *Perfect Soldiers,* 31.
72. For an excellent profile on Jarrah and Atta, see Terry McDermott, *Perfect Soldiers.*
73. McDermott, *Perfect Soldiers,* 1-4, 58-59, 86, 201.

74. Thomas H Kean, Lee H. Hamilton, et al., *The 9/11 Commission Report: Final Report of the National Commission on Terrorist Attacks Upon the United States*, Authorized Edition (Printed in the United States, W.W. Norton & Company July 22, 2004), 32-33, 285.

75. Bruce Lawrence, *Messages to the World*, 111, 150; reports do indicate that after the attack Wall Street went into a landslide amounting to some $1.2 trillion.

76. Gunaratna, *Inside Al-Qaeda*, 238.

77. *The 9/11 Commission Report*, Authorized Edition, 375.

78. Esposito and Mogahed, *Who Speaks for Islam?*, 47, 51.

79. Gunaratna, *Inside Al-Qaeda*, 52-53.

80. Gunaratna, *Inside Al-Qaeda*, 238.

81. Brisard, Jean-Charles, with Damien Martinez, *Zarqawi: The New Face of Al-Qaeda* (New York, Other Press, 2005), 12-13, 131, 142-16, 246-7.

82. Brisard, *Zarqawi*, 88-89.

Chapter 5: Bin Laden's Belief

Bin Laden and Islamist Jihad

It must be recalled that the word *jihad* does not inevitably mean "war", in spite of the fact that it is often used that way. The fact is it is most often used that way not only because the Western media does it, but because that is what the radical Islamists want. They want us and all Muslims to believe that this is a violent clash of religions, that it is inevitable, that there will be glorious rewards for those Muslims who die for jihad. We must remember, however, that the interpretation of *jihad* means "struggle", and it is in every Muslim's heart and mind to choose the kind of struggle to be committed to. In Bin Laden's home town, a man said his jihad was the welfare of his three-year old son.[1] Abdul Ghaffar Khan, a nonviolent Muslim who interpreted Islam in a much similar way to Gandhi's Hinduism had this to say about the word: "This is our *jihad*, our crusade. Before we can fight the British, we must first end the violence and murder in our own hearts. Remember that overcoming our personal weakness is the greater *jihad*, the greater crusade. It is what God wants of us."[2] If Abdul Ghaffar Khan were alive today (he passed away in 1988), he would have denied and offered refutation that jihad could have any violent meaning.

Yet Bin Laden is no less passionate about his concept of religion. Which is the better representative of the true spirit of Islam? Bin Laden believes that violent jihad is the only route open to Muslims at this moment. Muslims still have a choice, they can still interpret their duty to "struggle" for their religion how they will, but Osama bin Laden insists that there is only one viable alternative open to them: war and killing, in an indiscriminate fashion, upon those they perceive as their enemies. Bin Laden says: "There can be no dialogue with the occupiers except with weapons."[3] Bin Laden thinks it would be crazy to fight his war in the way of Gandhi. Perhaps it might seem crazy, but as King and Gandhi showed a nonviolent war is much more capable of penetrating the calloused mind of the opponent and striking a real blow to the moral conscience. It is, of course, never easy to do so.

Bin Laden has insisted upon jihad in numerous decrees, and having reviewed his life we can see how he incrementally moved towards this position.

He carried with him in youth an opposition to Zionism which was exacerbated by the Islamist propaganda he was exposed to at Abdul Aziz University. When the Soviets invaded Afghanistan, Bin Laden became further immersed in fighting jihad and mentored under Abdullah Azzam in support of the Afghan resistance. When he came home to Saudi Arabia, he found his country soon occupied by a perceived infidel and incapable of defending itself. Later he would become a man without a country, and only the flame of jihad in his heart. This radicalism was in fact mirrored by his later lieutenant Abu Musab al-Zarqawi. Zarqawi, who felt alienated by his home of Jordan once said: "I am global, and no land is my country."[4] Bin Laden declared war on the world because, in his mind, the world had declared war on him, and abandoned his concept of the true religion.

If Bin Laden's understanding of Islam is not legitimate, it is believed here that his agitation and anger is real. It is not put on for political purposes, he does not feign his beliefs (though he expresses it in the wrong way). Bin Laden has a very real sense of umbrage that makes him zealously committed to his cause. There were numerous opportunities for him to turn aside from his ways in Sudan, even appeals from his mother as we saw, but he rejected them all because he believed he was doing his religious duty. He has expressed that "The legal duty regarding Palestine and our brothers there — these poor men, women, and children who have nowhere to go — is to wage *jihad* for the sake of God, and to motivate our *umma* to *jihad* so that Palestine may be completely liberated and returned to Islamic sovereignty." Relating very much to the Islamic scholar Ibn Taymiyya, who was imprisoned for his Islamic protest and whom Bin Laden frequently cites as a source of inspiration, he upholds Taymiyya as a model for unwavering militancy. He cites Taymiyya, "There is no greater duty after faith than unconditionally fighting the attacking enemy who corrupts religion and the world. He must be resisted as hard as possible, as stipulated by our companions the scholars and others."[5]

Violent jihad is incumbent not only for Palestinians, but for all Muslims in the Bin Laden worldview. As we have seen before Bin Laden calls out for attacks on the U.S. and Israel:

> I say to our Muslim brothers across the world: your brothers in Saudi Arabia and Palestine are calling for your help and asking you to share with them in the jihad against the enemies of God, your enemies the Israelis and Americans. They are asking you to defy them in whatever way you possibly can, so as to expel them in defeat and humiliation from the holy places of Islam.[6]

On February 23, 1998, Bin Laden released his formal declaration of war upon America, Israel, and their allies. The reader will note a consistent theme in his thinking:

> Firstly, for over seven years America has occupied the holiest parts of the Islamic lands, the Arabian peninsula, plundering its wealth, dictating to its leaders, humiliating its people, terrorizing its neigh-

bors and turning its bases there into a spearhead with which to fight the neighboring Muslim people.

Some might have disputed the reality of this occupation before, but all the people of the Arabian peninsula have now acknowledged it. There is no clearer proof than America's excessive aggression against the people of Iraq using the Peninsula as a base. It is true that all leaders have rejected such use of their lands, but they are powerless.

Secondly, despite the great devastation inflicted upon the Iraqi people at the hands of the Judeo-Crusader alliance, and despite the terrible number of deaths — over one million — despite all this, the Americans are trying to repeat these horrific massacres again, as if they are not satisfied with the long period of sanctions after the vicious war, or with all the fragmentation and destruction.

Today they come to annihilate what is left of this people and humiliate their Muslim neighbors.

Thirdly, while these wars are being waged by the Americans for religious and economic purposes, they also serve the interests of the petty Jewish state, diverting attention from its occupation of Jerusalem and its murder of Muslims there. . . .

All these American crimes and sins are a clear proclamation of war against God, his Messenger, and the Muslims. Religious scholars throughout Islamic history have agreed that *jihad* is an individual duty when an enemy attacks Muslim countries. . . .

After faith, there is no greater duty than fighting an enemy who is corrupting religion and the world. On this basis, and in accordance with God's will, we pronounce to all Muslims the following judgment:

To kill the Americans and their allies — civilians and military — is an individual duty incumbent upon every Muslim in all countries, in order to liberate the al-Asqa Mosque and the Holy Mosque from their grip, so that their armies leave all the territories of Islam, defeated, broken, and unable to threaten any Muslim. This is in accordance with the words of God Almighty: 'Fight the idolaters at any time, if they first fight you;' 'Fight them until there is no more persecution and until worship is devoted to God;'. . . .

With God's permissions we call on everyone who believes in God and wants to comply with His will to kill the Americans and seize their money wherever and whenever they find them. We also call on the religious scholars, their leaders, their youth, and their soldiers, to launch the raid on the soldiers of Satan, the Americans, and whichever devil's supporters are allied with them, to rout those behind them so that they will not forget it.[7]

There are of course extreme claims throughout — the concept of the Judeo-Crusader alliance, the notion of responsibility for 1 million deaths, and that this is therefore a "proclamation of war against God, his Messenger, and the Muslims." The religious arrogance to suggest that the decree is "in accordance with God's will" also ignores completely every part of the Qur'an which condemns this kind of offensive violence. The Qur'an says, "Fight for the sake of God those that fight against you, but do not attack them first. God does not love aggressors (Surah 2:190)"[8], and while it goes on to suggest violence against idolaters, it again reiterates that one should break off violence from a non-aggressor.

The Qur'an also strongly indicates that life is precious, tying its own beliefs to that of the Hebrew scriptures: "That was why We laid it down for the Israelites that whoever killed a human being, except for punishment for murder or other villainy in the land, shall be regarded as having killed all mankind; and that whoever saved a human life shall be regarded as having saved all mankind (Surah 5:32)."[9]

Of course some violence is justified in the Qur'an, but it is always qualified as being in relation to self-defense. For example, the Qur'an says "You shall not kill any man who God has forbidden you to kill, except for a just cause. If a man is slain unjustly, his heir shall be entitled to satisfaction. But let him not carry his vengeance to excess, for his victim is sure to be assisted and avenged (Surah 17:33)."[10] One must ask the very obvious question — isn't Bin Laden's violence carried out to excess?! Bin Laden would argue in return that it is we who are in fact the first aggressors. In fact, however, though the Qur'an allows for retributive or defensive attacks and is very stern in its tones of judgment, it suggests also that mercy is better. This theme is not isolated in the Qur'an, but in fact repeated:

> "If you punish, let your punishment be commensurate with the wrong that has been done you. But it shall be best for you to endure your wrongs with patience." — [Surah 16:127]

> Twice shall their reward be given them, because they have endured with fortitude, requiting evil with good and giving in alms from what We gave them; and because they pay no heed to idle talk, but say 'We have our actions and you have yours. We wish you peace. We will have nothing to do with ignorant men.'" [Surah 28:54]

> "Let evil be rewarded with evil. But he that forgives and seeks reconcilement shall be recompensed by God. He does not love the wrongdoers." [Surah 42:38][11]

Of course there are parts of the Qur'an that can be produced and interpreted to create a contrary effect. The "sword verses" (for example, Surah 2:190-195 and Surah 9:5-7) of the Qur'an command the faithful to find and slay the idolaters, but they also say that this violence is not justified against those who are nonviolent, or who desists from violent ways.[12] It seems that to the contrary, no unambiguously violent interpretation of the Qur'an exists and that the text might be claimed for nonviolent ways inasmuch as it is claimed for violence. Even conversion to Islam at the point of force is forbidden, contrary to the misunderstandings of many. The Qur'an reads: "There shall be no compulsion in religion. True guidance is now distinct from error (Surah 2:256)."[13]

The point here is not to impose a final interpretation or meaning upon the Qur'an, but to show that, contrary to popular belief, it is very possible to interpret it nonviolently. In fact, many Christians would also prefer peace but allow for just war or violence in the extreme situations. Muslims would do the same.

Bin Laden's counterclaim, as we have indicated, is that it is we who pulled the first trigger — by supporting Israel and the violence against Palestinians, by our "occupation" of Saudi Arabia during the Gulf War with Saddam, and by our current actions in Iraq. We do not have to accept these interpretations, but we should at least know that is what Bin Laden and many other radical Islamists like him are agitated about. It deepens our own understanding and response to the problem.

The innocent women and children killed on 9/11 cannot be held accountable for violence in Israel, or Saudi Arabia, or Iraq. The connectivity is broken and absurd, and the act abominable. In Bin Laden's mind, unfortunately, the connection was real. Although Bin Laden weakly concedes that Islam does not allow for violence against the innocent, he always falls back upon a "tit for tat" logic that we struck first and that we bear responsibility.[14] He has had the gall to suggest that the victims of 9/11 were accountable and viable targets simply because they participated in American democracy:

> The American people are the ones who choose their government through their own free will; a choice which stems from their agreement to its policies. Thus the American people have chosen, consented to, and affirmed their support for Israel's oppression of the Palestinians, the occupation and usurpation of their land, and its continuous killing, torture, punishment, and expulsion of the Palestinians. The American people have the ability and choice to refuse the policies of their government, and even to change it if they want.
>
> The American people are the ones who pay the taxes which fund the planes that bomb us in Afghanistan, the tanks that strike and destroy our homes in Palestine, the armies which occupy our lands in the Arabian Gulf, and the fleets which ensure the blockade of Iraq. These tax dollars are given to Israel for it to continue attacking us and invade our lands. So the American people are the ones who fund the attacks against us, and they are the ones who oversee the expenditure of these monies in the way they wish, through their elected candidates.[15]

Of course this conception of democratic politics and accountability is seriously flawed, because it makes no discrimination between combatants or non-combatants, nor cares how close one is to the actual trigger that was pulled. It is a recipe for psychologically dysfunctional politics. If Gandhi had used the same logic, he could have said that the oppression, poverty, and starvation of Indians could have called for the throttling of British housewives or children. Thankfully, he did not, because Gandhi understood that eye-for-an-eye violence makes the whole world blind. *Satyagraha* does not declare a man evil in the core, only his actions to be evil, and appeals to his heart for reform. It seeks justice to be brought about by mercy. Mercy and justice is a potential source open in Islam, but Bin Laden has turned away from them and encouraged others to do the same. It is probably because the radicalized Muslims have taken such a dim view of the United States in recent years that they do not feel that the recourse to nonviolence is open to them. The might and power that the U.S. has *in the Is-*

lamist mind has deafened us to their calls for justice, and they see the ways toward peace as closed. We must do our best to convince as many Muslims otherwise, and not to join the Islamist fringe.

Bin Laden and Muslim Exclusivity

Mohandas K. Gandhi threw the door open wide to members of all faiths and all backgrounds. All people could be saved, as all faiths captured part of the glimmer of the overarching religious truth. This is not the case with Bin Laden. Bin Laden has closed many doors in his mind, and has remaining open only one: the path of Muslim exclusivity which puts him and those who would support him on the solitary path to righteousness.

While Gandhi emphasized that all religions should be respected, but are fallible, those who take the extremely exclusive religious view assert that their own traditions are infallible, and that they alone are respectable. Osama paraphrases the Qur'an in saying "Whoever believes in some of the book and doesn't believe in other parts of it is an infidel indeed."[16] The Qur'an itself does speak of its inerrant authority [Surah 2:1; 53:1-6, 56:74],[17] so in this we cannot fault Bin Laden much.[18] It is, however, the militant extremes to which he goes that has caused such problems. He portrays the conflict very much as a zero-sum battle between the righteous and the unrighteous: "This struggle is partly an internal regional struggle, but in other respects it is a struggle between global unbelief, with the apostates of today under the leadership of America on one side, and the Islamic *umma* and its brigades of *mujahidin* on the other."[19]

Bin Laden is so exclusive he would not even accept the presence of U.S. troops on the Saudi peninsula to ensure its defense. To be sure, this would be quite a cultural shame and a blow to one's national pride, as we discussed earlier. Bin Laden, however, endorsed the ancient *hadith* or tradition that claimed that no Jews or Christians should be present in the lands of Islam. The Caliph Umar was said to have carried this out, and Bin Laden passionately endorsed it:

> As the Prophet said, according to al-Bukhari: "Banish the polytheists from the Arabian peninsula." And "There can be no two religions in the Arabian peninsula." He also said "Fight the Jews and the Christians, take their sons' graves as places of worship — there can be no two religions on Arab lands." And "I am banishing Jews and Christians from the Arabian peninsula so that I preach only to Muslims.[20]

It should be pointed out here that these ideas are not found in the Qur'an and that the *hadith* are a secondary source of tradition in Islam. Muhammad al-Bukhari, an Islamic scholar of the 9th century, in fact culled through some 600,000 traditions or *hadith* reported to belong to the Prophet Muhammad and determined that only 7275 of them were authentic.[21] This amounts to 1.2%, indicating a highly unreliable medium of authenticity to all objective standards. It would seem that not too much weight should therefore be put in them, especially when they seem to be an egregious affront to good sense. If a person is not welcome in a country, even as a visitor, it seems prejudicial and detrimental to standards of diplomacy and international friendship. The Saudi royal government was willing to set these radical ideas aside and invited the U.S. troops onto its soil, even going so far as to get a religious *fatwa* to support them. Coerced or not, the position of the Saudi government in this instance is much more tenable than that of Bin Laden. Although this author is neither Muslim nor in a position to tell Muslims what is or is not authentic in their tradition, it is suggested strongly here that this particular hadith is not useful to any standard of morality or modernity.

Yet before 9/11 Bin Laden had said (in 1997): "In our religion, it is not permissible for any non-Muslim to stay in our country. Therefore, even though American civilians are not targeted in our plan, they must leave."[22] It should be noted that hospitality to guests can be quite important in many parts of the Muslim world. Guests may be honored and treated well, so in this sense, many Muslims may see Bin Laden as an aberration.

Hamid Mir, a Pakistani biographer of Bin Laden has also refuted the Islamic character of Bin Laden's declarations. Mir has stated: "When he (Bin Laden) started quoting from the Islamic Sharia and Islamic books and Koran, that the Koran says to fight against the non-Muslims for the supremacy of Islamic law, there was no thrill. Because you see he cannot prove through the Koran that the killing of Americans is Islam, that the killing of every non-Muslim is Islam. He cannot prove that."[23] It may be a moot point, as Bin Laden believes his view to be authentic, and he has convinced a militant minority of Muslims of the same claim.

The idea of exclusivity, of course, can be found in most of these strands of radical Islam that claim to have a monopoly on religious truth. Bin Laden was familiar with the works of Egyptian writer Sayyid Qutb. Qutb is the father of radical Islamism for many militants today. Qutb maintained that "Islam is the only system which possesses these values and this way of life."[24] Those who did not know the truth of Islam lived in ignorance of *jahiliyyah*. This could apply to Muslims guilty of apostasy (in Qutb's view) as well as all non-Muslims.

Qutb sketched out a kind of siege mentality in which "true" Muslims were confronting on all sides a world that was hostile and alien to their "true" values. Qutb (who visited the United States in the 40s and rejected our values) wrote, "If we look at the sources of modern ways of living, it becomes clear that the whole world is steeped in *jahiliyyah*.", and further, "This *jahiliyyah* is based on rebellion against God's sovereignty on Earth."[25]

Islamists who accept Qutb's logic believe that a great deal of the loss of power in Muslim lands is due to a loss of religious fidelity. They share with Qutb a triumphal hope to redeem themselves through a zealous devotion to the exclusive truth, as they see it, found in their tradition. Muslim society is portrayed by Qutb as in bondage to an inferior non-Muslim culture that has surrounded and asphyxiated it: "We must free ourselves from the clutches of jahili (non-Muslim or "ignorant") society, jahili concepts, jahili traditions, and jahili leadership." and that, "Our first step will be to raise ourselves above the jahili society and all its values and concepts."[26]

President Bush has called the radicals enemies of freedom, who do not share our values. In their own minds they perceive it to be the United States (and all other "jahili" societies) that are not free. In Qutb's own words, "All Jewish and Christian societies today are also jahili societies. They have distorted the original beliefs and ascribe certain attributes of God to other beings."[27] In Qutb's own mind, "the love of the Divine Law al-Shari'ah should be a consequence of pure submission to God and freedom from servitude to anyone else."[28] Hence for him Islam only frees, and all other cultures and societies provide mere obstacles that must be surmounted or destroyed: "Other societies do not give it any opportunity to organize its followers according to its own method, and hence it is the duty of Islam to annihilate all such systems, as they are obstacles in the way of universal freedom." For Qutb, *jihad* was a clear duty: "Jihad in Islam is simply a name for striving to make this system of life dominant in the world."[29] Qutb would not have rested until the whole world shared his view of Islam. He was executed for his militant opposition to the Egyptian government in 1966, but his martyrdom may have only elevated his status afterwards.

While Bin Laden does not directly cite Qutb much (he seems to prefer Taymiyya), the spirit of Qutb's exclusive militancy is there. The idea that Islam is true and the Qur'an is exalted above all other texts is a working assumption of many of these militants, so much so that they will spurn the range of non-Muslim works from Darwin or John Locke to Tolstoy. This idea however is *not* universal to all Muslims. While the Islamists believe it, many Muslims have respected and admired the religions of other cultures. There is in fact the concept that Jews and Christians are *dhimmi*, or "people of the book", who received a genuine revelation and should be granted religious freedoms. Admittedly this concept has had ambiguous usage and practice, much as *jihad* has, for at times the concept of *dhimmi* may have been used to relegate Jews and Christians to second-class citizens.

The Qur'an in some passages warns even against making friends with Jews and Christians, suggesting that they will lead the faithful astray [Surah 5:51].[30] Paradoxically, in other parts of the Qur'an, Jews and Christians are in fact exalted: "Believers, Jews, Christians, and Sabeans — whoever believes in God and the Last Day and does what is right — shall be rewarded by their Lord; they have nothing to fear or to regret. [Surah 2:62]" And elsewhere: "As for the true believers, the Jews, the Sabeans, the Christians, the Magians, and the pagans, God will judge them on the Day of Resurrection. God is the witness of all things [Surah 22:17]."[31] It is certainly *possible* for many Muslims to see the Christian and Jewish religions in a favorable light. Many Muslims in fact do so, and are engaged with the Jewish Tanakh and the Christian Bible. It is hoped that we can engage the Qur'an with a sense of mutual respect, openness, and toleration. Gandhi recommended it to be a lifelong duty to study religious scripture, to find the riddle of cosmic wisdom that was elusively concealed within.

Islamism — Religion and Politics

Can Islam practice the kind of tolerance which Gandhi deemed to be essential? Can there be a separation of church and state in the Muslim faith? Many would believe that there can be, that the idea that there simply should be "no compulsion in religion" decrees therefore that the Qur'an could not endorse a law in which religion was determined by political or legal force. Many Muslims have agreed with this, but it is not quite that simple. There is a competing interpretation in which it is suggested that the true nature of *jihad* is to get Muslim law fully realized in every aspect of society.

The Muslim Brotherhood is an organization dedicated to the realization of Muslim principles in society. Sayyid Qutb radicalized the Brotherhood, but before him the movement's true founder, Hasan al-Banna, had fused political goals with religious ones. His zeal for realizing Islam could sound quite militant:

> Every piece of land where the banner of Islam has been hoisted is the fatherland of the Muslims. . . . It is a duty incumbent on every Muslim to struggle towards the aim of making every people Muslim and the whole world Islamic, so that the banner of Islam can flutter over the earth and the call of the Muezzin can resound in all the corners of the world; God is greatest! This is not parochialism, nor is it racial arrogance or usurpation of land.[32]

Al-Banna may have avoided the extremes of violence,[33] while Sayyid Qutb and Bin Laden have not. Gandhi also asserted that there was a connection of religion and politics, but of course it was completely unlike the one which Bin Laden preaches. Osama has rejected the claims of Zionism, denying the right of a Jewish State of Israel to exist at all. In his own words:

> It brings us both laughter and tears to see that you have not yet tired of repeating your fabricated lies that the Jews have a historical right to Palestine, as it was promised to them in the Torah. Anyone who disputes with them on this alleged fact is accused of anti-Semitism. This is one of the most fallacious, widely circulated fabrications in history. The people of Palestine are pure Arabs and original Semites. It is the Muslims who are the inheritors of Moses (peace be upon him) and the inheritors of the real Torah that has not been changed. Muslims believe in all the Prophets, including Abraham, Moses, Jesus, and Muhammad. If the followers of Moses have been promised a right to Palestine in the Torah, then the Muslims are the most worthy nation of this.[34]

The extremes of militant Islamism on the one hand, and ultra-Zionism on the other, make it very difficult for any practicable peace in the Middle-East. Yet, the politics of Israel and Palestine as an ongoing conflict is a cornerstone behind all of the most radical grievances of radical Islamists. Bin Laden's complete inability to accept the existence of Israel makes it really impossible to find peace. Until such time when the extreme Islamists on the one hand reconcile themselves to the legitimate existence of Israel and the Zionists agree to rights and restitution for the Palestinians on the other, it is difficult to foresee any immediate end to the crisis there. Bin Laden's demands are in no way helpful and should be eclipsed by a moderate view that is accommodating to a compromise of Israeli Statehood. What imaginative solution and creative spark can get us past this historical impasse to peace is hard here to put forward in coherent form. What is only clear is that it will not deny Israel's right to exist, nor will it deny the Palestinians their fair place under the sun.

Bin Laden's program offers no solution, but he has convinced many otherwise. Bin Laden's program is a tit-for-tat game of inflicting injury for injury for any real or merely perceived injustice that has transpired between the West and the Islamic world. The Qur'an does not furnish us with this idea, nor does it seem to be a part of any mainstream Islamic idea, yet Bin Laden would argue otherwise:

> God the almighty, legislated the permission and the option to avenge this oppression. Thus, if we are attacked, then we have the right to strike back. If people destroy our villages and towns, then we have the right to do the same in return. If people steal our wealth, then we have the right to destroy their economy. And whoever kills our civilians, then we have the right to kill theirs.[35]

Religion and politics for Bin Laden are a grueling war of vengeful strikes and counterstrikes which, as we have said before, cannot possibly produce a lasting solution. We have debated Bin Laden with bullets and bombs more than words, however, and it is hoped that the clarity and wisdom in Gandhi's position has become much more vivid. Although nonviolence may not easily win or be readily applied to all political situations, it has the moral high ground in bringing that measure of peace and civility to any conflict that is requisite for its potential resolution. Until that measure of peace and civility is injected into the dialogue, no further possibility for a mutual reconciliation exists.

Bin Laden and Racial, Religious Inequality

Gandhi believed in the essential religious equality of all persons, but also in our racial equality as well: "In my opinion, there is no place on earth and no race, which is not capable of producing the finest types of humanity, given suitable opportunities and education."[36] While critical that some civilizations had gone down the wrong ends, none were essentially contaminated.

Could Bin Laden possibly share this belief? Amazingly, he does concede at one point the possible benevolence of those found in the West, or those found outside of Islam itself. Bin Laden observed: "Many in the West are polite and good people. The American media are inciting them against Muslims, but some of these good people are demonstrating against the American attacks because human nature is against cruelty and injustice."[37] Needless to say the suicidal piloting of civilian airliners into American skyscrapers is hardly an effective way of communicating that idea! Elsewhere, Bin Laden has made it clear that he agreed with Qutb, that American values (in their eyes) are an aberration. After inviting the American people to convert wholesale to Islam, he said, "the second thing we call you to is cessation of the oppression, lies, immorality, and debauchery that have spread among you. We call you to be a people of manners, principles, honor and purity; to reject the immoral acts of fornication, homosexuality, intoxicants, gambling, and trading with interest."[38] Foolishly, Reverend Jerry Falwell in one televised moment on September 13, 2001 diagnosed the event as punishment for sins similar to those Bin Laden rejected. Falwell apologized for the remark, but Bin Laden certainly will not.[39]

Western values, the allowance of alcohol, a sexualized media, pornography, the charging of interest, are all fundamentally incompatible with Bin Laden's understanding of Islam. Yet it really isn't the cultural or moral value differences which Bin Laden has foremost in mind. It is the exertion of military, political, and economic force in the world that Bin Laden complains about, which he has claimed to be unjust. It is very difficult to imagine him embarking upon his *jihad* because of the differences about sexuality, drinking, and usury. They are alienating to him to be sure, but they are by no means the things which pushed him over the edge. U.S. support for Israel, the U.S. presence in Saudi Arabia, and the U.S. policy in Iraq are really the three things he has claimed to be most offensive to him.

Bin Laden believes there is an essential inequality in the valuation of "Western and Muslim" blood. He believes that no one is concerned in the West when a Muslim child dies, but that the world comes to a grinding halt when one Westerner perishes. Osama has said, "in what creed are your dead considered innocent but ours worthless? By what logic does your blood count as real and ours as no more than water? Reciprocal treatment is part of justice, and he who commences hostilities is the unjust one."[40] We recall that the 1982 Israeli war in Lebanon outraged Bin Laden (again, making no concession of merit there, simply to state an observed fact). Osama said, "As I looked at those destroyed towers in Lebanon, it occurred to me to punish the oppressor in kind by destroying towers in America, so that it would have a taste of its own medicine and would be prevented from killing our women and children."[41] It is unfortunately not surprising that one nation counts its own dead before that of another; this is a part of the egocentrism of nations, perhaps an artifact of patriotism that cannot be wholly eradicated. We have been commanded to love our neighbors as ourselves, to see the common humanity in all, but this remains such a difficult thing to accomplish. If Bin Laden is right that Western culture has been at times indifferent to the plight of Muslims, his own methods and actions betrays all good and sensible ethics and makes dialogue all the more impossible.

Bin Laden betrays the cause of Muslims by dehumanizing and demonizing his enemies and by doing so in the name of Islam. His remarks have carried a powerfully anti-Semitic message that reflects intolerance in the extreme. Relating a traditional story about the days of final judgment, he suggested that Jews essentially should be killed. In the final judgment, he relates, "the Hour will not come until the Muslims fight the Jews and kill them. When a Jew hides behind a rock, or a tree, it will say: 'O Muslim, O Servant of God! There is a Jew behind me, come and kill him! All the trees will do this except the boxthorn, because it is the tree of the Jews."[42] Of course not all Muslims accept these views, but it is tragic that any of them do.

Bin Laden's views and those of radical Islamists are incompatible with democratic, pluralist nation-states. Of course the Islamists reject this model of politics as corrupt and insist upon states that are based upon only their interpretation of Islam. They have failed to see how an interpretation of any religious text itself can produce division and how a government based upon one religious view will invariably produce dissent amongst those who do not share this view. The West has lived out and rejected that historical experience in our own battles between Protestant and Catholic. Islam and the divisions between Sunni and Shia have not necessarily placed all Muslims on the same political and historical trajectory as the West.

It is a mild understatement to suggest that Bin Laden's model of conflict resolution in politics does not work. If adopted, one would imagine in this country that the Native Americans would exact bloody vengeance on whites (for crimes centuries past which whites living today had nothing to do with), that African Americans would then inflict similar pain and punishment for centuries of enslavement, that every Catholic or Protestant who felt abused by someone on the opposite side of the religious isle would begin a belligerent campaign of outrage. It is a simple fact that some measure of mercy and forgiveness is an essential component for resolving any historical conflict. This is why Gandhi did not exact any revenge for the massacre of Brigadier General Dyer at Amritsar, even though every measure of vengeance there was deserved. Forgetting and forgiving are indispensable aspects of any resolved conflict on the political or moral level. This is why Gandhi embraced these values, why Martin Luther King Jr. and Abdul Ghaffar Khan embraced them, and why Judaism, Christianity and Islam have all called for these values of mercy and forgiveness. They are an essential part of human morality, whether one affirms a God or does not.

Gandhi wrote at the conclusion of his *Autobiography*, "My uniform experience has convinced me that there is no other God than Truth. And if every page of these chapters does not proclaim to the reader that the only means for the realization of Truth is Ahimsa, I shall deem all my labor in writing these pages to have been in vain."[43] Your life was not in vain, Mohandas. It is simply this world with its entrenched political conflicts and volatile human tempers that finds it so hard to learn an eternal truth.

Bin Laden's Views of Civilization

Samuel Huntington erred when he said, "the underlying problem for the West is not Islamic fundamentalism. It is Islam, a different civilization whose people are convinced of the superiority of their culture and are obsessed with the inferiority of their power."[44] Really, the problem is more exactly Islamic fundamentalism, known as Islamism. Huntington has, however, hit upon part of the problem. The idea of being "obsessed with the inferiority of their power" hits a nerve. Most Islamists have seen the failure of their countries and misdiagnosed it as a failure of not being "religious enough", instead of not having the right political or economic reforms. Radical Islamism is a retreat into the Qur'an and a drastic restructuring of the Islamic faith in response to a feeling of powerlessness that has been created by political and economic, not religious, factors.

In many respects the model of the "clash of civilizations" is not helpful, because it creates a false paradigm that it is "our religion versus theirs" or "our values vs. theirs", and this creates a contest for cultural supremacy which can only deepen misunderstandings and exacerbate our problems. An unthinking "our culture / their culture" view dichotomizes the crisis in ways that are really too simplistic and unhelpful. In short, for Islamists to think that they only need to be "more Muslim" or for Westerners to insist that they must duplicate our democracy and values is not going to solve anything. The West is never going to adopt Islam wholesale, as Bin Laden asked, and Muslims need not mimic the ways of the United States or any other country.

There is a clash of some sorts going on here, and it related to Islam and the colonial-imperial legacy of the 19th and 20th centuries. Islam once compassed a wide civilization, technologically sophisticated, learned, and wealthy. When that civilization went into decline and Western civilization supplanted it as the technological and economic superpower, there was undoubtedly a clash of interests. Muslims resented foreign powers dividing up their lands and exerting profound influence in their territories, just as an American would resent Russia, China, France or England, or any other country dictating the thrust of our politics.

The existence of Israel is here fully supported, but it is that very existence that has agitated so many Islamists like Bin Laden. When Israel was created, many Palestinians were certainly thrust out of their homes and into exile. Israel has become for many Arab Muslims a kind of a whipping-post, however, to focus the grievance of their own internal disputes and problems that have also been created by the neo-colonial or imperial legacy. After the end of World War II, the colonial era came to a screeching halt, and the power of U.S. capitalism and political might supplanted Europe as the next "imperial" power; for though we neither have nor want any permanent occupation of any Middle-Eastern nation, our impact there has still been profound. Israel is here to stay, and U.S. might in that region will continue to exist for an indefinite period. If we can carefully renegotiate the tensions that uneven power relationships invariably cause, it will make the cultural differences between us seem much less marked.

Osama bin Laden and other Islamists have also simplified the crisis as one between two civilizations, between "good and evil" powers, failing to contritely acknowledge that every political system is some combination of both. The idea of forming a "pure Islamic" state, and that by doing this all problems will melt away, is their illusion. The idea that all Muslims are bad or that Muslim culture and religion is inherently dysfunctional is our illusion. Culture (including religious culture) is flexible and subject to change, but no amount of religious dedication is simply going to make moral and social problems go away. The most ardent theists await for God to do that. As long as we remain frail, flawed, and human creatures, the political systems we erect will reflect the imperfections in ourselves.

Even Gandhi, in his wisdom, at times mischaracterized and oversimplified the problem, saying "the British Government in India constitutes a struggle between modern civilization, which is the Kingdom of Satan, and the ancient civilization, which is the Kingdom of God. The one is the God of War, the other is the God of Love."[45] Osama bin Laden has said, "I say that there are two sides of this struggle: one side is the global Crusader alliance with the Zionist Jews, led by America, Britain, and Israel, and the other side is the Islamic world. It is not acceptable in such a struggle that he [the Crusader] should attack and enter my lands and holy sanctuaries, and plunder Muslims' oil, and then when he encounters any resistance from Muslims to label them terrorists."[46] He has elsewhere added: "I say that the battle isn't between the al-Qaeda organization and the global Crusaders. Rather, the battle is between Muslims — the people of Islam — and the global Crusaders."[47]

It is easy to accept many aspects of this dichotomy — we speak a different language, they speak a different language. We have one system of government, they have alternatives. We have a set of customs and cultural norms, and they have a variant one. Bin Laden sums it up again as a religious difference and conflict: "I say that there is not doubt about this. This [Clash of Civilizations] is a very clear matter, proven in the Qur'an and the traditions of the Prophet, and any true believer who claims to be faithful shouldn't doubt these truths, no matter what anybody says about them."[48]

Undoubtedly, there are many differences that do set us apart. Yet differences do not by themselves cause conflict. How many neighbors do you have on your street from differing national backgrounds, religious affiliations, political views, or ethnic or racial heritage? These differences can be overlooked, ignored, or they can even be an enriching source of daily life. It is when fundamental interests clash in politics or economics that suddenly these neighbors become "That damn . . . . . (insert national or religious heritage here: Christian, Jew, Muslim, Black, White, Latino) . . . . failed to take the trash out!" Cultural and religious differences become highlighted and more prominent when there are also underlying political and economic factors antagonizing them. When there is no basic antagonism, cultural and religious difference can become more like a benign curiosity.

There is, however, the factor of radical Islamism, here. Islamism is a particular interpretation of Islam, which most Muslims would likely reject. It is exclusive, it is militant, it is combative, it has misdiagnosed the problems besetting the Muslim world, and it is a set of ideas that must be challenged in order to reduce their effect. Westerners can help by becoming educated about Islam and the differences in the mainstream view and that of the radicals. There are of course many Christian and Jewish radicals also, but they do not speak for the whole religion either. Often they are merely the most noisome, and so get the most attention and hence the misperception that they are representative of religion.

There is a clash going on here, but it is not a simple one to resolve. The radical jihadists are under the misconception that militant dedication to their exclusive view of Islam can solve their problems. Some of us may still think that if we only kill the last terrorist, there will be no more terrorists. As long as we are in the business of killing and finding targets to kill, we will be creating further broken families, discord, anger, resentment, and hence a greater potential reservoir for more terrorist to be formed. That is exactly why we should be paying more attention to men like Gandhi or King, two of the greatest peacemakers of recent times; to seek the wisdom and nonviolent solutions we will need to remedy this problem. As long as we respond to violence with violence we may in the short term increase our security (not always or invariably!), but we will in the long term keep fighting the same tireless game of blood and belligerency in which there are no happy winners.

Understanding is light, and light casts out darkness, deceit, anger and hatred. Men of understanding like Gandhi and King can easily be gunned down, but the principles for which they stand cannot be destroyed.

The Strengths and Weaknesses of Jihad vs. Satyagraha

Does Osama bin Laden really have "ideas", or anything like a sophisticated ideology that can coherently be reconciled? That is certainly a highly debatable point. Some believe his ideas have no coherence. What is not in debate, however, is his impact. Substantial or no, wise or completely foolish, Bin Laden and Islamism has had substantial resonance. Radicalism has been appealing as an answer, perhaps because many other political or economic remedies have been wanting. The puzzling thing, however, is that the appeal is so broad. It is not limited to the disenfranchised or downtrodden, nor does it necessarily begin there. The London bombers showed no great material deprivation. The 9/11 hijackers were not poor and not even fully radicalized until they entered the non-Muslim nation of Germany. Islamism is a movement of wide appeal, and Bin Laden is only one of the figureheads. He may disappear tomorrow and the movement would still carry on, not merely because the underlying cultural, political, and economic circumstances are right, but because there are large groups of persons preaching that these ideas are true. The movement feeds upon itself the more its propaganda is believed.

As unpopular as Bin Laden is in the non-Muslim world, he has been popular with many Muslims. Abu Jandal, who once lived with Osama, described him as an ascetic, sacrificial figure who was very generous and would give his last dollar to those in need. Jandal noted the simplicity of Bin Laden's life, his love of horses, and his stern expectations for his sons. In person, Bin Laden does not come across as a raving madman, but as more soft-spoken. Jandal said, "so we never really felt afraid as long as we were with that man."[49]

Bin Laden was demanding with his sons in a way not wholly unlike the asceticism of Gandhi. Gandhi had high expectations of his sons to follow his cause, and Bin Laden also has high expectations. Of course the moral and political foundations of those expectations are extremely different, this must be noted. Bin Laden wanted his sons to follow his lead and refused to spoil them. His son Saad, asking for financial help in getting married and starting a family, was told to be self-sufficient and to fend for himself. Reportedly, Osama told them: "Sons, your father's millions about which you hear are not for your father's to use. This money is for the Muslims and I hold it as a trust for the cause of God. Not one riyal of it is for you. Each of you is a man. Let him rely on himself."[50]

If one were to subtract all the negative things we know about Bin Laden (a tall order!) — his terrorism, his intolerantly exclusive religious view, his anti-Semitism among them — and instead look at his personal sacrifice, the charisma of the man becomes more apparent. He is viewed as one who has sacrificed great wealth for his cause and his religion, as a lone man who has stood up to an imperial power. None of this is said with any intent to praise him, but to make his popularity to third-parties become more intelligible.

Bin Laden's sons, like Gandhi's, also rebelled. Bin Laden entered a radically rebellious service to Islam, calling for the life and blood of those loyal to his cause. In that course his living style has retreated from the luxuries of Saudi wealth to the harsh simplicity of existential living. Gandhi also called upon his sons and servants for great sacrifice, even of life, albeit under a very different moral banner. Some of Bin Laden's sons rebelled and rejected his cause, as did at least one of Gandhi's. As leaders of rebellious movements against dominant imperial or capitalist powers, their lives bear some striking similarity inasmuch as their moral and religious passion is totally different.

Bin Laden has some strength in his tactics. A line of nonviolent *satyagrahis* would make an easy target for a lone suicide bomber. Bin Laden has gone covert, and suicide bombers strike unpredictably from those shadows. Nonviolent satyagraha is not effective at targeting subterranean organizations such as this, for its targets have really always been powerfully visible, prominent governments and institutions. Yet the methods of satyagraha are honest, transparent, and moral. It gives them legitimacy in mainstream politics which allows them to be open participants in political change. This should be a very attractive and clear advantage to them. Osama bin Laden will never be able to run for any political office openly and will never have any legitimacy tied to any of the claims or demands he hopes to realize because of the immorality of his methods.

Terrorism in the short-term, then, has a tactical advantage over non-violence in that it can strike without easily suffering a counter-strike. The courage of the satyagrahi, however, to openly invite the blows and suffering of his or her enemies brings with it the strategic advantage of long-term political legitimacy. To stand in broad daylight is more courageous, as Gandhi observed, "terrorism and deception are weapons not of the strong but of the weak."[51] Anyone running with the political and moral authority of a Gandhi or a King for any office has a strong possibility of being elected and accepted. Of course these types of men never run for political office, as they are more effective reformers by agitating and campaigning from the margins of politics and not from the political center. Bin Laden, by contrast, is so far outside of the mainstream that he has condemned himself to remain there permanently.

Gandhi's universal moral view is in my mind, hopefully, the wave of the future. Remember Gandhi's optimism: "the time has now passed when the followers of one religion can stand and say, ours is the only true religion and all others are false. The growing spirit of toleration towards all religions is a happy augury of the future."[52] Given, of course, the religious and political fighting since he said that, we know that Gandhi's prediction was premature. But the hope that all religious traditions have an invaluable and indispensable seed of moral wisdom in them is widely compelling, yet also troubling.

The frank facts indicate that many religious observers still grow up with some form of a milder, but still traditionally exclusive view. It might go something like this: "I see the wisdom and truth of my own texts and religious traditions up close, but I only see a remote reflection of that in other traditions. I am not interested in oppressing or denying others the right to follow their religion, but I can see no greater truth before me than the one I have grown up with." Gandhi himself could coexist with that view, though he would not prefer it. He said that we should make Hindus better Hindus, Christians better Christians, and Muslims better Muslims. We should not expect to convert others, but show them the best truth and beauty contained in their own religious traditions, and to embrace all humanity.

Admittedly, many will still find Gandhi's broadly-minded views very troubling. "What do you mean my tradition or my sacred text is flawed? How *dare* you make such an assumption!" To my mind, the assumption is neither a radical nor arrogant assumption. Common humility forces us to admit the errors of our own ways and thought, if we are to acknowledge ourselves as part of this flawed reality. As Gandhi believed, to submit that religions, their texts, or their views may be flawed is to admit that any belief-system or ideology may be flawed; to admit a basic fact demonstrated to us every day that we have limitations of knowledge, of wisdom, and of perception. This is not equivalent with asserting that all or any religious tradition is bereft of truth or meaningless. Nor is it to say there is no metaphysical truth. While making the struggle to piece together an overarching meaning of religious truth more difficult (but in my view, much more compelling), it never discounts the essential viewpoint that any tradition has to offer to the construction of that truth. In the absence of any Final Judgment, Gandhi's wisdom includes all and condemns none in a contrite admission that it does not have all the facts.

The kind of traditional, mainstream, exclusive view expressed two paragraphs above will likely continue indefinitely, and I neither need nor intend to make any case against it here. But what must be criticized is the type of militant exclusivism represented in Islamism by Bin Laden, which claims to have a monopoly upon all facts, worldly and otherworldly, and will arrogantly invoke the name of God to accomplish its own political ends. The kind of religious view that acts as if it has privileged access to Divine Wisdom which the rest of us are not privy to really has always been a tragic dysfunction of the religious view, and it is not unique to any religion but unfortunately all too common. Secular creeds such as Soviet Communism and Nazism have also arrogated to themselves far more insight than they had with far less evidence than they could ever supply. The monopolist, "I have the truth and nobody else does", is afflicting the Islamists now. And while they may argue that we suffer from some other form of that intellectual malaise, knocking over civilian buildings with commercial airliners is hardly the way to go about making that case.

There is no expectation that any measure of rational argument or academic scholarship can resolve the crisis nonviolently, but to abandon totally that endeavor is to give up hope completely. What can be hoped for is that a message of greater mutual understanding and tolerance can be proliferated, and it is essential that this message be combined with better political and economic relations. Nothing is more destructive to a message than to say one thing and do another. What can be hoped for, and expected then, is that this message of greater tolerance and understanding will reach those niches and corners where radical militancy is yet brewing in young minds, but as yet not come to a boil. Nonviolence can diffuse violence and belligerency in the minds and hearts that are still possibly open to it, but it was Gandhi's lifelong frustration that it was difficult to sell to those who had turned a cold heart to it for too long.

Satyagraha is more powerful than violence, but its methods are slower, require more sacrifice, and are not invariably crowned with success. *Violent* jihad has a dark and sexy appeal, its destruction produces visible effects now, but in the void of its aftermath, it has no constructive program, only the broken pieces of humanity that must then be picked up and stitched back together. Satyagraha compared to the extremely violent approach of a radical jihadist, seems at times to pale by comparison, but we recall that Gandhi said the strongest forces in the world seemed to be the weakest: "Love is the strongest force the world possesses and yet it is the humblest imaginable."[53] He added, "the law of love governs the world. Life persists in the face of death. The universe continues in spite of destruction incessantly going on. Truth triumphs over untruth. Love conquers hate."[54] Violent jihad when contrasted to satyagraha is ideologically bankrupt. We know we want peace, and we are only seduced by our own pervasive inner darkness to want war. Bullets can claim lives permanently and irrevocably, and the glee and vengeance in striking back can be quite intoxicating. Words of peace, love, and wisdom do not have this immediate impact, but they do have a more lasting and permanent one. We hear the call of truth, but then become confused by other voices. Action is always necessary, as Gandhi said, "one has to speak out and stand up for one's convictions. Inaction at a time of conflagration is inexcusable." He hoped that action would be nonviolent, and that "When the practice of *ahimsa* becomes universal, God will reign on earth as He does in heaven."[55]

Notes

1. Bergen, *Holy War Inc.*, 194.
2. Jean Akhtar Cerrina, *Islam's Peaceful Warrior: Abdul Ghaffar Khan* (USA, Xlibris Corporation, 2003), 104.
3. Lawrence, *Messages to the World*, 217.
4. Brisard, *Zarqawi*, 153.
5. Lawrence, *Messages to the World*, 9.
6. Bruce Lawrence, *Messages to the World*, 30.
7. Lawrence, *Messages to the World*, 59-61.
8. N.J. Dawood, translator, *The Koran* (New York, Penguin Books, 2003); p. 29 or Surah 2:190.
9. Dawood, translator, *The Koran,* 83, or Surah 5:32.
10. Dawood, translator, *The Koran,* 199 or Surah 17:33.
11. Dawood, translator, *The Koran,* 196, 275, 342.
12. Dawood, translator, *The Koran,* 29, 133-134.
13. Dawood, translator, *The Koran,* 38. Of course forcible conversions have existed in Islam, contrary to the intent of this verse. This is no more unusual than Christians or Jews misinterpreting or misapplying their own scriptures. The simple intent of this writing, however, is that Islam is not unambiguous about violence, but that its potential way for peace remains open to those who will interpret it in that light.
14. Lawrence, *Messages to the World*, 117-118, 147.
15. Lawrence, *Messages to the World*, 165.
16. Lawrence, *Messages to the World*, 235.
17. Dawood, translator, *The Koran*, 11, 371, 380.
18. Whether Islam can or needs to accept the "liberal" view that many Jews and Christians have of an authoritative, but still flawed text, is one that can and should be a matter of ongoing concern and debate.
19. Lawrence, *Messages to the World*, 250.
20. Lawrence, *Messages to the World*, 263-4.
21. Lawrence, *Message to the World*, 155.
22. Lawrence, *Messages to the World*, 47.
23. Bergen, *The Osama I Know*, 201.
24. Qutb, *Milestones*, 8.
25. Qutb, *Milestones,* 10-11.
26. Qutb, *Milestones,* 21.
27. Qutb, *Milestones*, 81.
28. Qutb, *Milestones*, 36.
29. Qutb, *Milestones*, 75-76.
30. Dawood, translator, *The Koran,* 85.
31. Dawood, translator, *The Koran*, 15, 235.
32. Brynjar Lia, *The Society of Muslim Brothers: The Rise of the Islamic Mass Movement* 1928-1942, (UK, Ithaca Press, 2006), 80.
33. Lia, *The Society of Muslim Brothers*, 255-259.
34. Lawrence, *Messages to the World*, 162.
35. Lawrence, *Message to the World*, 165.
36. Gandhi, *Satyagraha in South Africa,* 33.
37. Lawrence, *Messages to the World*, 142.
38. Marlin, *What Does Al-Qaeda Want?*, 65.
39. Falwell's remark regarding the 9/11 tragedy as divine punishment: Falwell began, "I really believe that the pagans, and the abortionists, and the feminists, and the gays

and the lesbians who are actively trying to make an alternative lifestyle, the ACLU, People for the American Way, all of them who have tried to secularize America. I point the finger in their face and say 'you helped this happen." Reproduced in Goldberg, Michelle, *Kingdom Coming: The Rise of Christian Nationalism* (New York, W.W. Norton & Company, 2006), 8.

40. Lawrence, *Messages to the World*, 234.
41. Lawrence, *Messages to the World*, 239-240.
42. Lawrence, *Messages to the World*, 125.
43. Gandhi, *Autobiography*, 503-504
44. Samuel P. Huntington, *The Clash of Civilization and the Remaking of World Order* (New York, Touchstone Books, Simon & Schuster, 1996), 217.
45. Gandhi, *The Selected Works*, vol. 6, 282-283.
46. Lawrence, *Message to the World*, 73.
47. Lawrence, *Message to the World*, 108.
48. Lawrence, *Messages to the World,* 124.
49. Bergen, *The Osama I Know*, 267.
50. Bergen, *The Osama I Know*, 267-8.
51. Fischer, *The Essential Gandhi*, 154.
52. Narayan, *The Selected Works*, vol. 6, 272.
53. Fischer, *The Essential Gandhi*, 206.
54. Fischer, *The Essential Gandhi*, 190.
55. Merton, *Gandhi and Nonviolence*, 37, 42.

Chapter 6: Abdul Ghaffar Khan

If one were to take a random selection of popular media representations of Islam, my strong suspicion is that it would be predominantly negative. Even among many scholars, you will find writings that suggest Islam is inherently unlike Christianity and that it has strong propensities for violence. The truth, however, will lie somewhere else. If one looks, there is also evidence of very important Muslims who have taken an essentially nonviolent view of Islam. The subject of this chapter, Abdul Ghaffar Khan, shows a prominent example of Islamic interpretation of *jihad* as nonviolent! This may come as a shock to many Western readers, nonetheless we must remember that *jihad* does mean "exertion" or "struggle", and that confronting his or her own religious tradition there is no reason that a Muslim should not be free to interpret Islam non-violently, certainly no more than a Christian is free to interpret his or her religion as one of pacifism or "Just War."[1]

Abdul Ghaffar Khan in fact took a thoroughly pacifist view of Islam and convinced thousands of Muslims to do the same. His story is largely forgotten amongst Westerners today, however. There are a few books and only one video documentary about him. In discussing major religious leaders of nonviolence his name is unfortunately forgotten. It is hard to find an explanation for this. Abdul Ghaffar Khan's life and history seem to have been forgotten (in the West) or blended into the independence movement that led to India and Pakistan.

A more modern reason is that after 9/11, the burning need for revenge (beyond that of apprehending or killing Bin Laden) has produced a tendency that is very critical of Islam, in that our televised and written media has been captivated and focused so exclusively on the Islamist-Jihadists that they have framed and dominated our conception of the religion. But that is not the whole story of Islam. A new look at the religion and an examination of Abdul Ghaffar Khan and his life should suggest a much more nuanced and complex understanding of the Muslim faith.

Biographical Overview

Who was Abdul Ghaffar Khan, and what did he accomplish? Born in 1890 in the city of Utmanzai (what is today a small town north of Peshawar), Pakistan, "Badshah" Khan, as he came to be affectionately known, lived until the ripe age of 98 and passed away in 1988. Of that long life, he spent some thirty years in prison protesting the injustice of the governments of British India and Islamic Pakistan. Inspired by two figures — the Prophet Muhammad and Gandhi — he devoted his life to the cause of nonviolent civil disobedience. Ghaffar Khan could be called learned in terms of the Qur'an, and Islamic history, but his view of Islam was simple and uncomplicated. He preferred the non-violent interpretation of his tradition, and he rejected all violence in the name of Islam.

Abdul Ghaffar Khan grew up in an Islamic context, accepting the Qur'an and the traditions of the Prophet Muhammad.[2] He was taught to memorize the Qur'an by a local mullah, apparently well known for his cruelty and beating of students, Khan included.[3] The Islamic mullahs of his immediate area did not seem to have any positive impact in teaching him a non-violent Islam. There mullahs seem to have been more intolerant and exclusive in their outlook, refusing even Christians as legitimate *dhimmi* or "people of the book." One mullah reluctantly let local Pathans read textbooks in English, but rejected the Christian Bible: "Let the boys read English, so long as they do not read the Christian scriptures; for the Christians have tampered with these books and it is no longer lawful for Muslims to read them."[4] This reading of exclusive Islam we have become all too familiar with, but it is not the only interpretation of Islam. Badshah Khan's more tolerant, benevolent outlook seems to have been a natural endowment. Khan would challenge and reject the intolerant view of some of the local mullahs.

Abdul Ghaffar Khan did not set out to be part of the non-violent movement. He was a six foot three inch Pathan, prime material for a rugged soldier. In fact, he left his high school final examinations in order that he might join "The Guides", a corps composed of Sikhs and Pathans that he expected would give him privileged access to a career as a British Officer. After witnessing an incident of British racism against a fellow Pathan in that same corps, however, he realized nothing was further from the truth. He resigned from the Guides, and refused to accept a commission, much to the displeasure of his father.[5]

In the next few years, he gravitated towards the social education of his fellow Pathans. Inspired by his former high school teacher, Reverend Wigram, he realized he felt the impulse of a social reformer, and proceeded to open schools, and challenge Pathan custom and tradition. Abdul Ghaffar Khan believed that his fellow Pathans were kept ignorant and badly needed education and enlightenment. Illiteracy rates in the region were reported to be as high as 98%, and even A.G. Khan's own parents could not read or write. Despite the opposition of both the British, and the local mullahs (who perhaps feared losing a source of their own Islamic donations), he began to establish schools for Pathan boys and girls.[6]

The story of his love life is a painful one. Khan was married twice, but lost his first wife during an epidemic of influenza and lost his second wife while traveling in Jerusalem. He had been on the *hajj*, the religious pilgrimage to Mecca, when in Jerusalem his second wife fell from a staircase and was killed. At least two sons came from these marriages, but after the tragic death of his second wife, he determined not to remarry and to dedicate the rest of his life to public service. Abdul Ghaffar Khan viewed Islam in terms of selfless love and service: "It is my inmost conviction that Islam is *amal, yakeen, muhabat* — selfless service, faith, and love."[7] In his own eyes and interpretation, the Prophet Muhammad taught peace. This is a refreshing departure from what we have frequently feared and imagined about the religion.

"Badshah" Khan did not immediately come to prominence in the Indian movement for independence. As early as 1920, however, he was attending conferences and becoming politically aware, but it was not until several years later that he would first meet Nehru and Gandhi, and he was increasingly pulled into the orbit of the latter. Khan for a number of years was essentially a social reformer, taking pride in his own Pathan heritage but also realizing it was badly in need of reform.

One of the most important aspects of Pathan culture that Abdul Ghaffar Khan wanted to change was that of the *badal*, or the blood-feud honor code. If one person had been killed, it was laid upon the honor of his relatives to avenge that killing to maintain one's pride and tribal self-esteem. It was a brutal code of justice, and one that invited constant retribution. The code was not inherently Islamic, for many things that are mistaken as "mainstream Islamic teaching" today are in fact hybrids of belief systems based on tribal cultural values inasmuch as they are based on Islam. Eknath Easwaran commented that the code of *badal* blood-vengeance was so strong that it largely defined Pathan manhood: "[there are] two supreme arts of the Pathan life: how to kill and how to die. Through these he becomes most fully a Pathan."[8] Note the defining term was *Pathan,* and not Muslim. Pride in tribal values and codes can at times supplant and take precedence over religious creeds. Abdul Ghaffar Khan would reject the tribal values as un-Islamic, but his Pathan people were still feared. Gandhi himself commented that Hindu boys and girls often grew up in fear of the Pathans as a people with a reputation for violence.[9]

Abdul Ghaffar Khan was much influenced here by his father, who also disliked the *badal* blood-feud code, who kept no enemies, and yet stood out as one highly esteemed amongst the Pathans. Abdul Ghaffar Khan also concluded that the *badal* code was dysfunctional, and when he read the Qur'an and heard Gandhi's message of non-violent resistance, he became increasingly gravitated towards it. In his own words:

> As a young boy, I had violent tendencies; the hot blood of the Pathans was in my veins. But in jail I had nothing to do except read the Koran. I read about the Prophet Muhammad in Mecca, about his patience, his suffering, his dedication. I had read it all before, as a child, but now I read it in the light of what I was hearing all around me about Gandhiji's struggle against the British Raj . . . .When I finally

met Gandhiji, I learned all about this ideas of non-violence and his Constructive Program. They changed my life forever.[10]

To further illustrate the context of the culture, we must remember that the Pathan (also variously written or spelled Pakhtun, or Pashtun) culture is the same one that contributed large numbers of *talibs* or Islamic students to the Taliban movement. The Pathan culture straddles the boundary of the Durand line, which was established by Sir Mortimer Durand as far back as 1893 to demarcate the boundaries of Afghanistan and Pakistan.[11] The Taliban of course advocated everything that Abdul Ghaffar Khan spurned. The Taliban approved of *purdah*, or the seclusion of women, and prevented their education. Badshah Khan opposed *purdah*, fought for women's equality, and opened schools for girls.[12] The Taliban banned music, except for male voices singing in praise of the Taliban, while Badshah Khan celebrated the use of drums and bagpipes when he started his non-violent army, the *Khudai Khidmatgars*, or "Servants of God." If the Taliban took Islam in the direction of exclusivity and repression, Badshah Khan took the religion in the direction of openness and equality.

The very existence of Abdul Ghaffar Khan and his movement suggests that a more careful and nuanced understanding of Pathan culture (and Islam itself) must emerge. Khan's Islamic values (if he had lived longer — the Taliban came to power a few years after his death) would reject and repudiate those of the later Taliban. Men such as Abdul Ghaffar Khan, *from the same region as the Taliban, and existing within the span of a few decades of each other*, requires more scholarly attention be given to the possible flexibility of Islamic political theology, at least pertaining to this region. Clearly the understanding of Islam in the area has not been entirely belligerent or uniform.

Parallels of the Two Gandhis

Abdul Ghaffar Khan and Mohandas Gandhi were kindred religious spirits in many respects, though one was raised a Muslim and the other a Hindu. Khan would apply the concept of *dhimmi*, or favored "people of the book" in the Qur'an, not only to Jews and Christians, but also to all believers. Khan also asserted that non-violence was the essential heart of Islam. Non-violence was not a mere strategy to him or to Gandhi, it was an essential principle of life. Non-violence, or *ahimsa*, was elevated to the level of God, and in Gandhi's formulation: "Truth is God, gives me the greatest satisfaction. And when you want to find Truth as God the only inevitable means is Love, i.e., non-violence."[13] From an Islamic perspective, Khan would come to affirm much the same beliefs, seeing both himself and Gandhi as equals and humble servants of God.

Both Khan and Gandhi remained emphatic in their devotion to non-violence. While Gandhi himself once affirmed, "I do believe that where there is only a choice between cowardice and violence, I would advise violence"[14], it must be remembered that he was talking very theoretically. Non-violence was not a method for cowards. Indeed, those who lacked the stomach or capacity for it might resort to violence, which Gandhi abhorred. Gandhi at no time in his career personally embraced or accepted a violent response, and we find that Abdul Ghaffar Khan, who became one of his closest friends and allies, also maintained that consistent pledge. When the Indian National Congress took a more limited and policy-oriented approach towards non-violence under the threat of Japanese aggression in 1939, Gandhi rejected their advice, and he and Abdul Ghaffar Khan resigned from the council that had considered the issue. Khan and Gandhi believed in non-violence as an unwavering principle, and not a mere policy or stratagem.[15]

Khan affirmed, as did Gandhi, a more universal and inclusive understanding of religion. No person was regarded to be unholy or an "infidel" simply because of the label of their religion. Gandhi refused to accept that any one religious tradition had a monopoly on truth, and insisted: "For me all the principle religions are equal in the sense that they are true. They are supplying a felt want in the spiritual progress of humanity."[16] Gandhi's hope that a growing, inclusive spirit of religion would be the "happy augury of the future" is one that we find in Badshah Khan as well.

This belief in the inclusive spirit was probably a main reason for their deep and lasting friendship. Their views were naturally compatible, as the course of their religious pursuit led them to affirm that religious truth can be grasped from all corners of the world and all sorts of religious traditions. Gandhi himself noted about Badshah Khan: "I was struck by their transparent sincerity, frankness, and utmost simplicity. He was consumed by a deep religious fervor. I found him to be universalist."[17] Author and biographer Attar Chand also described A.G. Khan: "He was a devout Muslim but had genuine love for all religions, and he firmly believed in the brotherhood of man."[18] If he were alive today, Badshah Khan would have strenuously condemned the 9/11 attacks.

Abdul Ghaffar Khan established an army of Pathans committed to non-violence. This very remarkable fact is one too often neglected today, as we have been captivated by what we mistake to be the violent character of Islam. Although the media sometimes does exonerate the tradition of Islam from accusations of violence, the importance of men such as A.G. Khan is now overlooked.[19] Khan himself affirmed a universal outlook towards humanity in creating this band of non-violent Islamic warriors:

> The Prophet has said that the most pious and God-fearing youth is he who brings comfort to the creatures of God. Remember this also that the Muslims alone are not the creatures of God. The Hindus, Sikhs, Muslims, Jews, Christians, and the Parsis, in short, all the creatures that live in this world are the creatures of God. The mission of the Khudai Khidmatgars is to give comfort to all creatures of God.[20]

Affirming a universal regard for all religions as an essential duty, Khan's concept of dhimmi, or "people of the book", would have invariably been extended to Hindus as well as to Jews and Christians. A.G. Khan (reporting from prison) admired Hindus and Sikhs for their religious spirit and dedication to God.[21] The view of the essential equality of human beings and our religions was a basic tenet of this faith.

Martin Luther King Jr. once commented about Gandhi: "Non-violent resistance had emerged as the technique of the movement, while love stood as the regulating ideal. In other words, Christ furnished the spirit and motivation, while Gandhi furnished the method."[22] Khan actually understood Gandhi's contribution in a similar regard. In Khan's interpretation, Gandhi was speaking no less of the core values of Islam, and he might have suggested that it was Muhammad that furnished the spirit and Gandhi who had revived the Prophet's message.

Scholars of Khan's life also generally affirm that he could not separate religion and politics. Here we see obvious connections with Gandhi, who also affirmed very similar ideas about religion and politics. Gandhi believed:

> Politics bereft of religion are absolute dirt, ever to be shunned. Politics concerns nations and that which concerns the welfare of nations must be one of the concerns of a man who is religiously inclined, in other words, a seeker after God and Truth.... Therefore in politics also we have to establish the Kingdom of Heaven.[23]

Abdul Ghaffar Khan would echo much the same sentiment: "It is my inmost conviction that Islam is *amal, yakeen, muhabat* [work, faith, and love] and without these the name Muslim is sounding brass and tinkling cymbal. The Koran makes it absolutely clear that faith in One God without a second, and good works, are enough to secure a man his salvation."[24] This quote reflects possibly the Christian influence in his life, as Khan received education from Reverend Wigram, who encouraged and fostered his outlook as a social reformer.[25] Khan's view of religion was profound but simple — "have faith and do good works" — and show that commitment by your words and your actions. For Khan, dogmatic assertions that one religion occupied an exalted or privileged status would have been empty of real heart and soul. Controversial as that may be with some, it is what he and Gandhi believed.

In review, the "Frontier Gandhi" was non-violent, universal in outlook, religiously and politically engaged, and finally, of course, rooted in the belief of Islam. Many sources confirm Khan's piety and dedication to the Muslim way of life, not the least of whom was Gandhi, who never saw Khan miss a prayer, except when illness prevented it.[26] One of the most remarkable achievements of Khan's religious devotion culminated in his political efforts to establish non-violence as the proper Islamic response to oppressive rule. This would of course lead to the creation of the *Khudai Khidmatgars*.

The Khudai Khidmatgars

Abdul Ghaffar Khan must be remembered for the conversion of his own Frontier Afghans — the Pathans or Pashtuns — to the service of non-violence. The Pashtuns had an historic reputation as warriors. The tribal code of *badal* or blood vengeance prepared them not only to strike back within their own society, but against foreign aggressors. Based upon Abdul Ghaffar Khan's own testimony, many Pathans were born, bred, and raised with a fighting spirit dedicated to maintaining pride and honor. Badshah Khan decided, however, that violence was not really the solution; rather, it was just part of the problem. The very belligerence that was part of the Pathan culture made it all the more remarkable that Abdul Ghaffar Khan was able to teach them non-violence. Jawaharlal Nehru observed:

> There is nothing so surprising about our Frontier Province as the conversion of a war-like people to the doctrine of non-violence. That conversion is, of course, far from complete and the Pathan does not worry himself about philosophical or metaphysical speculations. But it is patent that in action he has been remarkably non-violent. The man who loved his gun better than his child or brother, who valued life cheaply and cared naught for death, who avenged the slightest insult with the thrust of a dagger, has suddenly become the bravest and most enduring of India's non-violent soldiers. That was due undoubtedly to the influence of one man — Abdul Ghaffar Khan — whose word was almost law to his people, for they love him and trusted him.[27]

Nehru made more favorable comments about Khan in his own *Autobiography*,[28] and he was not alone in his observations. Joan Bondurant wrote that the Pathans with no prior exposure to *ahimsa*, to non-violence, showed a remarkable capacity to adopt and practice it.[29] The miracle of the conversion of the Pathans to non-violence would seem almost surreal to Mohandas Gandhi: "That such men who would have killed a human being with no more thought than they would kill a sheep or a hen should at the bidding of one man have laid down their arms and accepted nonviolence as the superior weapon sounds almost like a fairy tale."[30]

Yet it was not a fairy tale; it was historical reality. Khan was able to convert some 80,000 to 100,000 of his own Pashtun people to the belief in non-violence. This, as evidenced by the Pathan cultural appetite for battle and *badal*, was certainly no easy task. Yet in 1929, he was able to first form the non-violent brigade of Pathans, the *Khudai Khidmatgars*, (also known as the "Red Shirts" for the particular dye they used on their garments) or the "Servants of God." Appealing to the Pathans on the grounds of practicality, and of Islam, Abdul Ghaffar Khan became known as the "Badshah" Khan, the "King" of Khans and as great a leader to his Pathans as Gandhi had been to much of the rest of India. The solemnly sworn oath is a serious thing in Pathan culture, and so it was that the Pathan "Red Shirts" or "Servants of God" were convinced by the force of Khan's personality, perseverance, and argument to take the following vow:

> I am a *Khudai Khidmatgar;* and as God needs no service, but serving his creation is serving him, I promise to serve humanity in the name of God.
> I promise to refrain from violence and from taking revenge. I promise to forgive those who oppress me or treat me with cruelty.
> I promise to refrain from taking part in feuds or quarrels and from creating enmity.[31]

But how was this accomplished? What arguments could Khan appeal to? Gandhi had observed that the dream of a non-violent Pathan was something more like a fantasy, but Khan had made it a reality. It was not, as Gandhi suggested, something out of a fairy tale. This was a hundred thousand Pathan Muslims; a very significant portion of the total population of the Frontier region at the time. Badshah Khan persuaded them to pledge their lives to non-violence, traveling some 25 miles per day on foot, going from village to village to promote non-violence, education, and social uplift.[32] As Martin Luther King Jr. suggested that non-violence was the only practical solution for American blacks, Badshah Khan evaluated his own historical reality and suggested that non-violence was the better strategy to be pursued by Pathans:

> Two types of movements were launched in our province. . . . The violent movement [the uprisings before 1919] created hatred in the hearts of the people against violence. But the nonviolent movement won love, affection and sympathy of the people . . . . If a Britisher was killed [during the violent uprisings] not only the culprit was punished, but the whole village and entire region suffered for it. The people held the violence and its doer responsible for repression. In the nonviolent movement we courted self-suffering . . . . Thus, it won love and sympathy of the people.[33]

Based upon his experience and his religious convictions, Khan told the Pathans that non-violence was their best hope. It was not only their best hope, it was also their greatest weapon: "I am going to give you such a weapon that the police and the army will not be able to stand against it. It is the weapon of the Prophet, but you are not aware of it. That weapon is patience and righteousness. No power on earth can stand against it."[34] Badshah Khan's faith and confidence in non-violence was based upon a personal creed and sincere devotion, but extended to an analysis that it was also the superior tactic.

The Khudai Khidmatgars helped to keep the Frontier Province out of violent conflict when elsewhere in India violence had erupted. Their service and the memory of Abdul Ghaffar Khan continues to be held high today in India, but it is a bitter fact of history that the movement was systematically pulled apart after the Independence and partition of India and Pakistan. Upon Badshah Khan's death in 1988, some authors point out that India may have mourned his loss more than Pakistan. A misfortunate but realistic fact about non-violence is that it does not always or inevitably prevail. Indeed, after partition, Badshah Khan felt as if he and his Khudai Khidmatgars were "thrown to the wolves" in Pakistan, that he was alone in an unsympathetic political climate (he had opposed partition, and later Muhammad Ali Jinnah in pursuing Pathan freedom).[35] Khan did not have the victory of independence with which Gandhi is credited, though he helped achieve it. He did not have the credit to civil rights that King had, so perhaps that is why he is less remembered today than he should be. He fought for an independent state for the Pathans, but did not get it. He chose to pay a very high price in his dedication to non-violence, spending a third of his life in prison for his principles. As one steadfastly loyal to nonviolence, however, this should not discredit his service to peace.

Gandhi had once promised that he would never abandon Badshah Khan and that he would always be there to struggle non-violently beside him. Gandhi once said, "We will fight Pakistan if they maltreated you. It is true that I believe in non-violence, but it will be for the Government of India to help the Pathans to keep their honor and the right of self-determination."[36] Sadly, however, the Mahatma was not able to keep that promise because a militant Hindu assassinated him on January 30, 1948. Instead of "two Gandhis", one in India and the other on the Frontier (now Pakistan), there was only one. Badshah Khan now wrestled with the unresponsive government of Pakistan, while sympathetic Indians such as Jawaharlal Nehru looked on, without intervening in the internal affairs of Pakistan. Perhaps because of his extensive time in jail in Pakistan, and the failure to keep his mission alive there, we know less of the Islamic Frontier Gandhi then we know of the Mahatma.

Badshah Khan and Gandhi

We typically understand *jihad* as violent struggle, as advocated by Osama bin Laden and practiced by Muhammad Atta, amongst others. Such men, however, would be in Badshah Khan's eyes apostates who had actually abandoned the true spirit of Islam. Badshah Khan saw in Gandhi and in the Prophet Muhammad his role models for non-violence. Operating in complete opposition to the concept of radically violent jihad which we know today, he elucidated his own concept of *jihad*:

> This is our *jihad*, our crusade. Before we can fight the British, we must first end the violence and murder in our own hearts. Remember that overcoming our personal weakness is the greater *jihad*, the greater crusade. It is what God wants of us.[37]

Substitute *satyagraha* for *jihad* in the above context, and these words might easily have been spoken by Gandhi. Replace *jihad* with *non-violence*, and the British with "American racists", and the quote might be put in Martin Luther King Jr.'s mouth. Yet it is odd that in cataloguing the heroic efforts of non-violence, the name of Badshah Khan so rarely comes up. Too much time and effort is put into showing the dysfunctional side of Islam. And while one cannot deny it is there (that would be to pretend that Bin Laden did not exist, or 9-11 never happened), one must appreciate that Islam is not alone in having a historical legacy of bloody conflict — Christianity has had its share, without argument. Hopefully men like King, Gandhi, and Badshah Khan can point to the more redeeming and positive aspects of political theology in the future.

Badshah Khan became a staunch proponent of non-violence and an equally staunch supporter of Gandhi. It is important, however, to re-iterate that he saw this as a *Muslim* duty. That the ideas of non-violence and Islam are essentially compatible is something that may seem jarring for many people today, but for

Badshah Khan and his converts to non-violence, it became the truth of their life and the truth of their religion.

Was Ghaffar Khan's interpretation of Islam genuinely based in Islam? Or did Ghaffar Khan just affirm everything the Mahatma said? Badshah once did say that he placed a great deal of trust in Gandhi's decisions, even going so far as to see them inspired by one who had devoted himself to God:

> Whenever a question of great pith and moment arises in Gandhi's life and Gandhi makes an important decision, I instinctively say to myself, this is the decision of one who has surrendered himself to God, and God never guides ill. I have never found it easy to question his decision for he refers all his problems to God and always listens to His Commands. After all I have but one measure, and that is the measure of one's surrender to God.[38]

In this statement, we see a Muslim interpretation of Gandhi as one who has submitted to God. It shows also how Badshah Khan equated the God of Islam with that of Hindus, a remarkable extension of the notion of "dhimmi." Badshah Khan did think in terms of Islam, but he *did not think narrowly* in terms of Islam. His Islam was a universal calling to faith, devotion, and non-violence. If one lived up to those callings, one could infer that Badshah Khan would have thought Allah was well pleased.

But serious attention must be given to the critics who have pointed to the violence that they see in the Qur'an and in the tradition of Islam. How do we reconcile these, and how did Badshah Khan also reconcile them?

The Qur'an and Jihad In Islam

Abdul Ghaffar Khan knew the Qur'an, as he had been required to memorize it by his mullah. Do we find non-violent messages in the heart of Islam, in the Qur'an itself? The Qur'an does distinguish right and wrong, and accordingly rewards or punishes: "What! Do those who seek after evil ways think We shall hold them equal with those who believe and do righteous deeds — that equal will be their life and their death?" (Qur'an 45:21).[39] Further the Qur'an speaks of love and doing good deeds: "Allah gives glad tidings to his servants who believe and do righteous deed. Say 'No reward do I ask of you for this except the love of those near kin." (Qur'an 42:23) Good deeds are superior to evil deeds: "Nor can goodness and evil be equal. Repel (evil) with the better, then will he between whom thee was hatred become as it were thy friend and intimate"[40] (Qur'an 41: 34).

The patient, enduring non-violence of Mohandas K. Gandhi is one that Badshah Khan saw as essentially inspired by God. To Badshah Khan, Gandhi was no less a holy person than any given Muslim, and indeed it was Gandhi's non-violence which he took to heart and interpreted at the essence of his own Islam. Believing this, Badshah Khan himself became known as the "Frontier Gandhi."

There are of course, troubling verses in the Qur'an that run against this grain. Particularly, the sword verses which plea for making war against the unbelievers when the holy months have passed (Qur'an 9:5), or to lop off the heads of the unbelievers on the battlefield (Qur'an 47:3). The Qur'an has comments which speak critically of Jews and Christians but also seem to uphold them as *dhimmi*, "people of the book", who have received a genuine revelation and whose Prophets are acknowledged. In my own assessment, the Qur'an does not have an unambiguous interpretation. While it speaks in terms of stern judgment and awaiting hellfire for the unbelievers and those who doubt, it also speaks consistently of God as merciful and kind and favoring persons who "do good works, and have faith." That last phrase is incessantly repeated and reiterated in the Qur'an, and it appears to have made a lasting impression on Badshah Khan.

But can we look to the Prophet Muhammad as a role model for non-violence? How could one reach this conclusion, given the fact that we know the Prophet Muhammad also fought in combat? The Qur'an states the need to "lop off the head of the unbeliever" (in Muhammad's case, the opposing Meccans) in combat, when peace has failed. The Prophet Muhammad was indeed no Gandhian, he physically did take up a sword and he did not just speculate as Gandhi did that violence was preferable to cowardice. The Prophet was a warrior, and as even Gandhi once complained, "The sword is too much in evidence among the Muslims. It must be sheathed if Islam is to be what it means — peace."[41] Badshah Khan certainly agreed with the Mahatma that Islam meant peace and did his best to live out that example. If the Prophet Muhammad had to defend the Muslim faith, Ghaffar Khan must have thought it had been an unpleasant or necessary duty, and not the pinnacle or intent of Islam.[42] I have not yet come across an extended Qur'anic exegesis by Khan on this matter, though it may exist and would help clarify his interpretation of Islam. Ghaffar Khan did not appear to be a systematic theologian any more than Gandhi was. Both were campaigners, and pragmatists, who desired to see their faith put into positive action.

Badshah Khan *might* have simply not accepted that the Qur'an was an infallible document, as Gandhi assumed his own Hindu tradition was not without flaws. No definitive statement, writing or reflection, however, has so far come to this writer's attention to suggest how Ghaffar Khan read the Qur'an — literally, or liberally. If the Qur'an is thought to be fallible, objectionable parts of it might be dismissed just as objectionable parts might be dismissed in the Judeo-Christian tradition. If Abdul Ghaffar Khan did object to parts of the Qur'an or of his Muslim tradition, it certainly seems that it was his prerogative to do so, despite that being a controversial standing in his religion.

How Abdul Ghaffar Khan reconciled the textual ambiguity of these verses and traditions in Islam is not fully known by this writer, but what is clear is that he decisively concluded that the proper interpretation of Islam, in his own eyes, was thoroughly non-violent. As before noted, Badshah Khan said:

> It is my inmost conviction that Islam is *amal, yakeen, muhabat* [work, faith, and love] and without these the name Muslim is sounding brass and tinkling cymbal. The Koran makes it absolutely clear

that faith in One God without a second, and good works, are enough to secure a man his salvation.[43]

Badshah Khan took a simple, peaceful, and very universal understanding of his religion. It seems possible to extend the idea that *any man, of any religion* — Christian, Muslim, Jew, Sikh, or Hindu — who had good faith and did good works would be accepted by the over-arching mercy and forgiveness of Allah, who in his mind was God of all. Whatever our petty differences amounted to upon this Earth, it was keeping the good faith and doing good-works in the spirit of peace and non-violence which would essentially count towards our salvation here and in the hereafter. This was his simple view of Islam.

Conclusion: The Legacy of Badshah Khan

The legacy of Khan's life is that with the partition of India and of Pakistan, new forces and new voices came to power that were very much opposed to Abdul Ghaffar Khan. His greatest potential friend and ally, Mohandas Gandhi, was assassinated shortly after independence, and Khan's own *Khudai Khidmatgars* either began to leave his movement or were repressed by the authorities in the new Pakistani government. Scholarship has also suggested that Khan's non-violent appeal to Islam and *ahimsa* was simply not sustainable without his leadership. Even Badshah Khan's own son was reported to dissent from his pure dedication to non-violence. In short, the conversion of Pathans to non-violence was not permanent.[44] Some may view this as failure, and it must be conceded that not every *satyagrahi* is a success. In my view, it does not detract significantly from his heroic stature or accomplishments. Khan's legacy, while very relevant ideologically and theologically, is sadly now in neglect.

Opposing his new government, Khan would spend another fifteen years in prison for his political agitation, earning him truly the title of "Badshah Khan" — King of Khans — whether he accepted it or not. In fact, if one adds the total time Badshah Khan spent in prison fighting for freedom for the Pathans, it adds up to some thirty years (accounts do vary of exactly how much time he spent in prison, but thirty seems a supportable figure); this is more than Martin Luther King Jr., Jawaharlal Nehru, and Mohandas Gandhi combined. Certainly that should qualify A.G. Khan as one of the great, *Islamic* non-violent resistors in our time. Mistakenly, the West constantly omits Khan's name in the legendary halls of those who dedicated their lives to peace and non-violence. If one looks for popular documentaries, magazines, articles, or even movies about the lives of Mohandas Gandhi, Martin Luther King Jr., or Mother Teresa, an abundance of material is to be found. Only one video documentary has recently been produced about Abdul Ghaffar Khan. This inexplicable imbalance should be remedied, for if the West wants to appreciate that Muslims can be non-violent, it has to start turning its television cameras and media in that direction.

It seems as if we are determined to believe otherwise, in the terribly mistaken words of Franklin Graham: "Islam attacked us. The God of Islam is not the same God. He's not the son of God of the Christian or the Judeo-Christian faith.

It's a different God, and I believe it is a very evil and wicked religion."[45] Nothing could be further from the truth, as the very life and existence of Abdul Ghaffar Khan plainly makes clear. It is high time we take a more honest and thorough look at Islam, and of religion itself. It is time we put the likes of Abdul Ghaffar Khan back on our radar.

A tragic fact is that since the terrorist attacks of 9/11, the call to violent *jihad* has imbued Islam with a new and bloody spirit that really betrays the more peaceful nature that it has been proven to sustain. The violence of terrorist *jihad* is a bloodstain that will not easily wash clean. Sullied by the reputation of those who have perverted its spirit, what is most urgently needed now is a *second* Islamic Gandhi, of equal or greater renown to Abdul Ghaffar Kahn. In particular, if such an Islamic Gandhi were to arise in Palestine and was able to reconcile peace between Israeli and the Palestinians, this would go a long way to restoring the reputation of Islam in the West, and reclaiming it from the terrorists who have done it a great disservice. This may seem far-fetched, this may seem idealistic, but recall the words of Eknath Easwaran: "If Badshah Khan could raise a nonviolent army out of a people so steeped in violence as the Pathans, there is no country on earth where it cannot be done."[46]

This is perhaps too optimistic. Favorable political and cultural factors are essential for the realization of non-violence. In terms of political factors, we have to have a government or a nation with some residual level of moral conscience that can be appealed to.[47] A totalitarian government — such as existed in Nazi Germany — would make non-violent *satyagraha* — be it Muslim, Christian, or Hindu, very difficult. Similarly in terms of culture, the people have to be ready for or persuaded to nonviolence, and willing to pay the very high price that might be paid to follow it patiently, enduring with great risk and an even greater heart. Perhaps most important, *satyagraha* needs powerful leadership.

Some seeds of non-violent resistance are already present in Israel-Palestine. Mubarak Awad, a Palestinian Christian, was called briefly by the press a "Palestinian Gandhi" for his efforts to support non-violent civil disobedience amongst the Palestinians. The title, however, is one he has been too humble to claim. Mr. Awad has made some remarkable accomplishments, but it is difficult to say with conviction whether he has or will equal the impact of Gandhi, King, or Badshah Khan. The greatest impact a nonviolent "Muslim Gandhi" would have would be to counterbalance the influence of Osama bin Laden, and to become a more effective and benign spokesman for Islam to the West.

Magnetism and charisma are undoubtedly qualities not to be underestimated and are especially valuable to give direction, hope, and popular energy to nonviolent religious movements. Such charisma is not something Khan or Gandhi would have voluntarily owned up to (both were somewhat embarrassed by their titles of "Badshah Khan — King of Khans" and "Mahatma or Great Soul"), but it is arguably indispensable for giving the necessary motivation and inspirational leadership that non-violence requires. Such leaders are always imaginative, optimistic, universalistic in their thinking, and unfortunately in many regards, far too rare, and far too unique. It is, however, a long century, and with patience we wait. Perhaps only a Muslim Gandhi, able to convict the conscience of Muslims, and non-Muslims alike, will have the patience and fortitude to wash the bloodstains out of politics, and restore it to a path hopefully in accord with its own Prophet. Abdul Ghaffar Khan would have wanted no less.

Notes

1. Christians differ on whether Christ's example and teachings compel one to take a completely nonviolent approach to religion, or whether force can be justifiably used, as in the "Just War" tradition. This chapter should help illuminate a similar split in Islam. While many Muslims affirm that the Qur'an allows them to use force under justifiable circumstances, Abdul Ghaffar Khan believed that Islam (which means "submission") meant that Muslims must be completely nonviolent.
2. Attar Chand, *India Pakistan and Afghanistan: A Study of Freedom, Struggle and Abdul Ghaffar Khan* (New Delhi, India, Commonwealth Publishers, 1989), 8.
3. Jean Akhtar Cerrina, *Islam's Peaceful Warrior: Abdul Ghaffar Khan* (USA, Xlibris Corporation, 2003), 32-34.
4. Eknath Easwaran, *A Man to Match His Mountains: Badshah Khan, Non-Violent Soldier of Islam* (Berkeley, California, Nilgiri Press, 1984) 56.
5. Eknath Easwaran, *A Man to Match His Mountains: Badshah Khan, Non-Violent Soldier of Islam*, 55-59.
6. Attar Chand, *India Pakistan and Afghanistan: A Study of Freedom, Struggle and Abdul Ghaffar Khan*, xliii, 27, 37.
7. Eknath Easwaran, *A Man to Match His Mountains: Badshah Khan, Non-Violent Soldier of Islam*, 12.
8. Eknath Easwaran, *A Man to Match His Mountains: Badshah Khan, Non-Violent Soldier of Islam*, 99.
9. Attar Chand, *India Pakistan and Afghanistan: A Study of Freedom, Struggle and Abdul Ghaffar Khan*, 55.
10. Eknath Easwaran, *A Man to Match His Mountains: Badshah Khan, Non-Violent Soldier of Islam*, 141.
11. Stephen Tanner, *Afghanistan: A Military History From Alexander the Great to the Fall of the Taliban,* (Cambridge, MA, Da Capo Press, 2002), 218.
12. Eknath Easwaran, *A Man to Match His Mountains: Badshah Khan, Non-Violent Soldier of Islam*, 104.
13. Shriman Narayan, editor *The Selected Works of Mahatma Gandhi*, Volume 6 (Ahmedabad-14, India Navajivan Publishing House, 1968), 100.
14. D. Mackenzie Brown, *The White Umbrella: Indian Political Thought from Manu to Gandhi* (Berkley and Los Angeles, University of California Press, 1964), 148.
15. Eknath Easwaran, *A Man to Match His Mountains: Badshah Khan, Non-Violent Soldier of Islam*, 167.
16. Shriman Narayan, editor *The Selected Works of Mahatma Gandhi*, Volume 6 (Ahmedabad-14, India Navajivan Publishing House, 1968), 266.
17. Jean Akhtar Cerrina, Islam's *Peaceful Warrior: Abdul Ghaffar Khan*, 126.
18. Attar Chand, *India Pakistan and Afghanistan: A Study of Freedom, Struggle and Abdul Ghaffar Khan*, 175.
19. One video biography of A.G. Khan exist, while multiple biographies can be found of King, Mother Teresa, or Mohandas Gandhi. Additionally, books about A.G. Khan's life are becoming older, or more frequently are out of print.
20. Attar Chand, *India Pakistan and Afghanistan: A Study of Freedom, Struggle and Abdul Ghaffar Khan*, 185.

21. Jean Akhtar Cerrina, *Islam's Peaceful Warrior: Abdul Ghaffar Khan*, 87-90. See also Attar Chand (above), 36, 178.

22. Martin Luther King Jr., *A Testament of Hope: The Essential Writings and Speeches of Martin Luther King Jr.*, edited by James M. Washington (New York, Harper Collins Publishers, 1986) 17.

23. Shriman Narayan, editor *The Selected Works of Mahatma Gandhi*, Volume 6 (Ahmedabad-14, India Navajivan Publishing House, 1968), 435.

24. Eknath Easwaran, *A Man to Match His Mountains: Badshah Khan, Non-Violent Soldier of Islam*, 63.

25. Eknath Easwaran, *A Man to Match His Mountains: Badshah Khan, Non-Violent Soldier of Islam*, 63.

26. Attar Chand, *India Pakistan and Afghanistan: A Study of Freedom, Struggle and Abdul Ghaffar Khan* (New Delhi, India, Commonwealth Publishers, 1989), lvi.

27. Attar Chand, *India Pakistan and Afghanistan: A Study of Freedom, Struggle and Abdul Ghaffar Khan*, 107.

28. Jawaharlal Nehru, *An Autobiography*, Centenary Edition, (New York, Oxford University Press, 1989) 265, 274, 556.

29. Joan V., Bondurant, *Conquest of Violence: The Gandhian Philosophy of Conflict* (Princeton New Jersey, Princeton University Press, 1988), 138-9.

30. Eknath Easwaran, *A Man to Match His Mountains: Badshah Khan, Non-Violent Soldier of Islam,* 20.

31. Jean Akhtar Cerrina, *Islam's Peaceful Warrior: Abdul Ghaffar Khan*, 96.

32. Attar Chand, *India Pakistan and Afghanistan: A Study of Freedom, Struggle and Abdul Ghaffar Khan*, 31, 63.

33. Eknath Easwaran, *A Man to Match His Mountains: Badshah Khan, Non-Violent Soldier of Islam*, 138.

34. Eknath Easwaran, *A Man to Match His Mountains: Badshah Khan, Non-Violent Soldier of Islam*,117.

35. Attar Chand, *India Pakistan and Afghanistan: A Study of Freedom, Struggle and Abdul Ghaffar Khan*, 86, 138.

36. Attar Chand, *India Pakistan and Afghanistan: A Study of Freedom, Struggle and Abdul Ghaffar Khan*, 13.

37. Jean Akhtar Cerrina, *Islam's Peaceful Warrior: Abdul Ghaffar Khan*, 104.

38. Attar Chand, *India Pakistan and Afghanistan: A Study of Freedom, Struggle and Abdul Ghaffar Khan* (New Delhi, India, Commonwealth Publishers, 1989), 175.

39. Abdullah Yusuf Ali, translator of *The Holy Qur'an*, Beltsville Maryland, Amana Publications, 1989.

40. Another translation by N.J. Dawood reads: "Good deeds and evil deeds are not equal. Requite evil deeds with good, and he who is your enemy will become your dearest friend. But none will attain this attribute save those who patiently endure; none will attain it save those who are truly fortunate."

41. Attar Chand, *India Pakistan and Afghanistan: A Study of Freedom, Struggle and Abdul Ghaffar Khan*, 177.

42. One finds actually a diametrical opposition in thought of Abdul Ghaffar Khan, and Osama bin Laden. The latter once stated that violent *jihad* was the peak of Islamic duty, see: Bruce Lawrence, editor, *Messages to the World: Statements of Osama bin Laden*, (New York, Verso / New Left Books, 2005), 49.

43. Eknath Easwaran, *A Man to Match His Mountains: Badshah Khan, Non-Violent Soldier of Islam*, 63.

44. M.S. Korejo *The Frontier Gandhi: His Place in History* (New York, Oxford University Press, 1993), 57-59.

45. Patricia Beattie Jung, and Shannon Jung, *Moral Issues and Christian Responses, 7th Edition,* (United States, Thomson / Wadsworth Publishing, 2003) 364.

46. Eknath Easwaran, *A Man to Match His Mountains: Badshah Khan, Non-Violent Soldier of Islam*, 189.

47. James L. Rowell, "Gandhi and Bin Laden: Polar Extremes" *Journal of Conflict Studies*, Volume 26, No. 1, 2006.

Conclusion

By now a few things have become very apparent. *Satyagraha*, as Gandhi and Abdul Ghaffar Khan practiced it, was completely opposite the tactics of violent Islamist-Jihadists. Both the *Jihadist* and the *Satyagrahi* were willing to exchange their lives for their beliefs and claimed religious principles in doing so, but that is where the similarity ends. While *terrorist Jihad* has an immediate tactical advantage in being able to strike in unpredictable places at unforeseen times, and while it can tear ranks of *satyagrahis* apart, it has no real moral legitimacy in any religion. Lacking the legitimacy of religious principles, it cannot do otherwise but marginalize itself in the long term, as the sober realization dawns that it is peace that people want. The brutal fact of our history is that this terrible drama has been repeated over and over — we constantly choose the shorter route of impatience, anger, and violence, and repress the higher calling of nonviolence, even when religious conscience tells us otherwise. Even Osama bin Laden has admitted that Islam does not allow for violence against civilians, but claimed that there are certain exemptions. These exemptions do not seem to have real justification in any religion, however, and the wisdom of Abdul Ghaffar Khan has been offered up as an alternative Muslim theology. He redeems the meaning of *Jihad* for peace. No doubt it may be difficult to convince some Muslims as well as Christians of its legitimacy, but Abdul Ghaffar Khan spent his life in dedication to that effort.

The inclusive perspective of Gandhi, universally welcoming and accepting, has a great many appealing advantages, and a few significant shortcomings. The advantages are clear — it is warmly democratic instead of woodenly dogmatic, it opens the path up to salvation and hope for many people. It does not reconcile well the competing truth claims of religions, as we have indicated. It may additionally seem very alienating if not threatening to those who seek exclusive salvation through Jesus, or Moses, or Mohammad. There seems to be no real threat here, however. Neither Gandhi nor Badshah Khan would have anyone give up his or her religion. A Christian could go on being a Christian, Muslims can go on being Muslims, Jews being Jews, Hindus being Hindus and so forth, and there would be nothing wrong with that and no effort to get them to abandon their views. It would simply insist that they see others as co-equals, as having also essential wisdom and hope to be found in their own respective traditions. This perspective would, however, dramatically reduce the "steam" and motivation behind the effort of conversion. And for religions such as Christianity and Islam, which have had such an active missionary and conversion effort, that may cause some troubling problems. Nonetheless, they could still preach their words and their theology. Neither Muslim nor Christian should expect the other to convert as a precondition for peace and it is hoped that the lives of Martin Luther King, Jr. and Abdul Ghaffar Khan would be instructive in that regard. The inclusive perspective simply democratically admits it has no monopoly on truth, and that one of its few dogmas is that all religions, as indeed all people, are not perfect. But as Gandhi said himself, being mindful of those faults it need not blind one also to the beautiful morals that religion has emphasized. Gandhi would not even exclude atheists in his assessments. Contemplating the person of Charles Bradlaugh, Gandhi said:

> I recall the name of Charles Bradlaugh who delighted to call himself an atheist, but knowing as I do something of him, I would never regard him as an atheist. I would call him a God-fearing man, though I know that he would reject the claim. His face would redden if I would say that 'Mr. Bradlaugh, you are a Truth-fearing man, and so a God-fearing man.' I would automatically disarm his criticism by saying that Truth is God, as I have disarmed criticism of many a young man.[1]

Christopher Hitchens' work *God is Not Great* makes some entirely baseless accusations about Gandhi and King. Gandhi did not increase sectarian division and King was not a secular humanist, as Hitchens maintains. It is clear that Gandhi would not have excluded atheists from having moral wisdom. Indeed, the formula "God is Truth" would seem to appeal to those not even looking for God necessarily, but for finding and being dedicated to what is true. It is unfair, however, to then reclassify atheists as being somehow religious or theistic. Though they may share moral principles and dedication that is very similar to that of a religious person, there is no need to subsume them under that category. It does seem evident, however, that the most inclusive direction of Gandhi's thinking would be open to atheists for fair and equal participation in pursuit of the Truth, and not to demonize them as lesser or unequal. I have as yet found no record of how Abdul Ghaffar Khan reacted to atheism.

The inclusive, universal view that privileges no religion and no philosophical perspective seems to be the most fair-minded and democratic. We are all passing through this existence, and we are raised in different traditions and different manners, yet none of us can furnish to the other an irrefutable concrete proof that our own tradition is best. Insisting that we can furnish that proof, or that we have it readily in mind, seems really to be taking a God-like view or an assumption of Divine Consciousness that none of us really have. Religious persons would probably even call this idolatry, to have such smug confidence in our own perspectives that we can really speak for God, and that such idolatry would be condemned. Atheists might call it madness, or speaking without facts, and as adherents to logical positivism or some similar doctrine, they just dismiss it as empty talk. Whatever one is to label it, from a religious or non-religious point of view, the moral absolutist who thinks his or her own view can be substituted for that of God or Final Truth has really lost firm grasp of his fragile humanity and limited perspective. We can have our views, and we can even think that they are competitively better than those of other views (many Christians think this about Jews or Muslims, many Muslims think this about Jews or Christians, and many atheists think this about all of the former), but to fall into the trap of this exclusivist, Absolutist mindset is really to go beyond the pale of reason. Religion must be reasonable, even as John Wesley once wrote "It is a fundamental principle with us that to renounce reason is to renounce religion, that religion and reason go hand in hand, and that all irrational religion is false religion."[2]

Karl Marx once wrote that "the criticism of religion disillusions man to make him think and act and shape his reality like a man who has been disillusioned and has come to reason, so that he will revolve around himself and therefore round his true sun. Religion is only the illusory sun which revolves round man as long as he does not revolve around himself."[3] When one becomes so convinced of the truth of one's perspective that it becomes an unquestioned absolute, this does seem to be a very bad and dangerous illusion that must be debunked. But the atheism of Marx became dogmatized in the Soviet administration of Stalin, and "truths" there became unchallenged and unquestioned also. It seems that the tendency to absolutize and mistake the self with an Infallible Truth occurs when we too zealously adhere to any ideology or religious creed.

Reinhold Niebuhr noted this, as well as the errors of Marxism which became akin to those of "bad religion." Religion speaks about the Absolute Truth, but in pursuit of that belief, or of what Truth is, we must never deceive ourselves into thinking that we are too near to it. Niebuhr wrote that "religion tends to absolutize everything it touches"[4] and that "bad religion can be worse than no religion."[5] In believing and letting the zeal of that faith grow inside us, Niebuhr cautioned, "we must not claim too much for our knowledge of God and His judgments. When we do, we merely make God the ally of our interested position in the scheme of things."[6] It seems Bin Laden has made these errors, but he will not admit them, and in fact would probably blame us. We, however, can look to Gandhi, King, Abdul Ghaffar Khan or Niebuhr for better judgments.

So what then is religion? Are Gandhi and Bin Laden to be considered equally religious persons? How can they be, given the fact that they are so polarized in many respects? How can a man who would lay his life down for others be psychologically and philosophically categorized with a man who has justified terrorist violence against women and children? Psychologically, philosophically, the one category of "religion" does not equally fit Gandhi and Bin Laden. Some conclusion remains left undetermined, for both men claimed religion in their cause and to be serving their understanding of the highest good. It is understandable in the midst of such polarizing religious attitudes why some grow fed up, or very cautious, about religion altogether. Yet I would maintain that religion is only one subset of a larger thing called human ideology, or rather "belief." Our beliefs can either assert there is no Divine God, or that there is, and if there is, they can further go on to suggest who and where that Divine comes from. It is in the overzealous dedication and exclusive insistence upon the content of this belief that really gets us into trouble and propels us to the extremes of militant delusion.

There may be a very subtle but dangerous paradox here. "Belief", or if you prefer to call it "ideology", may be something of a promising yet volatile character. For example, religious belief and conviction undoubtedly helped men like Gandhi, King, and Abdul Ghaffar Khan. Their movements and their ideas would have made no sense without religious belief, because it was an essential part of their world-views and their political programs. Yet religious belief might also become something explosive, something hazardous to handle. On September 11, 1906, a religious vow was taken by Gandhi, as well as other Hindus and Muslims in Africa, which produced the movement of *satyagraha*. On September 11, 2001 in New York City, a pledge of violent *jihad* was fulfilled that has focused our attention on religion and politics in an entirely different way. Yet I would admit that religion, in some form, was present in both acts — but it was of course religion of an essentially different character — "religion vs. irreligion" if you like to call it, or "good religion and bad religion", although this begins again to oversimplify.

Religion is not, and should not be thought about in static, easy to define terms. We should think of religion much like we think about chemistry — very complicated and capable of a wide variety of differing combinations. Take water for example, an essential component of our world which life cannot do without. Yet water can also drown us as it can keep us alive. The components of H_2O can be altered to produce the quite damaging H_2SO_4. Oxygen, another essential component of our lives, when combined with a carbon can become the lethal carbon monoxide (CO), or also the deadly CO_2. Yet oxygen by itself remains what it is — oxygen. It is when it combines in unique combinations with other elements that it takes on markedly different characteristics as mild as water or as deadly as carbon monoxide gas.

Belief systems — whether they be religious or not — can also be malleable and very flexible. Whether religion makes our belief better or much potentially worse, and what kind of religions or belief systems aid or abet that process will be debated from now until the end of our time as we know it. But if one were to substitute the above "O" or "Oxygen", with the idea of "R" for "Religion", and call that "Belief in God or the Sacred", you can see that this can produce a variety of results. Combine that essential belief with nonviolent attitudes and with inclusive views, and you get a Gandhi or an Abdul Ghaffar Khan. Combine that belief with militancy, and extreme rejection of the human "other" as something completely different from the self, and you get a belief system similar to Bin Laden. I would go beyond the idea of religion, however, and suggest that the "free radical" of oxygen can be compared to a general free radical "B", human belief. That belief can be zealous, can push it forward in good ways perhaps if you combine it with "J" for Jeffersonian Democracy, or "L" for Lincoln's abolition of slavery, but it becomes quite different when you combine it with "N" for acceptance of Hitler's Nazism, or "S" for insistence upon the inflexible Soviet regime of Stalin. Our human mental chemistry, the stuff our belief is made of, is a variable and sometimes volatile mix of a few essential human aspects of mind and culture. We as humans are all free to choose to believe something and to amend it with other beliefs systems. It behooves us well to take a very self-critical and discerning view of the nature of that belief, as well as the beliefs of those around us. When the chemistry of our belief is subtly altered, sometimes we may be the last persons to realize it.

The above chemical analogy should be clear in its simplicity, but it is the murky depths of religious and ideological power that as yet have not and cannot be defined here. We know that believing passions can push our politics and morality in good directions, but these passions (especially when they become more volatile and appeal to absolutes) can push us in an extremely dark direction. They can make us humane, or inhuman.

Gandhi and Bin Laden have shown us some radical extremes. The extremes of Gandhi are of course obviously preferred. Yet Gandhi was human, and errors and criticism of his thinking can and have been pointed out. We have also seen that Bin Laden has no monopoly on interpreting the Qur'an but that Islam has been driven in a much different direction by him than it was by Abdul Ghaffar Khan. Abdul Ghaffar Khan's life and deeds repudiated most all of Bin Laden's beliefs, and he insisted that Islam and in fact *jihad* could be about peace and nonviolence. Abdul Ghaffar Khan was certainly no wimp, as legendary reports of his great physical prowess have suggested that he even had the bodily strength to bend the bars of his own prison.[7] He preferred not to use that method, however, and to bend the mental bars of violence, anger, and alienation which can imprison us all. His nonviolent Islam can help point us back to the more inclusive, benign religion of Gandhi.

The mainstream belief of Islam is nonviolent. Most Muslims want nothing to do with violence and mainly are facing economic frustrations and undemocratic governments. I was reluctant even to use the word "Islamist" to describe the more radical group of Muslims, or even "Islamist-Jihadist", because those terms can easily be confused and conflated with "Islam" and "Jihad", terms which themselves have a much deeper history and a much broader historical meaning. Nonetheless, "Islamist" and "Jihadist" seem to be the best terms available. Suffice it to say I believe Abdul Ghaffar Khan to be a more noble spokesman for Islam, who hopefully also appeals to mainstream Muslims inasmuch as Martin Luther King Jr. has appealed to Christians. And if we are to remember the lives of Gandhi and King in the hallowed halls of nonviolence, let us also remember the name and life of Abdul Ghaffar Khan.

Notes

1. Gandhi / Narayan, *The Selected Works*, vol. 6, 99.
2. Jung, *Moral Issues and Christian Responses*, 281.
3. Marx, Karl and Friedrich Engels, *Karl Marx and Friedrich Engels on Religion*, editor unknown, (New York, Schocken Books, 1964), 42.

4. Reinhold Niebuhr, *The Contributions of Religion to Social Work* (New York: Columbia University Press, 1932), 50.

5. Bingham, June, *Courage to Change* (New York and Canada: Charles Scribner's Sons, 1961), 7.

6. Bingham, *Courage to Change,* 94.

7. When Abdul Ghaffar Khan was once taunted by a British official in jail about what he would do if he were not nonviolent, it has been told that Abdul Ghaffar Khan physically bent the bars of his prison and suggested "that is what I would do." See Cerrina, *Islam's Peaceful Warrior*, 84.

Bibliography

Ahir, D.C. *The Legacy of Dr. Ambedkar*. Delhi: B.R. Publishing Corporation, A Division of D.K. Publishers, 1990.
Anand, Mulk Raj, *Untouchable*, New York, Penguin Books, 1940.
Ali, Abdullah Yusuf translator of *The Holy Qur'an*, Beltsville Maryland, Amana Publications, 1989.
Armstrong, Karen. *The Battle for God: A History of Fundamentalism*. New York Ballantine Books, 2001.
Aslan, Reza, *No God But God: The Origins, Evolution, and Future of Islam*, New York, Random House Trade Paperbacks, 2006.
Bergen, Peter L., *The Osama bin Laden I Know: An Oral History of al Qaeda's Leader*, New York, The Free Press, 2006
_____. *Holy War Inc: Inside the Secret World of Osama bin Laden*. New York, The Free Press, 2001.
Bingham, June. *Courage to Change*. New York and Canada: Charles Scribner's Sons, 1961.
Bodansky, Yossef, *Bin Laden: The Man Who Declared War On America*, New York, Forum Prima / Random House, 2001.
Bondurant, Joan V., *Conquest of Violence: The Gandhian Philosophy of Conflict*, Princeton New Jersey, Princeton University Press, 1988.
Brisard, Jean-Charles, with Damien Martinez, *Zarqawi: The New Face of Al-Qaeda*, New York, Other Press, 2005.
Brown, Charles C., *Niebuhr and His Age*. Philadelphia, Trinity Press International 1992.
Brown, D. Mackenzie, *The White Umbrella: Indian Political Thought from Manu to Gandhi*, Berkley and Los Angeles, University of California Press, 1964.
Cerrina, Jean Akhtar, *Islam's Peaceful Warrior: Abdul Ghaffar Khan*, USA, Xlibris Corporation, 2003.
Chand, Attar, *India Pakistan and Afghanistan: A Study of Freedom, Struggle and Abdul Ghaffar Khan*, New Delhi, India, Commonwealth Publishers, 1989.
Clarke, Richard. *Against All Enemies, Inside America's War on Terror*. New York, Free Press 2004.
Colaiaco, James A. *Martin Luther King, Jr.: Apostle of Militant Non-Violence*, St. Martin's Press, New York, 1993.
Coll, Steve, *The Bin Ladens: An Arabian Family in the American Century*, New York, The Penguin Press, 2008.
Collet, Sophia Dobson. *The Life and Letters of Raja Rammohun Roy*. Calcutta, Brahmo Mission Press, 1962.

Dawood, N.J., translator, *The Koran*, New York, Penguin Books, 2003.
Easwaran Eknath, *A Man to Match His Mountains: Badshah Khan: Non-Violent Soldier of Islam,* Berkley, California, Nilgiri Press – division of Random House, 1984.
Einstein, Albert. *Ideas and Opinions,* edited by Carl Selig, translated by Sonja Bargmann, Random House, New York, 1954.
Erikson, Erik. *Gandhi's Truth: On The Origins of Militant Non-Violence.* New York: W.W. Norton & Company, Inc., 1969.
Esposito, John, *Unholy War: Terror in the Name of Islam.* New York: Oxford University Press, 2002.
Esposito, John and Dalia Mogahed, *Who Speaks for Islam: What A Billion Muslims Really Think,* 2007.
Feuerbach, Ludwig. *The Essence of Christianity.* translated by George Eliot. New York: Prometheus Books, 1989.
Fischer, Louis editor, *The Essential Gandhi: An Anthology of His Life, Works, and Ideas,* New York, Vintage Books, a division of Random House, 1983.
Fischer, Louis. *Gandhi, His Life and Message for the World.* New York: Mentor Books/ New American Library, 1982.
_____, *The Life of Mahatma Gandhi,* New York, Collier Books, 1962.
Gandhi Mohandas K. *Hind Swaraj and Other Writings*, Edited by Anthony J. Parel, New York, Cambridge University Press, 2003,
_____. *Satyagraha in South Africa,* translated from the Gujarati by Valji Govindji Desai, Ahmedabad, Navajivan Publishing House, 6th edition, 2001.
_____, *The Bhagavad Gita According to Gandhi,* ed. & trans. John Strohmeir. Berkeley, California, Berkeley Hills Books, 2000.
_____, *Gandhi, An Autobiography: The Story of My Experiments With Truth*, translated from Gujarati by Mahadev Desai, Beacon Press, Boston, 1993
_____. *The Selected Works of Mahatma Gandhi.* ed. Shriman Narayan, volumes 4 and 6. India: Ahmedabad, Navajivan Publishing House, 1968.
_____. *My Religion* ed. Bharatan Kumarappa. India: Ahmedabad, Navajivan Publishing House, 1955.
Goldberg, Michelle, *Kingdom Coming: The Rise of Christian Nationalism:,* New York, W.W. Norton & Company, 2006.
Gore, M.S. *The Social Context of an Ideology: Ambedkar's Political and Social Thought,* New Delhi Sage Publications, 1993.
Greenawalt, Kent, *Religious Convictions and Political Choice*, New York, Oxford University Press, 1988.
Gunaratna, Rohan *Inside Al Qaeda, Global Network of Terror*, Columbia University Press, New York, 2002
Hitchens, Christopher, *God is not Great: How Religion Poisons Everything*, New York, Twelve/Warner Books, 2007.
Huntington, Samuel P. *The Clash of Civilization and the Remaking of World Order.* New York, Touchstone Book, Simon & Schuster, 1996.
Juergensmeyer, Mark. *Terror in the Mind of God: the Global Rise of Religious Violence.* Berkley: University of California Press, 2001.
Jung, Patricia Beattie, and Shannon Jung, *Moral Issues and Christian Responses, 7th Edition,* United States, Thomson / Wadsworth Publishing, 2003.
Keay, John, *India: A History,* New York, Grove Press, 2000.
Kean, Thomas H., Lee H. Hamilton, et al., *The 9/11 Commission Report: Final Report of the National Commission on Terrorist Attacks Upon the United States,* Authorized Edition, Printed in the United States, W.W. Norton & Company July 22, 2004.

Bibliography

Keer, Dhananjay. *Dr. Ambedkar, His Life and Mission*. Bombay: Popular Prakashan Press, 1990.
Kelsay, John. *Islam and War, The Gulf War and Beyond: A Study in Comparative Ethics*. Louisville, Westminster John-Knox Press, 1993.
Khan, Yasmin. *The Great Partition: The Making of India and Pakistan,* New Haven, Yale University Press, 2007.
Kimball, Charles. *When Religion Becomes Evil*. New York: HarperSanFranciso, 2002.
King Jr, Martin Luther. *The Essential Writings and Speeches of Martin Luther King Jr.*, ed. James M. Washington. New York: Harper Collins, 1986.
_____, *The King Companion,* selected by Coretta Scott King, New York, St. Martin's Press, 1993.
Korejo, M.S., *The Frontier Gandhi: His Place in History,* New York, Oxford University Press, 1993.
Lawrence, Bruce, editor, *Messages to the World: Statements of Osama bin Laden,* , New York, Verso / New Left Books, 2005.
Lewis, Bernard *The Crisis of Islam: Holy War and Unholy Terror*, New York, The Modern Library, 2003.
Lia, Brynjar, *The Society of Muslim Brothers: The Rise of the Islamic Mass Movement 1928-1942,* UK, Ithaca Press, 2006.
Marcello, Patrician Cronin, *Mohandas K. Gandhi*, Westport, Connecticut, Greenwood Press, 2006.
Marlin IV, Robert O. *What Does Al-Qaeda Want?* Berkeley: *North Atlantic Books*, 2004.
Marx, Karl, and Frederick Engels, *Economic and Social Manuscripts & Communist Manifesto*, translated by Martin Milligan, Prometheus Books, New York, 1988.
_____. *Karl Marx and Friedrich Engels on Religion*, editor unknown, New York, Schocken Books, 1964.
McDermott, Terry, *Perfect Soldiers, the Hijackers: Who They Were, Why They Did It*, New York, HarperCollins Publishers, 2005.
Merton, Thomas, editor *Gandhi on Non-Violence.* USA, New Directions Paperback, 2007.
Nehru, Jawaharlal. *An Autobiography*, New York, Oxford University Press, (Centenary Edition), 1989.
Niebuhr, Reinhold. *Moral Man & Immoral Society: A Study in Ethics and Politics*. Louisville, Westminster John-Knox Press, 2001.
_____. *The Contributions of Religion to Social Work*. New York: Columbia University Press, 1932.
Nojeim, Michael J. *Gandhi and King: The Power of Nonviolent Resistance*, Westport, Connecticut, Praeger 2004.
Qutb, Sayyid, *Milestones*, New York, Islamic Book Service, 2005.
Rashid, Ahmed. *Jihad: The Rise of Militant Islam in Central Asia.* New York: Penguin Books, 2002.
Rohan Gunaratna. *Inside Al Qaeda, Global Network of Terror.* New York: Columbia University Press, 2002.
Rowell, James L., "Gandhi and Bin Laden: Polar Extremes", *Journal of Conflict Studies*, Volume 26, No. 1, 2006.
Sangharakshita. *Amebedkar and Buddhism,* Glasgow, Windhorse Publications,1986.
Shivery, Micah L. and Christopher Serf. *The Iraq War Reader: History, Documents, Opinions.* New York Touchstone Books, 2003.
Spencer, Robert, *Islam Unveiled: Disturbing Questions About the World's Fastest-Growing Faith,* San Francisco, Encounter Books, 2002.
Stern, Jessica. *Terror in the Name of God: Why Religious Militants Kill.* New York: HarperCollins Publishers, 2003.

Tanner, Stephen, *Afghanistan: A Military History From Alexander the Great to the Fall of the Taliban,* Cambridge, MA, Da Capo Press, 2002.
Vassiliev, Alexei, *The History of Saudi Arabia,* London, Saqi Books, 2000.
Wilcox, Clyde and Carlin Larson, *Onward Christian Soldiers, third edition,* Boulder Colorado, Westview Press, 2006.
Wright, Lawrence, *The Looming Tower: Al Qaeda and the Road to 9/11*, New York Alfred A. Knopf, 2006.

Index

Afghanistan: 79-84
Al-Qaeda: 80-81, 84, 89-94
Ahimsa: 50-51; women as incarnation of: 58, 122
Ahmedabad strike: 31
Ambedkar, B.R.: 37-38, 60
Amritsar: 31-32
Andrews, C.F.: 29
Atta, Muhammad: 7, 91-93
Azzam, Abdullah: 78-84
Badal: 121, 124
Banna, Hasan al-: 107
Bashir, Omar: 86-87
Bhagavad-Gita: 21, 48
Bin Laden, Mohammed: 73-77
Bin Laden, Osama, Afghan Conflict: 8, 79-84; Anti-Jewish views: 78, 88-89, 107, 109; Anti-Zionism: 107; Asceticism of: 7, 114; Birth: 77; Clash of Civilizations view: 111-112; Childhood: 77-78; East Africa Bombings: 89; Education: 77-79; Fatwas of: 5, 6, 11, 88, 100-101; Gulf War / Kuwait War: 84-89; Hadith of Caliph Umar: 86; Jaji Conflict: 84; Jihadist views: 82, 89, 99, 103 108; Lebanese invasion, view of: 82, 109; Man without a country: 87-88; Religious Views, exclusive nature of: 5, 6, 11, 78, 104, 109' Scandinavian Vacation: 77; September 11 Attacks support: 82, 90-94; Sons support or rebellion: 8; Sudan: 86-87; Violence, justifying: 5, 6; Wealth: 77; Will of his father: 7; Violence justified – see Jihadist views of OBL
Bin Laden, Salem: 76, 81
Brahmacharya 19, 48, 65-66
Capitalism vs. Communism: 60-64
Champaran Indigo campaign: 30
Chauri Chaura – violence in: 32
Christianity: 28, 41, 51-52
Church-State issues: 56-57
Churchill, Winston: 39
Clarke, Richard: 6
Clash of Civilizations: 62, 111-112
Dyer Brigadier General Reginald Edward Harry: 31-32
Easwaran, Eknath:
Erik Erikson / *Gandhi's Truth*: 31
Feuerbach, Ludwig: 9
Fischer, Louis: 52
Gandhi & Bin Laden, comparative analysis: 1-2, 9-11, 13-15, 17, 47, 53-54, 67, 73, 88, 93, 95, 113-116, 137-8
Gandhi & A.G. Khan comparative analysis: 124, 128

Gandhi, Harilal: 19, 24, 38-39
Gandhi, Kasturbai: 18-19, 28, 38
Gandhi, Laxmidas:
Gandhi, Mohandas K.: Assassination: 39-40; Beaten by South Africans: 25; Beaten by Pathan: 26; Bhagavad-Gita: 21. 48; Birth: 17-18; Caste views: 18, 34-35, 58-62; Children's Alienation: 24; Childhood: 18; Civilization, views of: 34-35, 62-64; Constructive Program: 33; Economic Views: 33-34, 60-64; Education: 20-22; England: 20-22; 36-37; Equality / Inequality, views of: 28, 34-35, 58-62; Experiments in Youth: 18; Fasting: in Amhedabad 31; in Yeravda/Poona 37-38; in Calcutta 39; Film by Richard Attenborough: 26; "Great Trial": 32; Harijan: 18, 34-35, 37, 58-62; Hartal: 31-32; Himalayan Miscalculation: 32; Hindu-Muslim unity: 35; Hitler and Fascism, views of: 67-69; Human Nature, views of: 49; Imprisoned: 32-33; Indian, return to 22; Indian Swaraj: 30-40, 64, 66; India partition: 10, 38, 56-57; Khadi, homespun: 34; Lawyer, Failures as: 22; Machinery, views of: 33-34, 63-64; Mahatma title: 31, 65; Marriage: 18; Muslim Allies: 26. 35; Partition of India: 10, 38-39; Religion and Politics: 10, 56-58; Religiously Inclusive Views: 10, 11, 20, 51-55; Second Roundtable Conference: 36-37; South Africa, Arrival: 22, Asiatic Act: 25, Boer Wars: 25, Discrimination: 22-24, Train Incident at Maritzburg: 23; Salt March, 35-36; Sexuality: 65-66, Brahmacharya: 19, 48, 65-66, Guilt over: 19, 66; Theosophists: 21; Truth and God: 20, 21, 40, 47-48, 55, 109, 116, 122; Untouchables: see caste or equality; Vegetarianism: 21; Vows to a Jain Monk: 20; War, view of: 50; Women, views of: 58-59;World War II:

Godse, Nathuram Vinayak: 39-40
Gokhale, Gopal Krishna: 29
Grand Mosque Seizure: 79
Hadith, no Jews or Christians in Muslim lands: 104
Hamburg Four: 93
Hamid Mir: 105
Hatred, political and social aspects of: 6, 7
Hekmetyar, Gulbuddin: 84
Hitchens, Christopher: 41, 136
Houris / Virgins: 5
Huntington, Samuel: 62, 111
Hussein, Saddam: 6, 84-85
India and partition: 10, 38, 56-57
Islam, rejection of violence and terror: 4, 73; meaning of: 131
Islamism: 54, 79; and takfir ideology: 80: Islamist defined: 91; 109, 111
Jahiliyyah: 8, 11, 105-6
Jainism: 53
Jain Parable of Elephant: 53
Jarrah, Ziad: 91-93
Jesus and nonviolence: 28, 40, 52
Jihad Magazine excerpt: 80-81
Jihad, meaning of: 3, 99-100, 119, 127, 131; Greater or Lesser: 3
Jihadists: 2-4, 91
Jinnah, Muhammad Ali: 10, 38
Kallenbach, Herman: 28-29
Karbala, sack of: 75
Kenya and Tanzania attacks: 90
King Jr., Martin Luther: 14, 40-41, 62
Kimball, Charles: 4-5, 9

Khan, Abdul Ghaffar: 35, 38, 40-43, 119-134, 139; Badal: 121, 124; Birth and Origins: 120; Jail Time: 130; Jihad for Khan: 119, 127; Marriage: 121; Non-violence: 123, 126, 130; Reforms in Education: 120; Religious Views: 123
Khudai Khidmatgars: 40-41, 124-127
Kuwait War: 84-85
Lewis, Bernard: 62
Love, power of: 49
Malcolm X: 14
Marx, Karl: 137
Massoud, Ahmad Shah: 84
Mektab al-Khidmat: 81
Mohammed, Khalid Sheik: 76, 90-93
Muhammad, the Prophet: 3-4, 129
Mujahideen: 81
Muslim Brotherhood: 78, 107
Muslims, opinion poll surveys: 4, 94; rejection of violence: 73
Niebuhr, Reinhold: 69-70, 137
Non-violence: see Satyagraha.
Pakistan, reparations: 39
Pathans or Pashtuns: 40-41, 122
Poverty, political and social aspects of: 7-8
Qur'an: citations, Against Murder: 102; Dhimmi: 106; Faith and Deeds: 128; Infallibility of: 104; Mercy/Forgiveness: 102; No Compulsion in Religion: 102; Sword Verses: 102, 129
Qutb, Mohammed: 78-79
Qutb, Sayyid: 8, 11, 78-79, 105-6
Rahman, Sheikh Omar Abdel: 83
Rowlatt Act: 31
Religion, complex nature of: 9, 137-9; Universal concept of: 51-55
Ruskin, John and *Unto this Last*: 27-28, 60

Salt March: 35-36; Dharasana Salt Works: 36
Satyagraha: 3, 67
 Etymology: 3, 27, 48
 Origins: 3, 26-27
 Principles Of: 36, 48, 67
 Satyagrahis: 3, 49-50
Saudi Arabia: 85
 Founding Of: 74-75
 Royal Saudi Family: 74-75
Saudi Bin Laden Group: 76-77
September 11 Attacks: 26-27, 90-94, 103; Muslim rejection: 4
Smith, Adam and the *Wealth of Nations*: 66
Smuts, Jan: 25-26
Socialism: 61-62
South Africa, discrimination: 22-23
 Three Pound (£3) Tax: 24, 29
Suicide Bomber: 3, 5
Taliban: 122
Taymiyya, Ibn: 100
Tolstoy, Leo: 28, 52, 60
Turabi, Hasan al-: 86-87
Untouchables: 28, 34-35, 58-62
United States: Foreign policy and implications: 6-7
U.S.S. Cole: 90
Wahhab, Muhammad ibn Abd-al: 74-57
Wahhabism: 74-75, 79
Wesley, John: 137
WMD: 11-13
Yousef, Ramzi: 90-91
Zarqawi, Abu Musab al-: 6, 94-95, 100
Zawahiri, Ayman al-: 82-83
Zionism: 108

About the Author

Dr. James L. Rowell is an Assistant Professor of Religion at Flagler College and teaches classes in world religion, as well as courses related to religion, politics and science. His interests include finding a common ground of ethics in world religion and political discourse. Having a Christian background, he came to appreciate the message of ethics common to all religious traditions, and is a strong enthusiast for studying widely and broadly. He has published articles on Gandhi, Bin Laden, and Abdul Ghaffar Khan. He did his undergraduate work in anthropology and politics at UMass, and his graduate work in religion and politics at the Universities of New Hampshire and Pittsburgh. This is his first published book.